CITIES *of* GOLD

CITIES

of

GOLD

LEGENDARY KINGDOMS, QUIXOTIC QUESTS,
AND THE SEARCH FOR
FANTASTIC NEW WORLD WEALTH

*On the Trail to El Dorado, Manoa, Paititi,
the Seven Cities of Cibola, the Mysterious Quivira, and Beyond*

BILL YENNE

WITH DRAWINGS BY THE AUTHOR

WESTHOLME
Yardley

Frontispiece: A conquistador contemplates the end of the trail.

Westholme Publishing, LLC

904 Edgewood Road

Yardley, Pennsylvania 19067

Visit our Web site at www.westholmepublishing.com

First Printing November 2011

10 9 8 7 6 5 4 3 2 1

ISBN: 978-1-59416-144-5

Also available as an eBook.

Printed in the United States of America.

Gaily bedight,
A gallant knight,
In sunshine and in shadow,
Had journeyed long,
Singing a song,
In search of Eldorado.

But he grew old—
This knight so bold—
And o'er his heart a shadow
Fell as he found
No spot of ground
That looked like Eldorado.

And, as his strength
Failed him at length,
He met a pilgrim shadow—
"Shadow," said he,
"Where can it be—
This land of Eldorado?"

"Over the mountains
Of the Moon,
Down the Valley of the Shadow,
Ride, boldly ride,"
The shade replied—
"If you seek for Eldorado!"

—Edgar Allan Poe (*Eldorado*)

CONTENTS

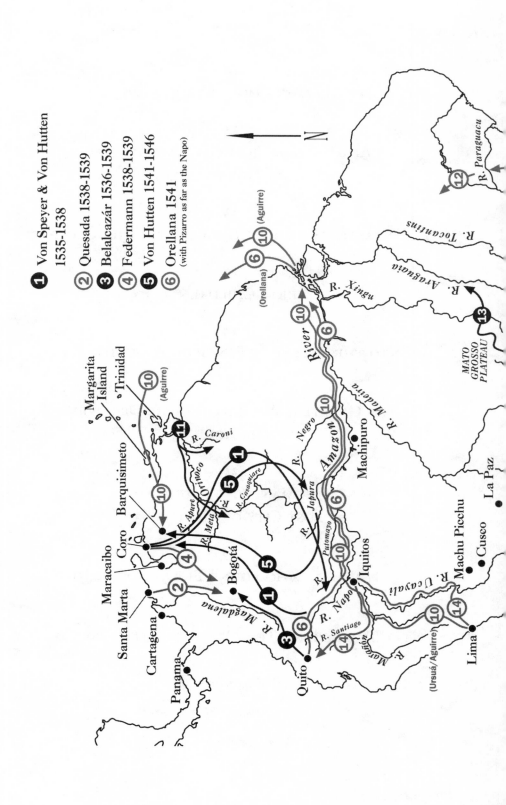

Von Speyer & Von Hutten 1535-1538

② Quesada 1538-1539
③ Belalcazár 1536-1539
④ Federmann 1538-1539
⑤ Von Hutten 1541-1546
⑥ Orellana 1541
(with Pizarro as far as the Napo)

N

Margarita Island
Trinidad
R. Caroni
Barquisimeto
(Aguirre)
Coro
Maracaibo
R. Orinoco
R. Casiquiare
R. Apure
R. Meta
Santa Marta
Bogotá
Cartagena
R. Magdalena
Panama
Quito
R. Santiago
R. Marañon
(Orellana)
(Aguirre)
R. Negro
R. Japurá
Amazon
River
R. Putomayo
R. Madeira
Machipuro
R. Xingu
R. Araguaia
R. Tocantins
R. Paraguacu
MATO GROSSO PLATEAU
Iquitos
R. Napo
R. Ucayali
Machu Picchu
Cuso
La Paz
Lima
(Ursuá/Aguirre)

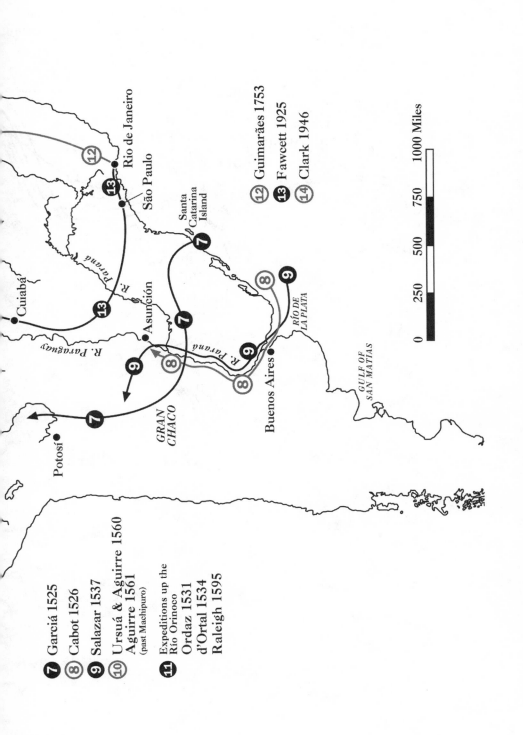

Río de Janeiro

São Paulo

Santa
Catarina
Island

Cuiabá

Asunción

R. Paraná

R. Paraguay

Potosí

GRAN
CHACO

R. Paraná

Buenos Aires

RÍO DE
LA PLATA

GULF OF
SAN MATÍAS

7 Garciá 1525
8 Cabot 1526
9 Salazar 1537
10 Ursuá & Aguirre 1560
Aguirre 1561
(past Machipuro)
11 Expeditions up the
Río Orinoco
Ordaz 1531
d'Ortal 1534
Raleigh 1595

12 Guimarães 1753
13 Fawcett 1925
14 Clark 1946

0   250   500   750   1000 Miles

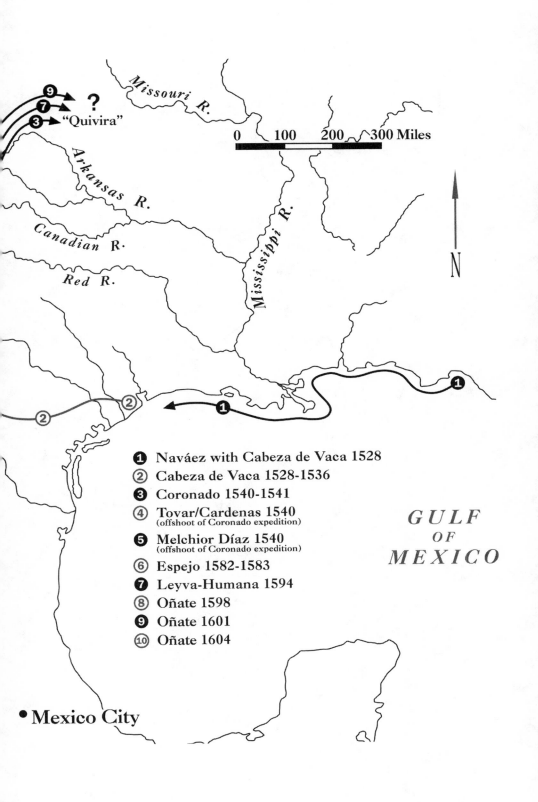

Missouri R.

⑨→
⑦→
③→ "Quivira"
?

0 100 200 300 Miles

Arkansas R.

Canadian R.

Red R.

Mississippi R.

N

②
②

①

GULF
OF
MEXICO

❶ Naváez with Cabeza de Vaca 1528
② Cabeza de Vaca 1528-1536
❸ Coronado 1540-1541
④ Tovar/Cardenas 1540
(offshoot of Coronado expedition)
❺ Melchior Díaz 1540
(offshoot of Coronado expedition)
⑥ Espejo 1582-1583
❼ Leyva-Humana 1594
⑧ Oñate 1598
❾ Oñate 1601
⑩ Oñate 1604

• Mexico City

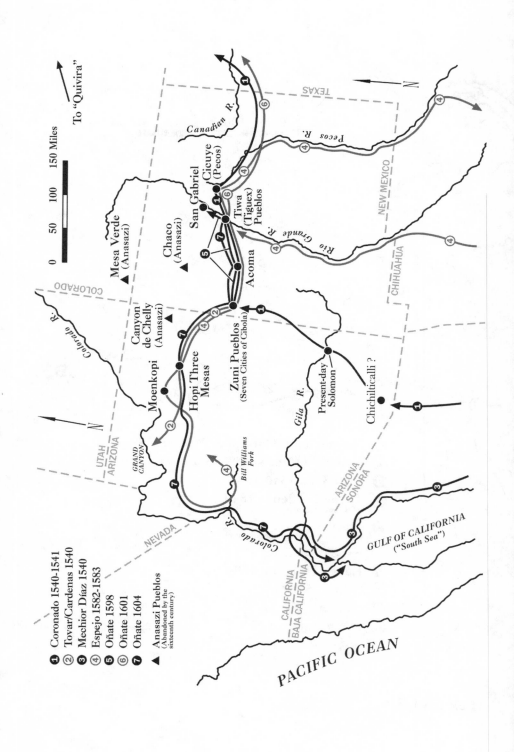

To "Quivira"

150 Miles

0   50   100   150 Miles

N

Canadian R.

Pecos R.

TEXAS

NEW MEXICO

San Gabriel
Cicuye
(Pecos)

Mesa Verde
(Anasazi)

Chaco
(Anasazi)

Tiwa
(Tiguex)
Pueblos

Acoma

Rio Grande R.

CHIHUAHUA

COLORADO

Colorado R.

Canyon
de Chelly
(Anasazi)

Moenkopi

Hopi Three
Mesas

Zuni Pueblos
(Seven Cities of Cibola)

Present-day
Solomon

Chichilticalli ?

Gila R.

GRAND
CANYON

Bill Williams
Fork

UTAH
ARIZONA

N

ARIZONA
SONORA

NEVADA

Colorado R.

GULF OF CALIFORNIA
("South Sea")

CALIFORNIA
BAJA CALIFORNIA

PACIFIC OCEAN

❶ Coronado 1540-1541
❷ Tovar/Cardenas 1540
❸ Mechior Díaz 1540
❹ Espejo 1582-1583
❺ Oñate 1598
❻ Oñate 1601
❼ Oñate 1604
▲ Anasazi Pueblos
   (Abandoned by the
   sixteenth century)

FIRE STOLEN FROM THE SUN

City of Gold!

The city sat high upon the bluff, like a jaguar crouched upon its throne, blazing in the glory of fire—fire stolen from the sun itself. It shimmered in the fading light with brilliance against the cold, steel-blue darkness of the surrounding storm clouds.

I watched the shadows creep up the towering sandstone cliffs toward it, like the lizards I had seen scrambling over the rocks nearer at hand.

I watched as the vivid colors of its rocky throne burned out and disappeared, first to the color of polished copper, and then to black, yet leaving the city still glowing like a spark floating in the heavens.

City of Gold!

This vision glowed so brightly that when I dared to glance away, I found that it had seared spots into my eyes.

As I watched, the heat and light of the city seemed to leap skyward, climbing on the jagged shafts of lightning which spit angrily from within the roiling thunderclouds.

Then, suddenly, it was gone, swallowed by darkness as the night swallows the day.

The hushed crowd hung on every word as he spoke.

In the great hall of the viceroy's palace, this city of gold seemed so far away, so alien, but so fabulous. The noblemen and women looked into the speaker's wide, bright eyes, which seemed fixed upon some unseen apparition, and which glowed like burning coals in his leathery face, well worn and of unknown age.

In the flickering light of the candles, it was hard to read this man. Who was he? Was he the respected Franciscan friar whom the viceroy had described, or was he merely a mad monk, a heretic relating tales seen only in a hallucination?

But they believed him. They believed what he described because he had been there, and because they had been told that others had seen it, too.

Mainly, though, they believed him because they wanted to believe him. They wanted to believe that he was telling the truth. They wanted to believe in the "Ciudad de Oro" which lay far to the north in a strange land that few had visited.

They closed their eyes, and they, too, saw it crouched upon its throne, blazing in the glory of fire—a fire seemingly stolen from the sun itself.

HALF A MILLENNIUM after this story was told in the viceroy's palace, we pass through the same timeless landscape where the friar had seen the apparition.

The late afternoon sky is cobalt blue, almost as dark as the blackness of outer space, or the eyes of a lover we have known, whose face, when seen once, resides forever in our memory.

The rugged cliffs of the Sangre de Christo Mountains are washed in the blood red of the setting sun. The midwinter snow that dusts this landscape is a luminescent, brittle white.

Stepping into the little adobe cantina at the side of the road we are greeted with an enveloping warmth. The aroma from the smoldering pine caresses our senses as our eyes adjust to the dim light of the room. The layers of soot which streak the old beehive fireplace built into the corner of the room have been more than a century in the making. The fire-place may perhaps be newer than the one inside the kiva at the pueblo up on the hill, but it has been around longer than the memory of anyone now living.

This tavern too is ancient and timeless, and soaked in the wild and distant history of the American Southwest that seems so real and tangible when you are here.

The tequila, dark and seductive, is poured from a bottle that has no label. It goes down smoothly, warming the throat the way the wood fire warms the soul. Our empty glasses are jewellike as the fire light shines through.

The stranger at the bar is no stranger. We are the strangers here.

"Where y'from?" starts the conversation.

Within moments, he knows a great deal about us.

We know nothing about him.

Another round of tequila, and the conversation twists and turns like the highway which brought us here.

"Lots of people who pass through talk about the lost mines and the old Spanish gold," he nods after he has heard us out. "No, I wouldn't exactly call it a myth . . . unless you want to use the word in a . . . well, a literary way."

"But, cities of *gold*? No way," we insist.

He shrugs with a wry smile which replies that there are no words to answer this question wrapped in an assertion.

We refill our glasses, and learn that our friend knows somebody who knows somebody, and with that he begins his story. The only way to answer our question is through parable.

Outside, it grows pitch black, and the temperature drops, but we are unaware. There is no one else in the cantina, except the bartender, and he is in the back doing something, but we don't notice.

We started out skeptical, as I suppose most people do. But now we believe the man at the bar. We believe what he describes because he has been there, and because we have been told that others have seen it too.

Mainly, though, we believe him because we want to believe him. We want so much to believe that at the core of the myth—and I use the word in a literary way—the stories which consumed the passions of so many for so long are real.

In his words, we can see it. We can look into his eyes in the flickering light of the old beehive fireplace and see it crouched upon its throne, the City of Gold.

✳

PEOPLE HAVE BEEN CHASING the shadow of the cities of gold across the Western Hemisphere for centuries. While it is the stuff of fairy tales to most, even today people devote their lives to searching, knowing that they will be the ones to find the elusive golden city. They have been chasing it across the mesas of the American Southwest, the cloud-shrouded peaks of the Andes, and through the inhospitable jungles of the Amazon watershed which explorers characterized as a "green hell."

They have been chasing it, not because there is a great body of rational evidence, but because, deep down in their heart and soul, they want it to be real.

The first men who lost themselves in the quest came to a place they called the "New World." It wasn't the "New Island," or the "New Place," or even the "New Continent." It was the New *World*.

They began coming as the fifteenth century was melting into the sixteenth, and as the Renaissance—with all of its lofty, liberating promises—was transforming Europe, and burning away the Dark Ages. They came with a change of mood, in which enthusiasm and ambition had edged out centuries of apprehension about the far horizon. They came at a time when the far horizon came to be regarded as a gateway, not as a barrier.

The New World was a land that went on and on, a land of which European common knowledge before 1492 had little inkling. It was a blank slate for the imagination.

Into this land, the dreamers could read all sorts of possibilities. As the dreams—specifically the dreams of wealth— really did start to come true, the possibilities seemed limitless. When the conquistadors first made contact with the Aztec and Inca empires, they found civilizations literally dripping with gold. This evidence made it easy to believe the stories of yet greater wealth just beyond the next horizon, and those stories continue to be spun.

In the myth and literature of the American West, there is an archetype, a stock character who appears in most treasure tales. He is the wily, grizzled old prospector who is the spinner of yarns, and the yarns usually speak of wealth.

Where? Just beyond the next horizon, of course.

Sometimes he has an old treasure map, or a yellowed manuscript that was old when your great-grandfather was young. Always, he has a story.

Though a fixture in Old West stories, the yarn-spinning prospector has inhabited the coffeehouses and cantinas of the New World from the moment that the first greedy European sat down willing to listen to stories of easy wealth. He is the man with a faraway look in his eyes, and fantastic tales on his lips—fantastic in all senses of the word. He is the man we believe because we want to.

He was, of course, alive and well long before that. Myths and rumors of fabulous wealth in some distant city had entered the stream of European popular consciousness long before the Spanish first set foot in the Americas. Stories of mysterious, wealthy kingdoms in Africa and Asia had always been alive in the castles and seaport taverns across Europe. Accounts of these astonishing places, such as the chimerical kingdom of Prester John, were told and retold so often that they were assumed to be true.

When the sixteenth century was still young, the great villain and conquistador Francisco de Pizarro sat down in a bar with a sea captain named Pascual de Andagoya, who recounted some fabulous tales. On the face of it, his stories were far-fetched, and improbable in the extreme. Pizarro had every reason to finish his drink and walk away, but the century was young, and he had nothing to lose.

Andagoya's ludicrous yarn brought Pizarro to the Inca city of Cusco, which revealed gold and silver beyond belief.

The Spanish stole from the Aztec and the Inca, then found their gold and silver mines. Later, the Spanish enslaved the indigenous people to work these mines. Thousands of tons of gold and silver were shipped to Spain through the seventeenth century. On the way, so much of it was lost in

Caribbean shipwrecks that finding this treasure is still creating wealthy people in the twenty-first century. Much more of the gold reached Spain, making it Europe's richest country and initiating the *Siglo de Oro*, Spain's Golden Age.

"This metal [gold] was rare in Europe," the historian Jean Descola writes. "When Christopher Columbus embarked for the West Indies, Europe's store of gold and silver did not exceed a thousand million gold francs. . . . Cast in a single ingot, all Europe's gold would have formed a cube only two meters in each dimension. . . . From 1503 (the year in which Columbus completed his fourth voyage) until 1560 (that in which Francisco Fajardo laid the first stones of Caracas), the New World sent Spain 101 metric tons of gold, or nearly 225,000 pounds."

Fernand Braudel, writing in *The Wheels of Commerce*, calculates that the reserves of New World gold and silver in the Spanish treasury had reached the modern equivalent of around $2 trillion by the middle of the sixteenth century—and that's only the reserves, and only the first half of that golden century.

The nineteenth-century anthropologist and historian Adolph Bandelier mentions the anecdote of four ships which arrived in Spain from Peru on December 5, 1533, January 9, 1534, and June 3, 1534. They carried, "without including golden vessels and ornaments, 708,590 pesos in gold and 240,680 pesos in silver." At the time, Spanish pesos were roughly equivalent to pounds sterling, making the total value of these four shipments worth at least $115 million in today's dollars.

Of silver, Descola points out that in just the four decades between 1560 and 1600, Spain mined, shipped, and received an amount that was double the total stock which had existed in Europe prior to the voyages of Columbus. There was so much of it that it had a heavy impact on the European economy. Bandelier reminds us that "the value of silver fell about 84 percent in Europe between 1514 and 1610."

Against the backdrop of the tons of gold and silver that had been plundered from the Aztec and the Inca, it was easy to believe those sweet stories of yet more cities of gold lying across the next range of mountains, just beyond the horizon.

*

OF COURSE, IT WAS NOT JUST the Spanish who succumbed to the venom of the gold bug. Some of the earliest treasure seekers were Germans, and as time went on, there were also the Portuguese, the English, and eventually the Americans. Though England's signature sixteenth-century soldiers of fortune, Francis Drake and Walter Raleigh, were arguably best remembered in the New World for pirating Spanish treasure ships, Raleigh later took up chasing the shadows of cities of gold.

Soon after Pizarro conquered the Inca, there were stories of yet another fabulous city of gold which was presided over by a king covered in gold dust who was called the "Gilded One," or El Dorado. Pizarro's own half-brother risked everything to find this place. The fact that he came up empty-handed was no deterrent to others, for El Dorado became one of the most enduring myths of the New World. In the twenty-first century, people are still seeking El Dorado.

Yet El Dorado is merely one of many sites of supposed riches. South America still holds as its secrets the mysterious cities of Manoa, Paititi, and others, while in North America there are those who still seek the Seven Cities of Cibola and Quivira—or at least the obscure sources of their rumored wealth.

There is an old axiom about how gold fever can turn men into fools, and that such fools do crazy things. Do the gold-seekers, once bitten, chase the shadows because they want to believe—or because they need to believe?

The twentieth-century explorer Leonard Clark wrote that "treasure hunters burn with a faith and trust incomprehensible to the man in the street. Once he sees a treasure map, he will believe even his worst enemy, let alone a friend. I was here [buying a treasure map] because of that belief, and here was a real map to substantiate that faith and hope."

This is the story of five centuries of quixotic quests based on rumor and innuendo, on fable and fantasy, which have captured the lust and the imaginations of many generations of treasure-seekers—not all of whom came home empty-handed.

It is their story, the story of those who have faced and over-come unimaginable adversity to cross that one last horizon, where they are sure they will come face to face with that golden city, crouched upon its throne, blazing in the glory of fire stolen from the sun itself.

I

THE MOST
EXCELLENT OF METALS

Gold is a thing so much the more necessary to your majesty, because, in order to fulfill the ancient prophecy, Jerusalem is to be rebuilt by a prince of the Spanish monarchy. Gold is the most excellent of metals. What becomes of those precious stones, which are sought for at the extremities of the globe? They are sold, and are finally converted into gold. With gold we not only do whatever we please in this world, but we can even employ it to snatch souls from Purgatory, and to people Paradise.

—Christopher Columbus, in his last letter to King Ferdinand (July 7, 1503) as quoted by Alexander von Humboldt

IT WAS ABOUT THE GOLD. Some have written that it was about politics or commerce, about adventure or even spices. Some have written that it was about religion, that it was about saving souls or about a diabolical plot to enslave the hearts, minds, or bodies of indigenous peoples.

To a greater or lesser degree it was about all of these things, but mainly it was about the gold.

What was "it" about which we speak?

"It" was the grand Spanish incursion, adventure, and colonization within the Western Hemisphere. It made Spain and its ruling elite richer and more powerful than any other of their European contemporaries, but at the same time fired an obsession for even more wealth.

It all began, as we were taught in American history class in school, in October 1492. It began, we have long been told, with an Italian navigator who had convinced two Spanish monarchs that he could get to the East by sailing west.

Why were they so interested in the "East"?

They were all looking for the shortest distance between two places, but they were, to use a twentieth-century phrase, following the money.

One of the first questions Columbus asked upon landing in the Western Hemisphere was, "where is the gold?"

The European obsession with the riches of the East went back centuries. Beginning with accounts written by the Apostle Thomas, popular tales had circulated in Europe and the Holy Land of a man named Prester John, also known as Presbyter Johannes, the mythical mystical patriarch who ruled a fantastically wealthy Christian kingdom somewhere out there beyond Asia Minor and the Euxine Sea (Black Sea). This kingdom was in a place so far to the east that it remained just out of reach, just across that next horizon, whenever someone went looking.

There were the myths and there were the realities. However, the realities that did crop up in tangible form—amulets, statuettes, fabrics, spices, and gems—only served to make the myths seem plausible. As trade goods from the East began to flow into Europe from Asia after the Crusades, it became evident that there were vast riches out there. Gold was rare in Europe and plentiful in the lands east of the Mediterranean. The stories, naturally embellished in the telling and retelling, made the precious metal seem more plentiful than it was.

Two centuries before Columbus sailed westward to the East, Marco Polo made his epic eastward trek to the East, where he met Kublai Khan and returned with tales of fantastic wealth. Soon, traders were plying the difficult Silk Road and further whetting the European appetite for gold, and the European willingness to believe tall tales about gold and golden kingdoms.

In China and India, the traders likely heard tales of places even farther to the east, places such as the golden kingdom of Suvarnadvipa. Like the empire of Prester John, its exact location was described only as "somewhere." It was said to have been on the Malay Peninsula, or in the East Indies, the islands which Columbus later thought he had reached.

Gold has long been a catalyst for exploration. As Adolph Bandelier of the Archaeological Institute of America pointed out in the nineteenth century:

> In every age gold has presented one of the strongest means of enticing men from their homes to remote lands, and of promoting trade between distant regions and the settlement of previously uninhabited districts. We have received from the earliest antiquity the stories of the voyage of the Argonauts, of the expedition of Hercules after the golden apples of the Hesperides, and of the settlement of the Phoenicians in Spain, the gold of which they carried to the Syrian coast. For gold the Semitic navigators sailed from the Red Sea to Tarshish and Ophir.

For all those willing to believe in tall tales and mythic lands to the east, there were those who believed in rich and mysterious lands in other directions. For more than a millennium, many people had believed in the existence of lost continents somewhere in the Atlantic. The Greek explorer Pytheas wrote in the fourth century B.C. of a land far to the north called Thule, while in his dialogues *Timaeus* and *Critias*, written that same century, Plato first revealed the story of Atlantis, the great seafaring civilization to the west which a cataclysm had sunk to the bottom of the sea in a single day. These were merely two examples of the myths of what lay beyond the horizon, "out there somewhere."

By the close of the fifteenth century, Europeans were about to alter the course of their history in pursuit of that "somewhere."

Even as Columbus sailed westward to bring light into the the sea Europeans feared for its darkness, the Renaissance was blossoming in the duchies and kingdoms of his homeland, the Italian Peninsula. Just as the Renaissance was an awakening of innovation and outlook in architecture, the arts, science, technology, and critical thought, a new generation of sea captains was about to begin redrawing obsolete maps in a search for a water route to the East.

As the Portuguese captain Vasco da Gama would sail south and east around Africa in 1497, acting on reports of gold being plentiful along the horn of that continent, Christopher Columbus sailed westward in 1492. While da Gama coasted southward, Columbus sailed straight into that dangerous and forbidding place which was labeled on the maps of the time as *Mare Tenebrosum*, the Sea of Darkness. It was the oceanic analog of the familiar terrestrial cartographic inscription *terra incognita*, the unexplored or obscured land. It was an uncharted place of mystery and legend, where sea monsters, whirlpools, and strange storms were thought to lie in wait to annihilate all comers. Historian Jean Descola described this Sea of Darkness as "the great devourer of lost paradises and sunken empires."

Descola was referring to mythical Atlantis, but he could well have been speaking of what lay in store for the population of this New World about to be "discovered." He could also have been describing what would lie in store for Spain, the European power destined to conquer and exploit most of the Western Hemisphere.

Columbus discovered America?

This truism, once taught in the textbooks, is not, of course, literally true. When Columbus landed in an island in what is now the Bahamas and called it San Salvador, in the Western Hemisphere there were tens of millions of people whose ancestors had lived in these continents for two dozen millennia or more. They had obviously discovered the place.

Though Columbus himself was not fully aware of what he accomplished, what he had discovered was that there were two hemispheres, or two "worlds." In turn, his discovery initiated a series of expeditions by others, who brought this into the mainstream of common knowledge in Europe within a

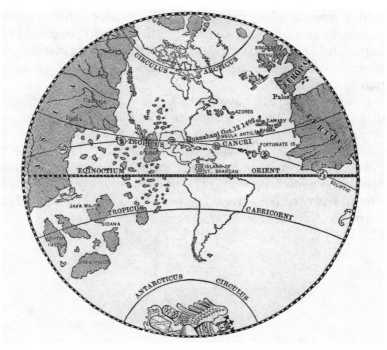

In 1491–1493, even as Columbus was at sea, Martin von Behaim of Nürnberg was creating a map of a spherical world, as well as a spherical globe. The Western Hemisphere is seen here superimposed upon the islands which legends supposed lay in the Atlantic Ocean between Europe and Asia.

generation. Before Columbus, though a few European explorers had crossed the Atlantic to stand on what we now call the Western Hemisphere, notably the Norsemen, there was no common knowledge on either side of the Atlantic that there was an opposite coast across the ocean.

Even those who believed that the earth was spherical did not imagine a land mass on the scale of the Americas. The prevailing theory, and that to which Columbus continued to subscribe, was that the land on the other side was actually Asia.

The voyage of Columbus altered the course of European thinking with regard to the size, the scale, and the shape of the world. After Columbus came others, and by 1522 the expedition of Ferdinand Magellan had circumnavigated the earth.

In a few decades, the true dimensions of what romantic Europeans came to refer to as the "New World" began to take shape, and it was vast beyond the wildest imagination, surpassing the most grandiose description of a lost continent such as Atlantis.

In describing the voyages of Columbus and the others of his generation, the storytellers told of human adventure, and conjured up the pure romance of venturing into the unknown. Yet, the driving force was gold. The tip of the spear in the vanguard of exploration may have included men—and even a handful of women—with a lust for adventure and probably a streak of madness, but the underlying desire was for gold.

2

INTO THE
BATTLEGROUND
OF AVARICE

The gold worn around the finger of an elegant lady or as a crown on the head of a king has more often than not passed through hands of creatures who would make that king or that elegant lady shudder. There is little doubt that gold is oftener bathed in human blood than in hot suds. A noble king who wished to show his high-mindedness could do no better than have his crown made of iron. Gold is for thieves and swindlers. For this reason they own most of it. The rest is owned by those who do not care where the gold comes from or in what sort of hands it has been.

—B. Traven, *The Treasure of the Sierra Madre* (1927)

IN RETROSPECT, IT IS AMAZING that only three decades, the years 1492–1522, separate Columbus's first timid step into the *Mare Tenebrosum* and the completion of the Magellan expedition. In that time, the notion that the "New World" truly was an enormous, continental-scale land mass was confirmed, and European expeditions along much of its coastline had been completed or were in progress.

Also amazing is how swiftly the Spanish moved to exploit their discovery of the New World. During those same three decades, outposts established on the islands of the Caribbean grew into Spanish cities. Initial disappointment in finding that the New World was not the opulent "East" gave way to a realization that the New World did contain potentially immense riches of its own.

The Spanish found that the love of gold was not restricted to Europeans and their trading partners back on the eastern side of the spherical earth. The people of the New World, whom Columbus dubbed "Indians," because he thought he had found the East Indies, were a great deal like the people of the actual East Indies. Like people throughout the "Old World," the Indians of the New World mined gold and used it for jewelry and precious objects.

Spearheading the Spanish exploration and exploitation were the conquistadors, meaning "conquerors." They were leaders of armies whose official status lay somewhere between that of paramilitary soldiers of fortune and instruments of official Spanish foreign policy. Among the conquistadors active in those three decades are several whose names have been quite familiar to us since elementary school. There was Vasco Núñez de Balboa, who was the first to claim the Pacific Ocean for Spain, and Juan Ponce de León, who explored Florida and the Caribbean in search of the Fountain of Youth. Then there was Hernán Cortés (also known as Hernándo Cortez), who subdued the Aztec Empire, which had been Middle America's dominant power for a century.

In defeating the Aztec in 1521, the year before the Magellan expedition returned to Spain, Cortés crushed a civilization so rich in art and scientific accomplishment that it could have stood shoulder to shoulder with its contemporary, Renaissance Europe. It was also rich in gold. Though the West Indies yielded some, but disappointingly little of the glittering metal, Cortés and the conquistadors who made the initial ventures into Mexico discovered that this was a truly gilded land.

Cortés had first arrived in the New World in 1504 at age eighteen, electrified by stories of the exploits of Columbus. He started out as a ranch hand on the island of Hispaniola, worked his way into land ownership, and in 1511, accompanied Diego Velásquez de Cuellar in his conquest of Cuba. In

1518, Velásquez ordered Cortés, now married to Velásquez's sister, to lead an expedition into the interior of Mexico. Though he later withdrew his order, Cortés went anyway, and set in motion major events.

Cortés briefly visited the Yucatan Peninsula early in 1519, but made a primary landing that summer at the harbor called San Juan de Ulua by the Spanish. This was near present-day Veracruz, and due east of the Aztec capital of Tenochtitlan, now called Mexico City.

Hernán Cortés (*Bill Yenne*)

Bernal Díaz del Castillo, who accompanied Cortés, penned a memoir of these escapades, entitled in part *A True and Full Account of the Discovery and Conquest of México and New Spain.* In this firsthand account, he writes of being greeted by Aztec and other indigenous people offering golden gifts, "to insure our good friendship." He adds that almost immediately, the conquistadors learned that the "newly-discovered country. . . . abounded in gold mines."

As much as the New World people valued gold, and they valued it a great deal, they also valued European trade goods, some of which they had never seen before. They were therefore willing, and often eager, to trade gold for objects as inconsequential to the Spanish as glass beads. This, in turn, led the Spanish to the misconception that the people of the New World trivialized the value of gold because they had it in such abundance and were so generous in trading it.

Díaz writes that they were met by emissaries of Moctezuma, the Aztec emperor, who

> produced the presents and spread them out on a mat, over which they had first thrown some cotton cloths. The first was a round plate, about the size of a wagon wheel, representing the sun, the whole of the finest gold, and of the most beautiful workmanship; a most extraordinary work of art, which, according to the account of those who weighed it, was worth above 20,000 gold pesos. The second was a round plate, even

larger than the former, of massive silver, representing the moon, with rays and other figures on it, being of great value. The third was the casque, completely filled with pure grains of gold, as they are found in the mines, worth about 3,000 pesos, which was more to us than if it had been ten times the value, as we now knew for certain there were rich gold mines in the country.

According to Díaz, upon meeting Cortés, Moctezuma was so generous with the conquistador that he offered to hand over "all the treasures contained in the secret chamber. There was such a vast heap of it that we were occupied three days in taking all out of the different corners of this secret room, and in looking them over; we were even obliged to send for Moctezuma's goldsmiths from Escapuzalco to assist us."

If it had not been before, it was certainly at this point that the Spanish lust for New World gold was whetted to the verge of madness.

Díaz later mentions that "on our proceeding to the great temple, and passing the courtyards adjoining the market, we observed numbers of other merchants, who dealt in gold dust as it is dug out of the mines, which was exposed to sale in tubes made of the bones of large geese, which had been worked to such a thin substance, and were so white that the gold shone through them."

Díaz also speaks highly of the skill of craftsmanship, writing of "sculptors, and the gold and silversmiths, who were clever in working and smelting gold, and would have astonished the most celebrated of our Spanish goldsmiths . . . the number of these was very great."

If the Spanish underestimated the Aztec value for gold, there was no obfuscating the greed of the Spanish themselves. In the story of the Cortés expedition included in his *General History of the Indies*, Spanish historian Francisco López de Gómara asserts that Cortés issued an order that Moctezuma should be led to believe that the Spanish cared little about gold.

However, Díaz, who was there, takes exception, writing that the emperor "knew very well how the matter stood on this point . . . he might also easily guess what we were after, when we begged of him to send us the casque full of golden

A copy of an Aztec drawing showing Moctezuma, seated, discussing his ransom with Cortés. Cortés's interpreter is standing by his side.

grains, and our daily bartering for that metal. The Mexicans, indeed, are not the kind of folks to be thus imposed upon."

The conquistadors had been overcome by the gold bug's venom and there was no disguising this fact. At first, this probably amused Moctezuma. In his accounts of the emperor's entertaining Cortés at his palace in Tenochtitlan, Díaz speaks of Moctezuma's willingness to discuss both the locations of his richest gold mines, and technical nuances of using sluices to extract gold from streams.

"Cortés and all of us were astonished at this generosity and great goodness of the monarch," Díaz effuses, "and we took off our caps very respectfully, and thanked him."

A year later Moctezuma was dead, having been caught up in an intrigue between his houseguests, the Spanish conquistadors, and elements among Aztec nobility who disliked and distrusted him for his cordiality toward Cortés. Whether he was killed by a Spaniard or an Aztec is still a subject of controversy.

In the war which then ensued, Cortés crushed the Aztec Empire, claimed it for the Spanish crown, named it "Nueva España" ("New Spain"), and became its governor. In the last year of those momentous three decades after the first voyage of Columbus, Hernán Cortés became the first European-born ruler of Mexico. Perhaps most important, this new lord of the erstwhile Aztec Empire knew where the gold mines were— or at least some of them.

New Spain, which became a Spanish viceroyalty fourteen years later, included not only the former Aztec Empire, but all of Mexico as well as Central America and what is now the western United States—despite most of this territory remaining a *terra incognita* unexplored by Europeans for many years to come. The fact of this claim would guide the course of the history of the region, and the Spanish exploration and exploitation of it, through the sixteenth century and beyond.

3

BLINDED BY
GOLDEN SUNS

Gold, generally speaking, is the great desire of man
. . . the more he possesses of it the more avaricious he
grows.
—Bernal Díaz del Castillo, *True and Full Account of the
Discovery and Conquest of México and New Spain* (1632)

IN THE SPACE of about a dozen years, Spanish conquistadors
defeated and subjugated the two most important empires in
the Western Hemisphere, perhaps the richest and politically
most powerful kingdoms which had ever existed on that side
of the globe. The Aztec Empire fell to Hernán Cortés, the
Inca Empire to Francisco Pizarro.

The empires of the Aztec and the Inca had both evolved
gradually, and each had stood at the height of its glory for
about a century when it was vanquished by the Spanish
sword. Both lost their independence to become a jewel in the
crown of the Flemish-born Holy Roman Emperor Charles V,
who also bore the titles of King of Spain, King of Italy, Duke
of Burgundy, and Lord of the Netherlands. His four-million-
square-kilometer empire eventually stretched from Vienna to
Manila Bay.

The empires of the Aztec and the Inca both succumbed
easily to Spanish troops wielding military technology previ-

ously unimagined in the Western Hemisphere. Each empire was overcome in battle by armies with fewer troops than George Armstrong Custer commanded during his milestone defeat by indigenous people at the Little Bighorn in 1876.

Even as the military technology of the conquistadors shocked and awed the Aztec and Inca, the Spanish found both empires' wealth in gold, silver, and precious gems almost beyond what they could comprehend. Indeed, each probably controlled more tons of gold at the beginning of the sixteenth century than all the countries in Europe combined.

It was Cortés, the conqueror of the Aztec Empire, who inspired his distant cousin. Francisco Pizarro was a decade older than Cortés, born to a poor, unmarried mother sometime in the early 1470s. Pizarro arrived in the New World in 1502, two years ahead of Cortés, and settled in Panama. At the time, Panama was part of the Spanish dominion of Nuevo Reino de Granada (New Kingdom of Granada), which also included what is now northern Colombia and Venezuela.

Pizarro was a member of Vasco Núñez de Balboa's expedition when he first saw the Pacific in 1513, but spent most of his first two decades in the Western Hemisphere as an underachieving petty bureaucrat.

By all accounts, Francisco Pizarro was a cruel man with a sour disposition who was liked by no one. However, he was a competent manager, because he rose through the bureaucracy, eventually becoming the alcalde, or mayor, of Panama City—which was evolving into an important crossroads of trade in Spanish America. Again, all accounts have him being one of those middle-management types who rules by intimidation rather than inspiration. They say he was ambitious, but his desire for wealth and glory did not truly manifest itself until he was approaching middle age. When it did, however, it was to the extreme.

During the early 1520s, stories were drifting back to Panama, telling of wealthy cities along the northern and western coasts of what is now South America, and being retold in the cantinas of every port city where soldiers of fortune gathered to drink, gamble, and exchange tall tales. At first, they were rumors related by Spaniards who had heard them from Indians, who had heard them from other Indians. Soon they caught the ears of alcaldes and generals.

In 1522, Pizarro crossed paths with Pascual de Andagoya, a sea captain who had been there (at least as far as present-day Ecuador), and who had seen the gold, or at least he had met people who *had* seen the gold. "There" was a place on the west coast which the locals called Virú or Pirú, and which the Spanish would later call Peru. For Pizarro, meeting Andagoya was the sixteenth-century version of the standard tale of the old prospector spinning yarns of a ledge of gold—so long as the shots of tequila keep coming. There was just enough fact to keep it interesting. However, in this case, the spinner of yarns was not lying.

Pizarro was hooked.

In 1524, inspired by the apparently easy victory by Cortés in Mexico, by Andagoya's tales, and by his own growing lust for the fame and fortune that had so far eluded him, Pizarro outfitted an expedition. When it failed due to bad weather somewhere off Colombia, he tried again two years later.

His second attempt made it farther down the coast, where Pizarro captured a trading vessel operated by some native people. Aboard, among the trade goods, he found gold, silver, and gemstones. Nothing fires the passionate seeker like a small taste of that which he seeks. Though forced to turn back again due to exhaustion, Pizarro returned a third time, and a fourth, making contact ashore with subjects of the Incan Empire.

By now, this empire had been the largest in the Western Hemisphere for more than eighty years. It was larger than the Aztec Empire, and probably the largest ever to exist in pre-Columbian America. The Inca civilization emerged around the twelfth century A.D., but it was preceded by other earlier cultures of note. These included the Ica-Nazca culture of what is now southern Peru, and the Moche, or Mochican, culture of northwestern Peru.

The Moche civilization, which flourished from around the first through eighth centuries A.D., reached its high point in about the sixth century. During this time, they developed an extraordinarily complex artistic tradition, manifested in pottery, textiles, and gold. Some of the most remarkable Moche archaeological finds and golden treasures would not be unearthed until the twenty-first century.

In the 1440s, the Inca under Patchacuti had expanded their holdings until they included virtually all of the west coast of South America from the Pacific to, and across, the Andes. At its greatest extent, it stretched for more than 5,000 miles from the frosty sub-Antarctic tip of Chile to the murky equatorial coastal jungles in southern Colombia.

The term Inca (spelled "Inka" under late twentieth-century Peruvian spelling conventions) actually meant ruler, or ruling class, in the local Quechua language. The Spanish initially referred to the empires as *Imperio Inca*, and the word came to be applied to the land and its people as well.

The people and the Inca rulers, however, called the empire Tahuantinsuyo (also written as Tahuantinsuyu or Tawantin-suyo), meaning "the four corners of the Earth." They had no conception of there being any significant earthly land beyond their control. As Jean Descola puts it, "this empire regarded itself as the world. Tahuantinsuyo—the four quarters of the world! In the Inca universe there was no place for a fifth. Space and time did not exist for the lords of Perú. The word 'tomorrow' was unknown to the people, and laws and statistics were for eternity."

Writing in *1491: New Revelations of the Americas Before Columbus*, Charles C. Mann reminds us that in that year Tahuantinsuyo was the largest empire in the world, "bigger than Ming Dynasty China, bigger that Ivan the Great's expanding Russia, bigger than Songay in the Sahel or Powerful Great Zimbabwe in the West African tablelands, bigger than the cresting Ottoman Empire, bigger than the Triple Alliance (as the Aztec empire is more precisely known), bigger by far than any European state." Tahuantinsuyo was even larger than the Holy Roman Empire when it was first inherited by Charles V.

Like the Aztec, the Inca had a complex culture. They were technically advanced in fields such as architecture and astronomy. They built cities with grand structures and vast public spaces that are often compared with those of ancient Egypt. However, unlike the Old World civilizations, both the Aztec and the Inca did it all without beasts of burden which could be ridden by adults, and without ever having developed the wheel.

The Inca were gifted metal smiths, but they never made use of iron for tools and weapons, even though iron ore was available. Their smiths, like their ruling class, were focused on the metals which were associated with, and used to celebrate, the centerpieces of their religion and cosmology—silver for the moon, and brilliant, gleaming gold for the all-powerful sun.

Francisco Pizarro.
(*Bill Yenne*)

In 1528, Francisco Pizarro returned to Spain, where he was received by Charles V. The monarch listened to the stories of the Inca Tahuantinsuyo and to the rumors of the extent of its wealth. Like any person, Charles was susceptible to the sweet seduction of the gold bug. So too was his young wife, Isabel of Portugal, who was the one who actually signed off on the paperwork authorizing Francisco Pizarro to take possession of Peru and Tahuantinsuyo on behalf of her husband's empire.

Unbeknownst, of course, to the Inca themselves, this decree called for their empire to be known as Nueva Castile (New Castile), and to be ruled in the name of Charles V by his designated governor—Francisco Pizarro.

The actual taking of possession finally began in 1532, with Pizarro winning his initial skirmishes, and founding the city of Piura, the first Spanish city in Peru, and the first south of Colombia. He then sent Hernándo de Soto, one of his lieutenants and a future explorer of North America, to scout the interior of Peru.

Meanwhile, Huayna Capac, who was the Sapa Inca (the "Great Inca," analogous to an emperor) had died, and there had been an internal power struggle between his son and heir Huáscar, and his illegitimate son Atahualpa. Huayna Capac had actually divided his realm between the boys, but after his death, each wanted it all.

By the time that Pizarro reached the interior of Peru with his small army, Atahualpa had prevailed in the civil war and was ensconced with his own army at Cajamarca. Through de

Soto, Atahualpa invited Pizarro to come see him. Initially, the meeting was cordial, with the Inca putting on a dazzling show of wealth and a lavish parade of costumed and decorated troops.

Atahualpa, as Pizarro first met him, is colorfully described by George Makepeace Towle in his book *Pizarro: His Adventures and Conquests.* Paraphrasing Pizarro's own account, *El Testamento de Pizarro,* published in 1539, Towle writes that Atahualpa appeared

> seated on a throne of massive gold upon a lofty litter, and surrounded by other litters on which sat many of his great nobles. It was a most imposing sight to see this mighty monarch seated high above the heads of those who surrounded him, the gorgeous plumes that adorned his diadem waving and nodding in the air, the blood red fringe covering his swarthy brow, his long robe falling in heavy folds over the sides of the glittering litter, and a wide collar of large and dazzling emeralds fastened about his neck; while on either side of the litter gathered a group of courtiers, more brilliantly arrayed than any who had yet entered the square, and wearing coronets of silver and gold. As Atahualpa was borne forward, his countenance betrayed the serene expression of true majesty, that disdained to show emotion even if he felt it. He glanced quietly around, and looked at the little group of Spanish chiefs, who awaited him at the farther end of the square, with an air of quiet and confident dignity.

But things turned bad. Pizarro was on a mission, and that was to take possession of Tahuantinsuyo. He offered to make Atahualpa his puppet, but it is not surprising that this preposterous proposal was rebuffed.

It was time for war.

The ensuing Battle of Cajamarca on November 16, 1532, was the turning point in the history of South America.

Pizarro had fewer than two hundred troops and fewer than one hundred horses. He was outnumbered by Atahualpa's army several hundred to one. However, the conquistadors had firearms, cannons, armored cavalry, and steel swords—all weapons unknown to the Inca. Pizarro began his surprise attack with an artillery barrage which stampeded the Inca troops. In turn, these people who were unfamiliar with animals as large as a horse, were then attacked by mounted swordsmen.

The meeting of Pizarro and Atahualpa drawn by Poma de Ayala in the sixteenth century.

The bloodbath wrought by the conquistadors decimated the Inca army, as well as much of the civilian population.

After the battle, Atahualpa gave Pizarro a room full of gold and two of silver to secure his release, but the conquistador kept him captive in deliberate emulation of Cortés having kept Moc-tezuma under house arrest. In July 1533, with no more use for Atahualpa, Pizarro had Tahuantinsuyo's last Inca Sapa executed.

In November 1533, one year after Cajamarca, Pizarro's invading army reached Cusco, the Inca capital city, essentially wrapping up his conquest of the Tahuantinsuyo. In his study of the conquistadors, Jean Descola reminds us that everything in the highly centralized world that was Tahuantinsuyo converged on Cusco: "defiles, roads, and canals, as well as thoughts and prayers. Cusco was for the Perúvians what Rome was for the Latins: the economic, political, and religious capital."

Centuries in the making and nearly a century at the apogee of its glory, it had fallen to a battalion-strength force in one major battle and a few skirmishes. In subduing the greatest empire in the Western Hemisphere, Pizarro had exploited its greatest weakness, the centuries-old political machine itself.

As Descola writes, "the machine, constructed for perpetual motion, was well oiled—too well—for to stop it Pizarro had only to capture Atahualpa and block the controlling lever. . . . The weakness of the regime was that by striking at the head, the entire organization could be crumbled. Separated from the Inca, the officials could no longer administrate and the elite were disoriented. To be sure, the people remained, but they had been taught only one thing, to obey, and they obeyed. Twelve million Perúvians, but ten million robots."

Of course, we are reminded by recent historical analysis of the period that the Spanish conquistadors had an important ally that even they did not understand. Disease, especially smallpox, would also ravage the Inca population, just as it would later impact the indigenous people of North America.

It was in Cusco that Pizarro's dreams of golden wealth were fully realized. Describing the Inca palaces, George Makepeace Towle writes: "If you had approached one of them, you would have seen a long, low building of stone, roofed with wood, and would not have been struck by its appearance. But, once within the doors, you would have been fairly bewildered and dazzled by its adornment. You would have observed that in the walls were fitted finely fashioned devices in silver and gold; and that in alcoves, at frequent intervals, statues of the same precious metals were placed. There were hangings of gorgeous cloths; and the Inca was served, when he dined in these palaces, upon heavy gold plate, and with pitchers and ewers thickly studded with large-sized gems."

Towle goes on to add that the

> noblest and most superb among these temples was that which stood in Cusco, the capital of the empire, and which was called both 'The Temple of the Sun' and The Place of Gold. . . . On one of the walls blazed an enormous effigy of the Sun, in burnished gold, the glittering rays shooting out from the central orb to the remotest corner of the ceiling, and down to the very floor. The orb itself was fashioned to represent the face of the Deity, and upon it appeared many brilliant jewels. The other walls were almost concealed behind the huge golden ornaments fastened into them, and the cornice of the temple consisted of massive bars of gold."

Pizarro also described another temple, dedicated to the Moon, in which a similar effigy was made of "shining silver."

A nineenth-century artist's conception of the Inca Temple of the Sun.

A looting spree then ensued, although by Pizarro's account, he made the looting of private homes off limits. Everywhere else in the capital was fair game, though. According to Mara Louise Pratt-Chadwick, referencing Pizarro's *El Testamento*, "the soldiers, eager for more treasures, ransacked the public buildings, tore the golden frescoes from the walls of the temples, and even entered the sacred vaults of the dead, robbing them of the funeral ornaments and golden urns."

To this, Towle adds that "all the treasure thus found was brought into the square, melted down, and divided, as before, proportionately among the officers and men; and, when this had been done, the humblest and most obscure Spaniard among them might count himself a rich man. The soldiers found themselves so rich, indeed, that they began to gamble furiously; and many a soldier thus played away in a week the fortune he had won by long hardship and suffering, and found himself a beggar again."

His conquest complete, Pizarro installed Manco Inca Yupanqui, another son of Huayna Capac, and a brother of Atahualpa, as his puppet. Pizarro also married their teenaged sister, Quispe Sisa, who had previously been the conquistador's concubine, and who had converted to Catholicism as "Ines Yupanqui." She bore him two children.

Because Cusco was too far inland and too high in the Andes to be conveniently supplied, Pizarro established the port city of Lima as the capital of Nueva Castile, and built his own palace there.

His reign was a short one, and dogged by political infighting between himself and his brothers on one side, and factions loyal to his former lieutenant, Diego Almagro, on the other. Pizarro prevailed, defeating Almagro in battle in 1538 and executing him. Three years later, in June 1541, a group of thugs, called "Almagristas," working for Diego Almagro II broke into Pizarro's palace and killed him.

In his final thoughts about the conquistador of Peru, Jean Descola notes that Francisco Pizarro died alone, both literally and figuratively: "From the first day to the last he had had no other love and no other companion but himself, and he remained constantly faithful to this austere solitude. Yet it must be emphasized that he desired this solitude. It had become, by the end of his life, the only climate in which his pride could live. When a man believes himself to be the elect of God and the interpreter of History, he can tolerate no one."

Late in the twentieth century, the trend toward revising history to paint all fifteenth- and sixteenth-century explorers as avaricious, rapacious scoundrels was ironically kind to Pizarro. By this, we mean that his *singular* historical infamy faded, and he was allowed to find camouflage in the crowd, just one among many.

To frame his despicable uniqueness, however, we can go back to his biographer, George Towle. Writing in 1879, in an era when explorers were still regarded as heroes rather than villains, Towle condemns him, writing that Pizarro invaded and conquered Peru "from motives of ambition, and greed of gold. . . . It is probable that higher motives than these seldom entered his mind. . . . He did not hesitate to carry widespread havoc among a peaceful race, to lay desolate a thriving land, to usurp a power to which he had not the shadow of a right, and to use means in achieving his purpose which were often barbarously cruel."

Meanwhile, his young royal child bride, Ines Yupanqui Pizarro, is often painted in her historic portrait solely as the victim of a dirty old man. However, in the spirit of a well-rounded picture, we must point out a certain document in the Harkness Collection of the Rare Book and Special Collections Division at the Library of Congress. It references a lawsuit brought by Ines and her daughter (by Pizarro), Francisca, in Lima in 1543. In it, Ines successfully asked the court to restore *native slaves* who had been her property when she was a member of the Tahuantinsuyo imperial family. She, like her husband and the Inca elite whom he overthrew, was an unrepentant slave holder.

As for the rest of the family, two of Pizarro's half-brothers, Hernándo and Gonzalo, survived his death. Displaying the familial fondness for teenaged wives, Hernándo married his young niece, Francisca, then returned to Spain, where he reputedly lived to the age of one hundred.

Gonzalo remained in South America, where Francisco had, in 1541, installed him as governor of Quito, a former kingdom that had been incorporated into Tahuantinsuyo in the late fifteenth century. He took up residence in its capital, the Spanish city of San Francisco de Quito, now Quito, Ecuador. The site had been a native trading site for centuries when it was captured in 1534 by Sebastian de Belalcázar, one of Francisco Pizarro's lieutenants and an ambitious soldier of fortune in his own right—who was destined to figure prominently in later quests for South American gold.

It was here in Quito that Gonzalo began hearing the fantastic stories of golden cities and yarns of a place called "El Dorado."

4

WHISPERS OF
EL DORADO

Eldorado! After Atlantis, the Fountain of Youth, Antilia, and the land of the Seven Cities, this was another of those Edens in which the conquerors had faith as hard as iron.

—Jean Descola, *Les Conquistadors* (1954)

SO GREAT HAD BEEN the score of gold and silver during the early decades of the sixteenth century that it was naturally logical to assume that as one continued, deeper and deeper into the hinterlands of this mysterious New World, yet greater wealth could be had.

There was no shortage of rumors to feed this supposition and the lust to which the greedy conquistadors subscribed. The fact that Francisco Pizarro wrapped his fingers around wealth beyond anyone's dreams by following such a rumor made the most fantastic seem probable.

In the late 1520s, even as Pizarro was probing the fringes of the coast of Tahuantinsuyo, conquistadors were already hearing of golden cities elsewhere in the Andes, as well as in the interior of present-day Colombia.

Among the legendary golden cities in the Andes which figured in the growing mythology was Paititi, which was presided over by El Gran Paititi, or the Great Paititi, who was also called the Emperor of Musus. This city was said to be located southeast of Cusco, across the Andes, somewhere in the rugged *terra incognita* where the borders of modern Peru, Bolivia, and Brazil meet. According to the legends, it was a city more glorious than any which the Spaniards had found, but so well hidden that they could never find it. In some retellings of the story, the city was the last refuge of the Inca, perhaps founded by the mythical Inkari, who was possibly the reincarnation of Atahualpa.

One of the biggest mysteries in the lore of lost Inca cities is why Machu Picchu, the fifteenth-century retreat of the emperor Pachacuti, never appears in any of the stories. Located in a breathtaking mountaintop setting, it is now a globally recognized archaeological site and tourist attraction—yet the Spanish conquistadors never found it and may never have even heard about it. This is despite the fact that it is only 50 miles from Cusco. Perhaps it was deliberately bypassed because it was not sheathed in gold, or perhaps whoever took the gold sheathing—if it was there in the sixteenth century—kept the secret.

However, of all the stories of golden cities, the one which seized the European imagination like no other was that of El Dorado.

Very soon after the conquest of Tahuantinsuyo and the Inca, the legend percolated prominently in the sixteenth-century rumor mill.

The term "El Dorado," sometimes written as "Eldorado," which means literally "the Golden One," was originally coined as "El Hombre Dorado," because it referred to a certain "golden man." This gilded man was the New World's Prester John, the man whose Old World kingdom in the East supposedly dripped with fantastic wealth. Like the shadowy Presbyter, the man called El Dorado lived in a place far away and just beyond reach.

Over time, the term "El Dorado" came to describe not just the man, but his mysterious city of gold. Ultimately, it came to symbolize the entire notion of fantastic yet elusive wealth.

Gonzalo Fernández de Oviedo y Valdes, the Spanish historian whose *La Historia General de las Indias* (1535) is considered one of the best of a handful of primary sources about this era, wrote at length about the golden man:

When I asked why this prince or chief or king was called Dorado, the Spaniards who had been in Quito and had now come to San Domingo (of whom there were more than ten here) answered, that, according to what had been heard from the Indians concerning that great lord or prince, he went about constantly covered with fine powdered gold, because he considered that kind of covering more beautiful and noble than any ornaments of beaten or pressed gold. The other princes and chiefs were accustomed to adorn themselves with the same, but their decoration seemed to him to be more common and meaner than that of the other, who put his on fresh every morning and washed it off in the evening. . . . The Indians further represent that this cacique, or king, is very rich and a great prince, and anoints himself every morning with a gum or fragrant liquid, on which the powdered gold is sprinkled and fixed, so that he resembles from sole to crown a brilliant piece of artfully shaped gold.

The legend apparently originated with stories about the Muisca people who lived deep in the mountains of central New Granada, far up in the headwaters of the Magdalena River. The Muisca were a group of linguistically similar tribes with a technologically complex culture who occupied a sizable area on the plateau in the Cordillera Oriental (Eastern Range) mountains of what is now central Colombia, encompassing the present location of Bogotá. The Quechua name for this area, "Cundinamarca," meaning "the condor's nest," certainly describes its elevation and its remoteness.

Specifically, these tales described the initiation rites of new rulers. An especially memorable portrait of the golden man was later penned by the conquistador turned lay preacher, Juan de Castellanos, in his epic poem, *Elegias de Varones Illustres de Indias*. Published in 1588 and now held in its complete form in the Lenox Branch of the New York Public Library, the work is considered to be the longest extant poem in the Spanish language. In it, Castellanos writes:

A chief was there, who, stripped of vesture,
Covered with golden dust from crown to toe,

Sailed with offerings to the gods upon a lake,
Borne by the waves upon a fragile raft,
The dark flood to brighten with golden light.

Though the story had been told around the Spanish colonies for a century when he chronicled it, the account written by Colombia-born Juan Rodríquez Freyle in his 1638 narrative *El Carnero* (*The Goat*) is considered as one of the better of the early prose summaries.

He reports that as a new Muisca ruler took office, the man would go to the shore of a great lagoon, subsequently identified as Lake Guatavita, near Bogotá, to "make offerings and sacrifices to the demon which [the Muisca] worshipped as their god and lord." He goes on to describe an elaborate ritual involving pomp, ceremony, incense, and the journey of the initiate out onto the lake on a balsa wood raft laden with gold and jewels.

According to Freyle, the priests officiating at the ceremony "stripped the heir to his skin, and anointed him with a sticky earth on which they placed gold dust so that he was completely covered with this metal. They placed him on the raft . . . and at his feet they placed a great heap of gold and emeralds for him to offer to his god. . . . [and] when the raft reached the centre of the lagoon, they raised a banner as a signal for silence. The gilded Indian then . . . [threw] out all the pile of gold into the middle of the lake, and the chiefs who had accompanied him did the same on their own accounts."

As he was completely covered with gold dust, the initiate himself became "El Dorado," the "Golden One." He then dived into the lake, leaving nothing but that which was described as "a flaming patch on the surface of the lake." When he had been washed clean of the precious coating, he was "recognized as lord and king."

The implication of this narrative, as perceived by the Spanish conquistadors, is obviously that the Muisca had so much gold they could simply throw it away as part of the ceremony.

Nor are stories of such an expansive display of wealth uncommon elsewhere in the literature of America's indigenous people. One is reminded of the potlatch ceremony of the Northwest Coast tribes, such as the Haida and Tlingit. The potlatch involves an elaborate feast at which the host or host family gives away immense quantities of wealth and costly personal property to his guests in an extreme demonstration of generosity. Of course, the notion of sacrificing valuable property to deities has been an integral part of numerous cultures and religions around the world throughout history.

The stories of this land of a golden man somewhere beyond the headwaters of the Magdalena had been discussed all across New Granada for some time, but daunting logistical challenges deterred any serious expedition into this *terra incognita*.

By an interesting twist of South American colonial history, the first conquistadors into the region would be German, not Spanish. How did this come about?

Going back for generations, the influential Welser banking family had been merchants and power brokers in the city of Augsburg, in the area of Schwabenland (Swabia) that is now part of the German state of Bavaria. In the sixteenth century, the generation in power included Anton and Bartholomeus Welser. As the story goes, Bartholomeus had loaned considerable money to Holy Roman Emperor Charles V, who was, of course, also the monarch of the Spanish New World. Finding himself a bit overextended financially, Charles was unable to keep up his payments to Bartholomeus, so he did what shrewd debtors have been doing throughout history, he put up some sight-unseen land as collateral. In 1528, he gave his banker a long-term lease on a large tract in New Granada.

The Italian cartographer Amerigo Vespucci, the namesake of America, had dubbed this area "Venezuela," or "Little Venice," because the native settlements along the coast were on islands, or on stilts in tidal estuaries. In German, "Little Venice" is "Klein Venedig," and so this became the name of Welser's territory.

In turn, Bartholomeus did what new property owners often do when acquiring distant land; he sent an agent to check on it. In this case, the agent and territorial governor was a German adventurer from Thalfingen named Ambrosius Ehinger, the son of Heinrich Ehinger, who was in upper-level management with the Welser business empire. Because of the family origins, the surname is also seen in various accounts as d'Alfinger, Dalfinger, or Thalfinger.

In 1529, shortly after setting up his base of operations for the Germans at the recently established port of Santa Ana de Coro in Klein Venedig, Ehinger started hearing the irresistible legends, legends of gold located somewhere in the interior of the Welser colony. Along with his right-hand man and fellow would-be conquistador Nicolaus Federmann, he ventured inland. Federmann himself wrote an account of their adventures, entitled *Fine and Agreeable Narrative of the First Voyage of Nicholas Federmann, the Younger, of Ulm, to the Indies of the Ocean Sea*, which was published in Haguenau in 1557. In this, he tells simply that "finding myself now in the city of Coro with a number of men who were unoccupied, I determined to undertake a campaign into the interior toward the south or the Southern Sea, in the hope of finding something profitable."

Few phrases better or more candidly describe the avaricious nature of the European adventurers and conquistadors who explored and plundered South America during the early sixteenth century. As Swabians, Ehinger and Federmann could trace their soldier-of-fortune heritage to the ancient Suebi tribe who had thwarted the legions of Julius Caesar during his brief and tenuous campaigns east of the Rhine back in the first century B.C.

Of the early Ehinger expeditions, the sixteenth-century historian Antonio de Herrera y Tordesillas writes, "He went up the country, keeping by the river and the hills, to the Río de Lebrija, the windings of which he followed as closely as possible. And when the way became barred by the numerous lagoons he went up into the hills, where he found a cool region (*tierra fria*) thickly populated. He was forced to fight with the people, and suffered severely from them."

Nevertheless, the Germans prevailed against determined opposition from the indigenous people in the vicinity of Lake Maracaibo, and established the settlement of New Nürnberg, which later evolved into the city of Maracaibo, now Venezuela's second largest.

Between 1531 and 1533, Ehinger and his conquistadors conducted extensive expeditions, traveling upstream on the Magdalena River and on the rivers which feed Lake Maracaibo. They penetrated as far into the interior of Klein

Venedig as Pizarro had by that time into the interior of Peru. In the steep mountains and thick jungles, the conquistadors suffered from cold, disease, and myriad other hardships.

Ehinger may have reached the Cordillera Oriental (Eastern Range) and though he crossed paths with many indigenous tribes, he probably had not yet made significant contact, if any, with the Muisca people.

He had found no civilization with golden cities to rival those of Tahuantinsuyo. Rather than greeting him in grand plazas with lavish entertainment as the Inca had Pizarro, the indigenous population in the Klein Venedig rainforests met Ehinger with hostility and ambushes. The terrain greatly benefited the defenders, who had no great cities to defend or to tie them down. They could attack at a time and place of their choosing and melt back into the jungle when it suited them. As with European armies fighting guerrilla bands throughout history, the Germans found the going tough. Indeed, the German governor himself met his own demise in the Colombian outback, cut down by a poison arrow to die a painful death in 1533.

Federmann briefly succeeded Ehinger in the governorship at Coro, but when Spanish colonists complained of his cruelty, the Welser family replaced him in 1535 with another ambitious German conquistador named Georg von Speyer. Born Georg Hohermuth, he had changed his surname to that of the Rhineland town of his birth. He is said in some accounts to have ruled with a more politically adept touch than his predecessors. Mainly, however, his rule was in absentia. No sooner did he land in South America than he, like Federmann, was bitten by the gold bug, which sent him marching deep into the interior.

According to Oviedo, the Welsers tolerated this activity, having authorized Rodrigo de Bastidas the Younger, the Archbishop of Santo Domingo and the son of the late conquistador Rodrigo de Bastidas, to act as administrator ad interim in Coro while the Germans were in the field.

Von Speyer made several short trips into the jungle soon after arriving, and in May 1535, he embarked on a three-year expedition. During this wandering sojourn, his was one of the first European parties to explore the headwaters of the Orinoco and Casiquiare rivers.

At the urging of his lieutenant, Esteban Martín, von Speyer probed as far south as what is now Ecuador. At every turn, however, he was met by strong resistance from indigenous tribes, including the Jivaro, who were still notorious as late as the twentieth century for "shrinking" the decapitated heads of their victims.

By August 1537, von Speyer was ready to turn back. Of the nearly four hundred men with whom he had started, all but fifty had been killed by Indians, or had been incapacitated by disease. Martín, the optimistic point man, was among those who

Gonzalo Jiménez de Quesada. (*Bill Yenne*)

was killed, ambushed by Indians while trying to find a pass through a steep mountain range somewhere in northern Ecuador.

Some of von Speyer's men had simply disappeared, swallowed into the rainforest. At one point, he left some of his sick troops at a place they supposed was safe. When he sent a contingent to get them, they had vanished.

Meanwhile, in 1536, even as von Speyer's Germans were battling their way into *terra incognita*, two Spanish soldiers of fortune had led *"entradas,"* as the Spanish described their expeditions, into the interior of New Granada in search of El Dorado. They were Pedro Fernández de Lugo, the *adelantado*, or military governor of the Canary Islands, and Gonzalo Jiménez de Quesada, who was not simply another conquistador, but rather the man who was called *"El* Conquistador." These men were initially impeded by the same sort of inhospitable local population and harsh conditions which had deterred the Germans, and they retreated to the Spanish coastal city of Cartagena.

Though Fernández de Lugo died before they could outfit another *entrada*, Jiménez de Quesada returned to the interior in 1537. Having lost a substantial number of his men to the elements, his team finally climbed the mountains of the

Cordillera Oriental. They reached the Cundinamarca Plateau and made contact with the Muisca.

Unlike the people who had so harassed and so vexed the European adventurers in the jungles below the mountains, the Muisca did have cities with grand plazas to defend. The sophisticated, city-dwelling Muisca were like the people of Tahuantinsuyo, and therefore at a greater defensive disadvantage than the people in the virtually impenetrable jungles.

Jiménez de Quesada shrewdly followed the same policy as had Pizarro in Peru. He approached the Muisca with apparent amity, extending the proverbial olive branch and ingratiating himself to them. Of course, the first question he asked of his new friends was the first question asked by Columbus on his first day, and by Pizarro when he first met the Inca— "where's the gold?"

Having been welcomed by the initial group of Muisca, the Spanish found themselves caught up in an intra-Muisca feud between their hosts and another group living in a place called Muequeta. The conquistadors were manipulated into attacking Muequeta, having been told that the people there possessed a great deal of the gold and emeralds. In turn, the Spanish took this invitation as a license to plunder.

As in the Andes, the Spanish prevailed militarily against the indigenous civilization. Their new enemies were terrified by the Spanish horses and by the arms of the conquistadors.

Having subdued the Muisca, Jiménez de Quesada established a settlement in 1538 which would ultimately evolve into Bogotá. He had now reached and plundered the land of the whispered El Dorado, but he had found far less gold than the El Dorado stories had suggested.

Though he found a hoard of golden objects at Tunja which reminded him of the stories that had been told of the pillage of Peru, El Conquistador realized that the value fell far short of that which Pizarro had taken from the Inca, or Cortés from the Aztec. The Muisca operated no gold mines, and occupied no golden cities. They had gotten their gold by trading for it. The conquistadors would have to keep looking.

As he prepared and organized for the continuation of his quest, however, he learned that he was not alone. Nicolaus Federmann, the former lieutenant of Ambrosius Ehinger, was still on the hunt in these mountains. So too was Sebastian de Belalcázar, the former Pizarro lieutenant and the conqueror of Quito.

Belalcázar had by now disassociated himself from Pizarro, and was setting out as a conqueror in his own right. Many accounts characterize his ambitions and actions in the 1530s as insubordination, or at least a snub to Pizarro's authority. Certainly, this drove Pizarro's decision to install his brother Gonzalo as his man in charge at Quito. However, in all probability, Belalcázar could have cared less about running Quito for Francisco Pizarro. He had his eyes on the gold of El Dorado.

Sebastian de Belalcázar. (*Bill Yenne*)

As Quesada and Federmann reached the Cundinamarca Plateau by following the rivers southward from the Caribbean, Belalcázar had marched north, overland from Quito. Indeed, on his way, he had founded the future Colombian cities of Cali and Popayan in 1536 and 1537.

By 1539, both Belalcázar and Federmann were in a position to challenge Jiménez de Quesada for control of the Cundinamarca Plateau, and the yet-undiscovered El Dorado. Jean Descola paints a romantic, and almost certainly embellished, picture of the three conquistadors meeting face to face on the Plateau:

> Belalcázar's column, coming from Quito, Federmann's, which had set out from Coro, and Jiménez de Quesada's, which had started at Santa Marta, had an unforeseen meeting in the plain of Bogotá. Who would have imagined that the three expeditions, originating in the south, east, and west, would have come together at the gates of the ancient Colombian city? It was a grandiose encounter and one that could have been bloody. But the three captains remembered in time that they were subjects of the same emperor. *Noblesse*

oblige! They saluted one another with their swords, slipped them back in their sheaths, embraced, and celebrated their meeting with a banquet of venison.

Indeed, in realizing that an armed confrontation served none of them, the three parties pursued a course that was very uncharacteristic for conquistadors—they agreed to take the question to court. Indeed, the three of them traveled to Spain to argue their respective positions. The decision, handed down by Charles V himself in 1540, granted the region to Belalcázar, who was named as its *adelantado*.

Quesada, meanwhile, never went back to the plateau. He remained in Europe until 1550, and when he finally returned to New Granada it was to settle down on an extensive land grant to play the role of colonial power broker. His brother, Hernán Pérez de Quesada, meanwhile, launched his own *entrada* in search of gold and emeralds in September 1541, but he came up disillusioned and empty-handed.

By now, Federmann's tenure in the New World had come to an end. While he was in Spain he was summoned back to Augsburg by the Welsers, who were apparently angry with his campaigning on his own behalf while on their payroll. Unlike many others, he lived to tell the tale, specifically in his 1557 memoirs, but he never set foot in Cundinamarca again.

Of course, such treasure-seeking distractions were not unique to Federmann among the German conquistadors. His successor, Georg von Speyer, had finally returned to Coro in May 1538 after spending three years absent from his post. He came back with a disappointing handful of gold, but had added much to European geographical knowledge of the Orinoco River drainage and the area that is now southern and western Venezuela. He died in Coro in 1540 while in the midst of plans to outfit yet another expedition.

A tantalizing sixteenth-century conspiracy theory surrounds von Speyer's demise. Most accounts, including that of the trusted Spanish historian Gonzalo Fernández de Oviedo y Valdes—who knew von Speyer personally—report that he died of natural causes, probably one of the many bacterial infections that plagued Europeans in the tropics. However,

Girolamo Benzoni, an Italian who spent fifteen years in the New World, wrote that he was murdered in his bed by unnamed Spaniards.

Benzoni was himself a mystery man insofar as there has never been a clear explanation of what he was doing for those fifteen years, and for whom he was working. He arrived from Milan in 1541, one year after von Speyer's alleged assassination, traveled widely from the Caribbean to Peru, but returned to Spain broke. His book *Historia del Mondo Nuovo* was published in Venice in 1565. Though it contains detailed accounts of political intrigues and commercial trading which are generally undisputed as to accuracy, there is no mention of how he was personally involved in any of these activities.

As his old friend, Francisco Pizarro, had found as ruler of Peru, Sebastian de Belalcázar would not have an easy time as *adelantado* of Cundinamarca. He had prevailed against Quesada and Federmann in court, but over the coming years, Belalcázar would find himself fending off challenges to his authority, and would-be usurpers of his domain from various challengers. Among them was none other than Pascual de Andagoya, the same man who had first told Pizarro about the gold in Peru. In 1550, Belalcázar was sentenced to death for ordering the murder of a neighboring governor in a land squabble, but he died of natural causes as he was preparing his appeal.

What about Lake Guatavita itself, the lake central to the basic El Dorado legend? This gilded lagoon now lay within Spanish control, but still it was out of reach. Beginning with Hernán Pérez in 1540, numerous attempts were made through the ensuing centuries to drain it, or otherwise to get at the gold within it. Though small amounts of treasure were found, no probe ever yielded more wealth than had been expended in engineering each of the searches. (The idea of gold winding up at the bottom of South American lakes is not limited to Guatavita. Between 1989 and 1992 Dr. Johan Reinhard discovered numerous Inca artifacts at the bottom of Lake Titicaca on the border of present-day Peru and Bolivia. The world's highest navigable lake, Titicaca was important in the mythology of the Inca in pre-Columbian times.)

By the 1540s, the Spanish had concluded that the true source of the fantastic "more and greater" wealth of the mythic El Dorado lay elsewhere than the Cundinamarca Plateau. Though nobody could say exactly *where* else, the general direction was, as Edgar Allan Poe later observed, "Over the mountains of the Moon, down the Valley of the Shadow."

5

INTO THE
VALLEYS OF SHADOW

Between the trunks, even enveloping whole trees, hung huge silvery spider nets. Enormous hairy yellow spiders ran in and out. Countless insects were trapped in these vast webs. I saw a rare type of Morpho butterfly, with wings measuring eight inches across; there were even small birds and lizards. While underfoot in this vile place was the mygale [a tarantula], a poisonous bird-catching spider some seven inches across. All this horrible mess of stiff and wiry spider webs covered us as we took turns cutting a narrow trail. Our clothes dripped with perspiration. All of us became caked with the whitish pepper-sized isango [red chigger], a minute blood-feeding insect. In the very midst of the spider webs we came upon a human skeleton, well gnawed by ants. The Indians fearfully examined it, and then explained what had happened—sounding a grim warning. . . . Here in the jungle [the same place Pizarro explored four hundred years earlier] the reaction psychologically was a chilling sense of incomprehensible mysteries and lurking types of malignant dangers.
—Leonard Clark, *The Rivers Ran East* (1953)

THE GERMAN AND SPANISH CONQUISTADORS had come into the mountains of New Granada searching for a repeat of Pizarro's amazing Peruvian payday. They got their hands on much gold, but less than Pizarro, and less than they expected, but they remained undeterred.

The archaeologist and ethnographer Adolph Bandelier, who studied the El Dorado legend in great detail in the nineteenth century, concluded that despite their optimism, the conquistadors really had reached their high-water mark. "With the conquest of Cundinamarca was secured the last great treasure of gold that awaited the Spaniards in America," he writes. "Their wild greed was, however, doubly excited by their success so far, and they thirsted for more and greater."

If not in Cundinamarca, they reasoned, El Dorado was certain to be out there somewhere in the unexplored vastness, just waiting to be found.

On the maps the Spanish—and Italian, German, English, and Portuguese—cartographers drew of what we know as South America, that "somewhere" was in a place that all languages rendered in Latin—*terra incognita*, the unexplored land of the continent's interior. Early in the sixteenth century, this encompassed an area about four times the size of Europe. El Dorado could be anywhere within this measureless mass. The consensus was that it was probably south of Bogotá, but it might be southeast or southwest. It had to be east of Quito, but it might be northeast or southeast.

Two decades after Francisco Pizarro started hearing stories of golden cities down on the western coast, his brother, reigning as governor at Quito, began hearing about El Dorado.

By the time that Gonzalo Pizarro set up shop in Quito in 1540, El Dorado was the talk of the town wherever greedy conquistadors gathered to drink their rum and scheme about quests to come. Some of what he heard probably came from those who knew Sebastian de Belalcázar, who was even then searching for the place himself.

Juan de Castellanos, in his epic poem *Elegias de Varones Illustres de Indias*, confirms our "old prospector" analogy, telling us that Belalcázar had learned "from a stranger then living in the city of Quito, but who called Bogotá his home, of a land there rich in golden treasure, rich in emeralds glistening in the rock."

When considering the Quito connection, one should also recall that in Oviedo's *La Historia General de las Indias*, he specifically mentions having heard the story in Santo Domingo on Hispaniola from "Spaniards who had been in Quito."

What is particularly intriguing about the El Dorado legend is that the basic elements of the story as it was told in the 1530s were the same, whether they were related by "old prospectors" in Cartagena, Bogotá, or Quito, or in any number of other places as far east as the mouths of the Orinoco River.

To take this a step further is to recognize that each of the "old prospectors" had ultimately learned the story from indigenous people, who communicated across the interior of South America in a vast polyglot of differing linguistic traditions. The fact that similar stories originated with various indigenous people all across the continent indicated to conquistadors and old prospectors alike that they *must* be true. Of course, they just as well could have been told by Indians who would like to see the conquistadors and old prospectors get lost in the rainforests.

In Quito, Gonzalo Pizarro also perked up his ears at another tale, this one being told around town by a man named Gonzalo Díaz de Pineda. In about 1539 he had explored the Andes, where he had discovered some cinnamon-smelling trees in a place he dubbed "La Canela," translated alternately as the Land of Cinnamon or the Valley of Cinnamon.

According to the chronicler and historian Pedro Cieza de León, whose *Cronicas del Perú* was first published in 1553, Pineda had also learned of a more advanced civilization somewhere to the east that possessed more cinnamonlike trees and much gold.

The combined allure of both gold and cinnamon was apparently the spark that Gonzalo Pizarro needed to get him going. A number of historians have pointed out that cinnamon may have been important because, after all, Columbus was sailing in search of spices, and cinnamon is a spice. However, as we well know, it was really about the gold.

Early in 1541, Gonzalo mounted an expedition, or *entrada*, that involved around four hundred Spanish troops and several thousand indigenous people brought along as porters. Riding with Gonzalo as one of his lieutenants, and his de facto second in command, was the thirty-year-old conquistador Francisco de Orellana. Like the Pizarro brothers, Orellana was from the Spanish city of Trujillo. He first set foot in the New World when he was seventeen and had campaigned with the Pizarros since around 1533. Some sources indicate that he may have been their cousin, or possibly a nephew.

Quito, like Cusco, is located high in the Andes (today it is one of the world's highest capital cities). Therefore, Gonzalo and Orellana were soon heading downhill into the Amazon basin. Descending out of the mountains about a month after they began, they followed the Coca River as it plunges and flows through steep canyons into the Napo, a tributary of the Amazon itself.

The conquistadors were utterly unprepared for the Amazon basin, an area the size of the contiguous United States that remained mostly unexplored well into the twentieth century and consists of impenetrable jungles and countless meandering waterways which later explorers would routinely refer to as the "green hell."

At the time, of course, the entire Amazon basin was in the heart of *terra incognita*. Except for a few timid expeditions in the vicinity of its sprawling mouth, Europeans had yet to explore the great river, and the true extent of the Amazon and its enormous web of tributaries was unknown to them. Today, even after half a century of satellite imagery, the length and source of the river remain open to debate. It may or may not be the longest river in the world, but its watershed absolutely contains more miles of streams and rivers than any other.

Indeed, even in the twenty-first century, much of the *terra* of the Amazon basin remains just as *incognita* as it was in the sixteenth century. It is unexplored to the extent that the government of Brazil reckons that there may still be as many as five dozen indigenous tribes who have yet to be contacted by outsiders.

In 1541, none of the tribes deep inside the Amazon basin had ever seen a European. The Spanish intruders were treated as such. As elsewhere in the Western Hemisphere, there was a balance of power between the tribes, and those who trespassed upon another's area were resisted, whether they were a rival tribe hunting for slaves, or clueless outsiders blundering through the unknown.

Whereas Francisco Pizarro and the other conquistadors had wielded modern military technology to shock and awe their New World opponents in the Andean deserts and mountains, the steamy jungles stripped Gonzalo of the European technological advantage. In the Andes, Francisco had astounded the Inca with mounted cavalry, but traveling in the Amazon rainforest was nearly impossible for horses and pack animals, as they struggled up hills and through muddy mazes of tangled vines and fallen logs. Both man and beast were stung mercilessly by insects, and

Gonzalo Pizzaro.
(*Bill Yenne*)

attacked by vampire bats by night. As Amazon explorer Percy Fawcett would observe in the early twentieth century, insects and spiders not only attacked people from the outside, but laid eggs in open wounds, leaving maggots to consume human flesh from within.

Finding clean water and edible food for the men and their horses proved astoundingly difficult. Eventually, the horses became the food for the troops.

Francisco's armor and steel weapons had made his men virtually impervious to Inca arrows in the Andes, but as the horses faltered in the Amazon, and men were forced to carry all their equipment, the weight of the armor became a painful liability. Artillery was discarded as impossible to move, and with damp powder, guns would not fire.

Francisco Pizarro had benefited from the heavily centralized political and military structure of Tahuantinsuyo. Once decapitated, it simply collapsed. In the Amazon, where a myriad of tribes dwelled, there was no unified command, only ambushes by unseen enemies who knew every nuance of the terrain. Even if the Spanish had managed to obliterate an entire tribe, which they never did, there would have been another self-contained tribe around the next bend who was unaffected by this.

Stripped of their armor and weakened by fever and infected insect bites, the Spanish were no match for a stealthy foe wielding blowguns with poison darts. Even if the conquistadors had managed to meet the Indians on an open battlefield, it would have been hand-to-hand combat.

When recalling the devastating effects of smallpox on the indigenous people of the Western Hemisphere, we are reminded that the toll was so great because these people had no natural immunity to diseases from the other hemisphere. In the Amazon, it was turnabout time. The indigenous people here had adapted over time to life in a harsh environment that literally consumed the Europeans. They had, for example, developed herbal remedies for malaria and many other maladies which would not be understood or successfully used by Europeans for more than a century.

About the only positive herbal discovery that was made on the 1541 *entrada* was that there were cinnamonlike trees—although they were few, and quite far between. In his *Dictionnaire Raisonné d'Histoire Naturelle*, published in 1765, the great naturalist Jacques-Christophe Valmont de Bomaré postulated for his European readers that it was *Canelle geroflée* or "black cinnamon."

By the time that Gonzalo Pizarro's men had reached the confluence of the Coca and Napo, the expedition was on the verge of collapse, if not annihilation. Disease, terrain, and hostile indigenous people had cost the lives of more than half of the personnel who had started out from Quito at the beginning of the year.

Adolph Bandelier colorfully describes the *entrada* as "an impotent groping around in a tropical wilderness, where, surrounded by an overwhelming profusion of impenetrable vegetation, man had to give up every other purpose than that of maintaining himself, and might in the end consider that he had done well if he escaped with his life."

However, Bandelier goes on to charitably acquit the ill-fated conquistador for his foolishness. Observing that his expedition was up against a foe of unimagined immensity, he writes that "it would be unjust to hold Gonzalo Pizarro responsible for this failure. The numerous rivers in these forest wildernesses are the only highways practicable to man, and his plan was from the beginning to use for his further movements one of the tributaries of the Amazon that is, one of the streams issuing from the eastern slopes of the Andes; of the existence of the Amazon itself, as well as of its magnitude, he had no knowledge."

In other words, his defense was that he was clueless.

Having found no gold, and fearing that he would soon have no life, Gonzalo Pizarro threw in the towel. He and Orellana had started downstream on the Napo when they parted company. By some accounts, it was decided that Gonzalo would take most of the troops and head back to Quito, while Orellana would take a handful of men and continue down the river. By other accounts, Orellana simply abandoned Pizarro.

Citing contemporary narratives, Bandelier reports that before they agreed to part, Orellana's contingent took to the river aboard boats, while Pizarro remained ashore with the main body of men. Orellana tried to keep pace with his leader, but the current was too much for him and the boats were swept along. When he finally put ashore, he waited for Pizarro, who never showed. He then made the command decision to head downstream, hoping to reach the great river which we now call the Amazon—then called the Marañón—whose mouth had been observed by conquistadors, if not fully explored, earlier in the century.

Even if Orellana believed that he could reach the Atlantic, he clearly realized that it was more probable that his small band of conquistadors would sail into the jaws of obliteration. Traveling eastward with the current was easier than fighting it by rowing westward, but they were sobered by the realization that they would have to gamble on treacherous rapids and deadly waterfalls.

For Orellana and those who took the chance with him, the decision had to have been driven by a belief that anything would afford better odds than trying to climb back across the Andes with Pizarro.

Nevertheless, Gonzalo Pizarro *did* beat these odds, though many who accompanied him did not. He made it over the mountains, but he returned to Quito only to discover that he was out of a job, and that his illustrious brother, Francisco, had been assassinated by the Almagristas in June 1541 while Gonzalo was still swatting flies and dodging blowgun darts in the Amazon headwaters.

One of the earliest accounts of the Pizarro-Orellana *entrada* was by Augustin (or Agustin) de Zárate, the treasurer of Peru in the 1540s. His book, *La Historia Extraña y Deliciosa del Descubrimiento y de la Conquista de las Provincias de Perú* (*The Strange and Delectable History of the Discovery and Conquest of the Provinces of Peru*), was published in Antwerp in 1555. As Zárate described Gonzalo Pizarro's men upon their eventual return to Quito: "All, the General as well as the officers and men, were nearly naked, their clothes having been rotted by the constant rains and torn besides, so that their only covering consisted of the skins of animals worn in front and behind, and a few caps of the same material. . . . Their swords were without sheaths, and all eaten up with rust. Their feet were bare and wounded by thorns and roots, and they were so wan and wasted that one could no longer recognize them. . . . They threw themselves upon the food with so much eagerness that they had to be held back and to be gradually accustomed to the taking of it."

Gonzalo's glory days (if any of his days had really been glorious) were almost over. When Blasco Núñez Vela, appointed by Charles V as the first Viceroy of Peru, reached his dominion in 1544, Gonzalo, along with the brutal Francisco de Carvajal, led a contingent of conquistadors in opposition, defeating and beheading him near Quito in 1546. Political and personal support for Gonzalo Pizarro soon ebbed and he was defeated and beheaded in 1548.

Meanwhile, Francisco de Orellana, who had parted company with Gonzalo in the last days of 1541 to embark on his impossible voyage, had succeeded famously.

He and his men arrived at the mouth of the Amazon on or about August 24, 1542, becoming the first band of Europeans to successfully cross South America by way of the Amazon basin. To do so, his men had constructed an ocean-going brigantine—sails included—in the middle of the rainforest using only tools that they had managed to carry on their backs across the Andes or fashion from locally available resources.

As chronicled by Gaspar de Carvajal, a Dominican friar who was on the expedition, the Spaniards managed to preserve themselves against the ravages of a hostile environment, and to defend themselves against attacks from indigenous people. The latter included the strongly matriarchal Icamiaba, whose ferocious women warriors particularly impressed the Spaniards.

Orellana received a warmer welcome from the Omagua, who lived in cities and had plantations and who fed and entertained Orellana's men generously.

Francisco de Orellana.
(*Bill Yenne*)

Carvajal wrote of making contact with the Omagua in May 1541 near the confluence of the Amazon and the Putumayo. He also mentioned that the people whom they met on the river spoke of a great city about 25 miles inland, which Orellana never investigated as a potential El Dorado. Apparently, at this point, his number-one objective was not cities of gold, but getting out of the green hell.

The fact that a civilization such as that described by Carvajal has never been found over the past few centuries has been attributed alternatively to tall-tale telling on his part, or to the Omagua having been especially susceptible to European diseases such as smallpox. If the latter, as the people had died out, the jungle would have reclaimed the architecture of the Omagua, as they would have constructed their cities of wood, rather than stone as did the Aztec, Maya, and Inca. Archaeological discoveries made since the late twentieth century have begun to confirm that Carvajal and Orellana were probably not exaggerating.

Orellana was almost certainly the first European to have had contact with the Omagua. The reports from his voyage put Omagua country on the treasure map.

Now known by the Portuguese term Cambeba, these upper Amazon people speak a language still referred to by linguists and ethnologists as "Omagua," which is part of the Tupi-Guarani linguistic group. Once a very large tribe, their numbers declined rapidly after later European contact to a twenty-first-century population of around one hundred. In the decades after their first contact with Orellana, their homelands north of the Amazon would come to play a prominent role in European theories regarding the possible location of El Dorado.

Having reached the Atlantic, the *entrada* coasted around South America to Venezuela, and proceeded to sail to Hispaniola. From here, Orellana returned to Spain to tell the amazed Emperor Charles V what had been accomplished.

It was Charles who named the river that Orellana had conquered. The tales of Icamiaba women warriors reminded the monarch of the Amazons of Greek legend, who were a race of women warriors who lived north and east of the Black Sea in the vast central Asian region known in classical times as Scythia. The earlier name, Marañón, survives today as the name of an important tributary of the Amazon.

If Gonzalo Pizarro had experienced failure as an explorer of colossal proportions, Francisco Orellana was just the opposite. His geographical discoveries made him the greatest Spanish explorer since Magellan. He had literally cut a slash of geographical knowledge across the center of *terra incognita*.

Orellana's accomplishments, his resourcefulness, and the odds against his success cannot be overstated. While he did discover both cinnamon trees and Amazon warriors, he did not find El Dorado.

6

UPRIVER
FROM THE EAST

Then rose again, like an avenging spirit, the legend of
the gilded chieftain, in the still unknown regions of
the South American continent. Transplanted by the
over-excited imagination of the white men, the vision
of El Dorado appeared, like a mirage, enticing, deceiv-
ing, and leading men to destruction, on the banks of
the Orinoco and the Amazon, in Omagua and Parime.
—Adolph Bandelier, *The Gilded Man* (1893)

AS BELALCÁZAR, QUESADA, AND FEDERMANN were rac-
ing for gold across the Cundinamarca Plateau, and as Gonzalo
Pizarro was sniffing the air for faint traces of cinnamon waft-
ing across the Andes, an ambitious man named Diego de
Ordaz was scouting the east coast of South America, and the
mouths of the eastward flowing rivers. The stories of the
cities of gold told to the conquistadors by native people were
not limited to Peru and New Grenada. Such stories were
being told all across the continent. At the same time the
Germans were ascending the Magdalena River, Ordaz was
hearing the same stories at the eastern end of the Orinoco.

A former Cortés lieutenant, Ordaz had taken part in the
overthrow of the Aztec Empire in 1521, and had made himself wealthy with confiscated gold. More than a mere com-

mand tent conquistador, he had reportedly established his reputation as a hearty adventurer by being the first European to climb the 17,800-foot volcano Popocatepetl, the second highest peak in Mexico.

Anxious to pursue a search for the cities of gold upriver on the Orinoco, Ordaz sailed to Spain where he sought and finally obtained a concession for a vast swath of the northeast coastline of South America, roughly from the eastern boundary of Bartholomeus Welser's concession in Venezuela to the Amazon Delta. This area included the three modern states of Guyana (formerly British Guiana), French Guiana, and Surinam (formerly Dutch Guiana). Including the Orinoco Delta which is now in Venezuela, the area was generally known in the sixteenth century as "Guiana."

Ordaz sailed from Europe in 1531 with high hopes, but according to sixteenth-century historian Antonio de Herrera y Tordesillas, he lost half of his expedition to Atlantic storms. Under the cloud of things already starting to go wrong, he sailed upriver as far as he could, hearing the usual tales from the local people as he went. They told him of a place in the interior called "Meta," which was, like El Dorado, said to be dripping with gold. It was said to be located on a lake, which the Spanish dubbed Laguna Parima (Lake Parime) and believed to be the source of the Orinoco.

Other stories, notably those told to Sir Walter Raleigh by the Carib people later in the sixteenth century, told of a city of gold upriver on the Orinoco which was known as "Manoa." Like Meta, it too was located near a very large lake.

Ordaz's golden paradise of Meta was suggested to exist somewhere in the vast watershed of the Río Meta, which comprises the Guatiquia, Guayuriba, and Humea rivers and their tributaries. The 500-mile Río Meta itself forms part of the present border of Colombia and Venezuela and flows into the Orinoco at the border town of Puerto Carreno, nearly 1,000 miles upstream from the Atlantic.

Coincidentally, it was in this same region that the German conquistador Georg von Speyer would be searching unsuccessfully for El Dorado less than a decade later, though he would be working his way south from the Caribbean, while Ordaz had traveled westward from the Atlantic.

Some of Ordaz's officers were in favor of an immediate overland expedition, but he cautiously overruled them because of the small contingent of men available. Returning to Spain for reinforcements in 1532, he was lost at sea.

In October 1534, Geronimo d'Ortal, a former Ordaz lieutenant, often called his treasurer, launched his own *entrada* up the Orinoco in the company of Alonzo de Herrera.

Diego de Ordaz.
(*Bill Yenne*)

The sixteenth-century El Dorado scholar Gonzalo Fernández de Oviedo y Valdes specifically notes that native people had confirmed for d'Ortal and Herrera that there was "a land of great wealth" in the headwaters of the Río Meta. For this reason, no doubt, their greed propelled them to foolishly pick the rainy season for their venture.

Oviedo tells that it took them twenty days to finally reach the mouth of the Río Meta, which indicates that they were making good time. However, at this point, their fortunes were reversed. The rivers were rising and d'Ortal's oarsmen found it impossible to row upstream, and it was hugely difficult to pull the ships by hand from the shore against the heavy current. After forty further days, they had managed to travel only 50 miles.

The land for miles around the river was now submerged by the floodwaters, and they saw few people. Had they known exactly where they were going, it would be possible to say that the conquistadors had gotten lost. However, they really had no idea where they were going—except somewhere upriver.

Finally, they met a woman who, Oviedo reports, "understood the dialects they had so far heard." She promised to guide the conquistadors to a large city farther upstream, but warned them that its inhabitants "would certainly eat up the Christians, seeing they were so few."

Apparently, Herrera was one of those who blamed messengers for bad news. He later "had her hanged" in thanks for her work.

The Spaniards continued overland from this point, following the course of the Río Meta through an area of open plains dotted with ponds and swamps. Oviedo writes, with tongue-in-cheek irony, that "I do not believe that any of those who took part in this expedition would have taken so much trouble to get into Paradise."

The only Paradise that Herrera saw as a result of the expedition was not an earthly one. A short time after he killed the Indian woman, the party was ambushed one night and a poison dart connected with Herrera. His death was slow and painful.

D'Ortal survived to tell the grim tale, and to try again the following year. This time, the conquistador abandoned the Orinoco to try reaching the mythical Meta by making an excruciating overland trek from the north. The distance to be covered by crossing the coastal mountains and hiking into the Llanos Orientales plains was much greater than that from Coro to Cundinamarca, and the terrain was every bit as daunting.

They reached the Orinoco somewhere downstream from the Río Apure, whose mouth is about 150 miles downstream from that of the Río Meta. However, as might have been predicted, given d'Ortal's past failures and the nature of the terrain, the venture foundered, and d'Ortal nearly lost his life in a mutiny.

Nevertheless, he survived and went on to spend his final years in blissful retirement in the Caribbean. As Oviedo writes, "God gave him a good wife, a respectable and virtuous widow of suitable age, who had means enough for him to live decently in our city of San Domingo on the island of Hispaniola, with more security and fame than could come to him in all these wars, or in hunting the fabulous riches of Meta, of which no one knows anything to this day, or can find the way there without its costing yet more human lives and leading to other troubles."

In the nineteenth century, after researching the folklore surrounding Meta, Adolph Bandelier concluded that this golden city and the mythical, notional El Dorado were one and the same. He wrote in *The Gilded Man* that "the story of Meta referred to the treasures of New Granada, and was the echo, in another shape, of the legend of El Dorado, which had been transported to the lower Orinoco. The gilded chieftain had vanished from the picture, and only the indefinite idea of a tribe in the highlands rich in gold was left; to this was joined the recollection of a lake [Laguna Parima], afterward transformed into the great lagoon of El Dorado."

In 1541, just a few years after d'Ortal's treasure-hunting career came to an end, Francisco Orellana coasted past the Orinoco Delta after his epic trek across the continental mid-section. Having spent a few years growing bored in Europe, Orellana couldn't stand it. He too was ready to go back to attack the El Dorado legend from the east.

While in Spain, though, Orellana met a young noble-woman named Ana de Ayala, whom he married on November 24, 1544, at the Iglesia de la Macarena in Seville. What makes their romance particularly compelling is that he married her despite her having no bountiful dowry, and that she seems to have become a true soulmate—accompanying her new husband on his next *entrada*. They sailed in May 1545 with four ships and made it to the mouth of the Amazon having lost at least one (accounts vary) of their vessels.

Francisco Orellana was unable to reprise his fantastic success of 1541, and he never again traveled far on the great river that had carried him into the history books. He succumbed to "fever"—likely malaria or some form of bacterial infection—in November 1546, while exploring the Amazon Delta. It is not clear what happened to Ana.

AT THAT SAME TIME THAT Orellana had been in the field on his second expedition, a contingent of German conquistadors from the north were farther west, heading out of *terra incognita* after having made contact with the city-dwelling Omagua people whom Orellana had met on his first trip in 1541.

According to Oviedo, this well-financed venture got under way in 1541, simultaneously with the Pizarro-Orellana *entrada*, but it lasted for five years. It was organized by Archbishop Rodrigo de Bastidas of Santo Domingo, who had functioned as interim administrator in Coro while Nicolaus Federmann and Georg von Speyer had been away chasing shadows. The archbishop himself did not go, but appointed Philipp von Hutten of Württemberg as the leader. He was a young German soldier of fortune (Oviedo describes him as a knight) who had come to the New World with von Speyer, and who had been one of his lieutenants during his bloody and disappointing 1535–1538 expedition.

The von Hutten party also included Bartholomeus Welser the Younger, who had come for adventure in the family's overseas territory. Also aboard was the highly regarded conquistador Pedro de Limpias, who had acquired a great deal of experience in the interior as one of Federmann's lieutenants on his earlier campaigns. He was also indispensable as a gifted linguist who had mastered many of the indigenous dialects.

The Spanish priest and historian Padre Pedro Simon later wrote in his *Noticias Historiales*, published in 1627, that Limpias had been the first man to tell Ehinger and Federmann about El Dorado back in 1529, but the legend was probably already in wide circulation before that.

Von Hutten headed into the South American wilderness in August 1541, the same month that Orellana completed his transcontinental trip. The Germans crossed, and for a time followed, the trail taken by Hernán Pérez de Quesada, who was traveling in the area south of Cundinamarca at about the same time.

For about a year, beginning in early 1542, they explored the drainage of the Río Apure, where Geronimo d'Ortal and Alonzo de Herrera had searched for the golden city of Meta back in 1534 and 1535.

As had been the case with all the previous expeditions, two years in the interior of South America, disease, poor diet, and natural obstacles were taking their toll on the bodies and spirit of the men. However, the terrain apparently did prove easier on the expedition's horses than had the Amazonian rain-forest that was encountered by the Pizarro-Orellana expedition two years before.

By 1543, von Hutten's contingent had traveled south as far as the mouth of the Río Guaviare, about 150 miles upriver on the Orinoco from its confluence with the Río Meta. This put them closer to the Amazon than any other European expedition other than Orellana in 1541.

It was here that the local Uaupe people whom they met warned them not to travel any farther because their weakened force would be no match for the Omagua. The latter were described to the Germans as the dominant tribe in that region. As both Orellana and von Hutten were told, the Omagua were a city-dwelling people who enslaved members of adjacent tribes to work in their large agricultural plantations.

Philipp von Hutten.
(*Bill Yenne*)

The warning was interpreted by the conquistadors as a dare, and they organized a forty-man cavalry contingent to scout the Omagua city. As the mention of such a city had failed to tempt an exhausted Orellana two years before, it only whetted the appetite of Philipp von Hutten and Pedro de Limpias. Observing the city from a hill-top, all they could think of was El Dorado. As Adolph Bandelier writes:

> They observed a settlement of considerable extent, regularly laid out, with large dwellings, and a high structure amidst them. The view was a surprise. Convinced by it that this was the long-sought city and that the high building was the 'palace' of the gilded chieftain, the Spaniards rode full speed down the hill; simultaneously the war drum sounded from out the village, and armed soldiers rushed into the streets and opposed the assailants with wild cries, letting fly a shower of missiles against them. Von Hutten at once saw that he could not accept battle on this ground. He therefore withdrew in good order to a level spot, hoping that he might find there compensation for his inferiority in numbers in the superior weight of his cavalry. Although pursued, he reached the position he sought without great difficulty.

According to accounts by the historian-priests Padre Pedro Simon and Padre José Gumilla, cavalry attacks the following day were repeatedly driven back. Both von Hutten and Limpias were wounded, von Hutten more severely. An acrimonious disagreement ensued between Limpias and young Welser over who should be in charge while von Hutten was convalescing. As a result, a furious Limpias split from the expedition and headed back to Coro with about a half dozen men.

The others followed when von Hutten had recovered sufficiently, but they moved more slowly. Though they withdrew from the Omagua city without having captured the supposed palace, von Hutten and his *entrada* did so convinced that they had found El Dorado.

By the early months of 1546, as von Hutten and Welser finally started heading back to Coro, five years had passed since they had departed, and major changes had taken place. Archbishop Bastidas was gone, and steps were in motion in Europe which would lead to the Spanish government terminating the Welser lease on Klein Venedig. The Spaniard Juan de Carvajal had been installed in Coro as governor in 1545, but von Hutten and Welser, still hacking their way out of the Amazon jungle, were unaware of this. Carvajal was justifiably concerned that von Hutten would attempt to regain power when he discovered he had been ousted.

Bandelier describes Carvajal both as "unprincipled and violent," and "the sworn enemy of the Welsers and their representatives." Meanwhile, he goes on to describe Limpias as "filled with hatred and thirsting for vengeance against the Germans."

When Limpias reached the European settlement at Tocuyo, about 120 miles south of Coro, he made contact with Carvajal and the two joined forces. Their mutual distaste for the Germans, combined with Limpias having "confirmed" the discovery of El Dorado, set the stage for what was to come next.

Young Bartholomeus Welser with an advance guard, reached Barquisimeto, about 30 miles northeast of Tocuyo around the end of April 1546, and Philipp von Hutten followed a short time later. Carvajal, now in Tocuyo, heard of their arrival and ordered them to appear before him, threatening von Hutten that he would send a fifty-man cavalry detachment to arrest him if he did not. Though stern in his summons, Carvajal greeted the Germans cordially when they did arrive in Tocuyo. He invited von Hutten and Welser to dinner and tried amiably to talk the German out of going on to Coro.

Carvajal proposed that von Hutten take him back to the Omagua El Dorado that both men were sure had been discovered. However, the German conquistador insisted on traveling to Coro to meet with the inquisitorial judge, the *juez de residencia*, about getting his job back. Also on his mind, arguably at the forefront, was the plan to organize a new and larger expedition and to go back to his Omagua El Dorado without Carvajal, and seize it for himself.

As the dinner conversation that night became a quarrel, Carvajal decided that it was time to play hardball. As with his German counterpart, El Dorado was his glittering, distracting, ultimate goal, but holding power in Coro was also important to him.

The following day was marked by an even more heated jurisdictional dispute between Carvajal and von Hutten over who was in charge in Klein Venedig. Carvajal ordered von Hutten's troops to swear allegiance to him in his role as governor, whereupon the German conquistador insisted that Venezuela, as Klein Venedig, belonged to the Welsers, and he was their chosen agent. In turn, Carvajal shouted that Venezuela belonged to the Spanish, hoping to convince von Hutten's Spanish troops that he was right.

Swords were drawn and the troops on both sides prepared for a fight. According to historian Antonio de Herrera y Tordesillas, Bartholomeus Welser personally attacked Carvajal with his lance three times before his horse collapsed. The poor animal, exhausted after being ridden across hundreds of miles of the Amazon basin, was simply worn out.

With this, both sides backed off from their armed confrontation. The following day Carvajal appeared to revert to his more conciliatory persona. He met with von Hutten again and agreed to permit safe passage for the Germans to Coro.

Herrera seems to believe that von Hutten did not suspect Carvajal of planning to set a trap, but in hindsight, it seems clear that he had every reason to do so. Herrera notes that the Germans hit the trail to Coro without even a modest concern for their own security. After five years in hostile country, they should have known better.

In the middle of the night about a week later, Limpias and Carvajal ambushed the Germans as they slept, taking both Philipp von Hutten and Bartholomeus Welser into custody. After a quick kangaroo court trial, Carvajal ordered the two men beheaded with a rusty machete just before sunset on May 17, 1546—six months before Francisco Orellana died in the jungle farther south. Once again, it is interesting to note how many well-documented searches for El Dorado were occurring simultaneously in the fifth decade of the sixteenth century.

As the heads of von Hutten and young Welser fell to the boggy ground, the nearly two-decade chapter of German rule in Klein Venedig effectively came to an end. Like the succession of German conquistadors who nominally ruled it—Ehinger, Federmann, von Speyer, and von Hutten—the Welser territory was a victim of both German and Spanish lust for El Dorado.

Through the years, many historians have rebuked the Germans for throwing away an opportunity to develop Venezuela as a functioning colony. However, the end was preordained in the nature of the German conquistadors themselves. The Germans who endured all the necessary hardships involved with coming to South America, like so many of the Spaniards who came during that era, were adventurers and treasure-hunters, not planters or administrators.

The dream of a Germanic Klein Venedig may have succumbed, but the shining vision of El Dorado certainly had not. While Ehinger, Federmann, and von Speyer died knowing they had never found it, yet they each lived their final days in the impassioned belief that it did exist. As for Philipp von Hutten, he died believing that his Omagua El Dorado was the city they all had sought. Even the historian Gonzalo Fernández de Oviedo presumed that von Hutten had actually found El Dorado, and said so in his history of European adventures in the New World in the sixteenth century.

7

THE WRATH OF GOD ON THE RIVER OF DESPAIR

The personal Dorado has vanished, but his elusive shade still floats before us. The valiant figures of the conquest, knights who were little inferior in bravery and adventurous spirit to those of the Round Table, went in pursuit of him. Their career, begun with violence, ended usually in crime, and the generation which called forth and bore the great figures of Cortés, Pizarro, Quesada, and Georg von Speyer expired in the iniquities of Carvajal and the revolting monster Lope de Aguirre.

— Adolph Bandelier, *The Gilded Man* (1893)

BY THE 1560S, THE INFORMATION gained by Francisco Orellana's discoveries along the Amazon and by Philipp von Hutten's supposed "discovery" of an Omagua El Dorado had flowed together into a tantalizing stew, seasoned of course by ever more delicious rumors. This naturally resulted in a renewed effort to find the fabled cities of gold. The new expeditions would feature a new cast of avaricious rogues who were, if anything, more perfidious scoundrels than those who came before.

As we read of the German conquistadors von Hutten and Bartholomeus Welser the Younger passing through the Venezuelan town of Barquisimeto in 1546 en route to their demise, we cannot help but think of Lope de Aguirre, himself a seeker of El Dorado, who was executed in that same place fifteen years later, only to be immortalized by a German five centuries later. Filmmaker Werner Herzog's 1972 film *Aguirre: der Zorn Gottes* (*Aguirre: The Wrath of God*) took its title from a name that Aguirre bestowed upon himself, and chronicles Aguirre's bloody obsession with El Dorado. It is without doubt the most disturbing depiction of a man's lust for the golden city that has ever been put on film, and for that reason, perhaps the most realistic.

The real Aguirre was not one of the more romantic sixteenth-century El Dorado-hunters. By all accounts, he was an unabashed sadist, and an obsessed madman. Indeed, this self-described "Wrath of God" was known to others as "El Loco," the madman.

Born in Spain's Basque country, Aguirre was among that stream of young soldiers of fortune who flowed into the New World in the 1530s. As the story goes, his interest was piqued, his greed ignited, when he saw the Inca gold brought back to Seville by Hernándo Pizarro. Shortly after he reached Peru, Aguirre coincidentally found himself as a foot soldier in the Peruvian power struggle involving Hernándo's brother Gonzalo.

As noted earlier, soon after Gonzalo returned from his ill-fated expedition to find El Dorado, he was involved in an open conflict with Blasco Núñez Vela, who had been appointed by Charles V as the first Viceroy of Peru. Counterintuitively, considering his later reputation, Aguirre fought on the side of Viceroy Vela, who had been sent to Peru to implement the Leyes Nuevas (New Laws).

Promulgated by Charles V to enhance the civil and human rights of the indigenous people of Peru, the Leyes Nuevas included provisions which curtailed the *encomiendas*, a system that "assigned" indigenous people to powerful conquistadors and landholders as slaves. In exchange for their Indians being "entrusted" to the Spaniards for protection, they had been compelled to return the favor in the form of indentured servitude or slavery. Ironically, this system by which the people of the former Tahuantinsuyo were enslaved was modeled after the same system by which the Inca leadership itself had previously kept their own people as slaves.

Gonzalo Pizarro and his cohort, Francisco de Carvajal, were heavily invested in the *encomiendas*, and openly battled with Vela. Though he was in his eighties and had been in Peru for only a couple of years, Carvajal had developed such a reputation for cruelty to Indians that he had earned the nickname "Demon of the Andes."

Lope de Aguirre.
(*Bill Yenne*)

All three men died violently, their heads sliced from their shoulders. Vela was decapitated in 1546, and both Pizarro and Carvajal met their demise two years later. With these three in their graves, Charles V's second Viceroy of Peru, Pedro de la Gasca, was able to wield his considerable political skills to restore, at least temporarily, a sense of order to the lawless colony.

With the wars over for the time being, Aguirre became a drifter, spending the next decade seeking his fortune up and down the coast and in the Andes, roaming as far north as Nicaragua, and south into present-day Bolivia and Chile.

Meanwhile, he was honing a reputation for ruthlessness in his dealing with the Indians that would have made the Demon of the Andes blush. At one point, he was convicted of a violation of the Leyes Nuevas and sentenced to a flogging. Afterward, he tracked down and brutally murdered the judge who had sentenced him.

In 1554, Aguirre was back in action as a mercenary on the side of the Spanish crown in Peru's ongoing series of civil wars. This is worth noting because in the Battle of Chuquinga, he was shot in the right leg with an arquebus while fighting with Alonzo de Alvarado against the rebel conquistador Francisco Hernández Giron. This injury would leave him with a permanent limp and constantly in pain, circumstances that doubtlessly contributed to his signature sour personality.

It was while Aguirre was back in Peru for these campaigns that he would cross paths with the man who would put him on the road to El Dorado—a conquistador named Don Pedro de Ursúa. Basque like Aguirre, Ursúa was born in Navarre, and the nephew of Miguel Díaz de Armendariz, the inquisitorial judge or *juez de residencia* for New Granada. He had arrived in New Granada in 1545 at age twenty as his uncle's aide, and he subsequently served as an enforcer for his uncle and other judges. In this role, he spent the decade between 1548 and 1558 in the interior south of the Cundinamarca Plateau. His objective here was not the cities of gold, but rather pursuing fugitive slaves and punishing Indian tribes who were harassing Spanish settlers. By this time, the Muisca people of Cundinamarca had submitted to the colonial power, but the people who lived in the forests and mountains farther to the south remained hostile.

One of Ursúa's tactics was regicide. At one point, as described by Adolph Bandelier, "when a large number of chiefs had come to him to conclude the treaty, he induced them to go inside of his tent, where they were murdered to the last man. He hoped by an act of such surpassing terror to paralyze the force of the tribe."

Among the people whom Bandelier credits Ursúa with subduing are the Tairona, who lived in the Sierra Madre de Santa Marta, and who were linguistically related to the Muisca. Like the Muisca, they had cities, and they had golden objects, though like the Muisca, they did not have the volume of gold of which the El Dorado seekers dreamed.

Unlike many conquistadors who had preceded him in New Granada and Venezuela, Ursúa attended to his assigned duty of murder and mayhem, and did not succumb to the temptation to drop everything and disappear into the rain forest for several years to look for gold.

Finally in 1558, Ursúa did leave New Granada, returning to Peru, where he went to work for Don Andreas Hurtado de Mendoza, the Marquis of Caneta, who had been appointed two years earlier the fifth Viceroy of Peru. It would be Mendoza who would be the man who sent both Ursúa and Aguirre on the road to El Dorado.

Though two decades had passed since Gonzalo Pizarro had made his failed but famous quest for the golden city, the El Dorado legend was as big a topic of conversation in Lima as always. If anything, it was more pervasive than ever. The viceroy himself is said to have been interested, and soon his interest turned to excitement.

An integral part of the whole El Dorado mythology had always been tales related to the Spaniards by Indians. These included old legends which involved a small quantity of gold that was inflated either by the

Pedro de Ursuá.
(*Bill Yenne*)

interpreter or the listener, and they included stories that were fabricated either as pranks or to curry favor with this conquistador or that. Some of these yarns were dismissed out of hand, while ones that seemed to have a degree of credibility entered the folklore, and a few became the catalysts for expeditions.

One of the specific El Dorado stories that was widely told, and widely believed, in Lima in the 1550s involved not one or two, but about two hundred Indians. Indeed, it found its way into Pedro de Cieza de León's *Chronicas del Perú* (*Chronicles of Peru*). Published in Spain in 1553, the first volume of this work became one of the most influential books in shaping the sixteenth-century view of the New World. (The second volume was not finally published until the nineteenth century, and the fourth volume appeared in 1909. The more conspiratorial of El Dorado-seekers still whisper guardedly about the fact that the "missing" third volume was discovered by happenstance in the Vatican Archives, and not published until 1979.)

A conquistador who had campaigned in New Granada with Sebastian de Belalcázar in the early 1540s, Cieza de León had later fought with the first viceroy against Gonzalo Pizarro, but he had settled down in 1548 in Lima as a chronicler of the Spanish experience in the New World. The first volume of his *Chronicas del Perú* and the story of the two hundred Indians were certainly well known in Lima by 1558 when Mendoza, Ursúa, and Aguirre all converged in the city. Of the visitors from the East, Cieza de León wrote: "In the year of the Lord 1550 there came to the city of La Frontera . . . more than two hundred Indians. They said that since leaving their home a few years before they had wandered through great distances, and had lost most of their men in wars with the inhabitants of the country. As I have heard, they also told of large and thickly populated countries toward the rising sun, and said that some of them were rich in gold and silver."

For the viceroy, however, the true affirmation of the existence of El Dorado came when he too met personally with a group of Indians from the East. They told of their remarkable journey across the continent all the way from the Atlantic to Peru. Theirs was essentially the Orellana *entrada* in reverse. This adventure interested the viceroy less than did their stories of having seen a place which met the description of El Dorado.

As they told it, the location was within the Omagua country north of the Amazon. Naturally, the fact that this was in the same general area as the golden city reported by Philipp von Hutten's expedition seemed to provide the proof that the story was true.

In their detailed description, these people from the Atlantic explained that there was another tribe on the south side of the Amazon, the Ticuna, who possessed some gold, but that the Omagua had it in abundance. They also repeated the story that had first been heard in New Granada about a king encrusted by gold dust. Again, as so often in the El Dorado lore, it was a case of the same tale cropping up in widely separated places.

Indeed, the story of the Indians from the Atlantic having seen El Dorado became a widely reported part of the evolving folklore of the cities of gold. These people from the Atlantic were also described in detail by Padre Pedro Simon, the respected Spanish historian, in his *Noticias Historiales*, which was published in 1627. "Those Indians brought accounts from the province of the Omagua, which Captain Francisco de Orellana mentioned when he went down the Marañón [Amazon] River," Padre Simon writes. "In that province, of which the Indians told when they came into Peru, lived the gilded man."

These accounts are in turn, supported by Toribio de Ortiguera in a 1561 manuscript about a journey through the Amazon (Marañón) basin entitled *Jornada del Marañón*. Ortiguera goes on to confirm that these people had come all the way from the Atlantic coast. He wrote of their tribe having a population of between 2,000 and 4,000, originally living near the mouth of the Amazon. He spoke of a chief named Viraratu who led his people up the river, fighting many difficult battles against other tribes living along the shore, traveling to the Andean foothills, and crossing into the Viceroyalty of Peru.

It was at this point, having interviewed eyewitnesses personally, that the fifth Viceroy of Perú was bitten by the gold bug and contracted what the old chroniclers called "Dorado fever."

To lead the expedition, the viceroy chose Pedro de Ursúa, promising him a title, and the rights to govern the places which he discovered and conquered. To take him to El Dorado, Ursúa would bring some of the Atlantic coast Indians as guides. The viceroy apparently did not take a hands-on approach to organization, for he gave Ursúa free rein to pick the men for the *entrada*. For this, Ursúa seems to have dragged the taverns and cantinas for the roughest bunch of misfits and mavericks that he could find. This should have been the first clue that the expedition was headed for trouble.

Among these outcasts swept up from the proverbial barroom floor was Lope de Aguirre. This should have been the second clue, as Aguirre's reputation was no secret. Bandelier calls him "the most detestable character" in the group, and adds that Ursúa ignored "earnest warnings" about the malevolent nature of this notorious sociopath, presumably thinking himself capable of handling El Loco.

Rather than starting out on horseback as had the last major expedition from Peru into the Amazon, that of Gonzalo Pizarro a decade earlier, the viceroy took a page from the triumph of Gonzalo's lieutenant. As Francisco Orellana succeeded by water rather than overland, it was decided to construct boats to be used to sail downriver into the Amazon and beyond.

In the spring of 1560, after a year of boat building and preparations, Ursúa assembled his troops in the headwaters of the Río Huallaga, across the crest of the Andes about 200 miles north by northeast of Lima.

"It was really a 'picked company,' that met there." Bandelier writes. "The scum of Peru formed the principal part of it; the majority, men accustomed to everything except order and morals; and with them were women."

He charitably does not say that the women were unaccustomed to order and morals, but merely suggests it. Among the women in the company was Ursúa's own girlfriend, Inez de Atienza, whom Bandelier describes as a "young and beautiful widow," with whom Ursúa "lived intimately." Lope de Aguirre brought his daughter, Elvira.

Padre Simon observes in his description of this merry band of adventurers that those in charge, Ursúa's officer corps, were "all doughty champions with elastic consciences."

Among these officers, Juan de Vargas was to be Ursúa's second in command, while Fernando de Guzman, described by Padre Simon as a young knight from Seville, was named as the ensign, while Aguirre is listed as a sergeant. Though Aguirre was not among the highest ranking, his influence, wielded from the shadows, would prove considerable.

Given the irascible nature of the troops, it was necessary for the officers to establish through intimidation an understanding of who was in charge. Not all of the officers were able to gain such a "rapport" with the crew. Indeed, one of them, Pedro Ramiro, was murdered while the expedition was still getting ready. When Ursúa had the perpetrators hung, it cast a literal and figurative shadow over preparations.

The advance party under Juan de Vargas finally shoved off in a brigantine on July 1, with the plan being to launch the rest of the *entrada* shortly thereafter. However, it was discovered that among their boats, only three flatboats and another brigantine were seaworthy. What Orellana had done in the middle of the jungle with a handful of men and second-rate tools, Ursúa and company had failed to do with access to the best shipwrights from the port of Lima and all the resources of the viceroy's treasury. This was another ominous sign.

Meanwhile, Ursúa had agreed to transport a number of colonists to Moyobamba, and this outstripped the capacity of his ships. The process of building additional rafts and canoes delayed the departure of the overloaded armada until September 26. Even with this additional capacity, they were forced to leave 85 percent of their horses, and the entire herd of beef cattle upon which they had hoped to depend for food.

About 500 miles downstream, at the mouth of the Río Ucayali, they caught up to Juan de Vargas's party, whose ship had deteriorated to the point where it was no longer watertight. With each passing day of the annals of Ursúa's debacle, one grows more impressed with the skill of Francisco Orellana and his team.

Ursúa patched his ships together and they finally reached the confluence of the Amazon and the Río Napo. This was the same river whose banks Pizarro and Orellana were following when Pizarro decided that he would turn back to Quito, and near where Orellana built his brigantine.

Here at the mouth of the Napo, they encountered a series of indigenous settlements whose people greeted them cordially. Padre Simon writes that they were able to disembark and trade for fresh vegetables, including beans, corn, and yams. They were also afforded an opportunity to drag their disintegrating fleet ashore to attempt repairs.

Also here, Don Pedro de Ursúa turned to the Atlantic people traveling with him as guides, and asked that question asked by travelers since time immemorial: "Are we there yet?" To this, they pointed eastward, nodded toward the Omagua country on the north side of the Amazon, and replied, "No, not yet."

In his account, written after having interviewed people who were on the expedition, notably Francisco Vásquez, Padre Simon reports that shortly before Christmas 1560, they reached the land known as Machiparu. Located in what is now the Brazilian Territorial Prelature of Coari, Machiparu was around 600 miles downstream from the mouth of the Río Napo, and about 250 miles upstream from the present city of Manaus. Today, the name is rarely used, although it appears occasionally on the blogs of environmental activists who use it as a reference to the ancient cultural roots of the area.

Here at Machiparu, the answer to the age-old question appears to have been "yes." They were now in the region populated by the Omagua, and had found a broad path leading into the jungle from the shore of the Amazon. This path, writes Simon, "led to a large city and province." This, Ursúa reasoned, *had* to be the road to El Dorado.

His eyes glazed over by thoughts of being at last so near the city of gold, the enforcer failed to pay attention to trouble that was brewing under his nose. His crew, exhausted by the physical exertion of rowing on the Amazon for three months, and smelling the same gold as Ursúa, were reverting to their previous incarnation as an unruly gang of miscreants. Perhaps it was because of their having been little more than this, that Ursúa did not see the discontent within his ranks. Some, though not all, were on the edge of mutiny. The man who could, and would, push them over that edge was Lope de Aguirre.

On December 26, as Ursúa sent a contingent of his most loyal men to scout the road to the Omagua El Dorado, a scheme was being hatched at their camp near the shore. The plan was to murder both Ursúa and Juan de Vargas, and to install young Fernando de Guzman, who was well liked among the men, as the new commander. In addition to his popularity, Guzman was, as Bandelier called him, a "simple minded youth." Over time, though not immediately, it would become evident that he won Aguirre's support because he was a man whom the shrewd El Loco could manipulate from the shadows.

On New Year's Day 1561, Ursúa was in camp planning for the overland expedition to the Omagua El Dorado when the conspirators struck. That evening, just after sunset, a group of men led by Alonzo de Montoya and Cristoval de Chavez, came to his tent.

"What are you looking for here at so late an hour?" Ursúa asked, according to the account recorded by Padre Simon and related by Adolph Bandelier.

They responded, demanding that he prepare to meet his maker, shouting *"Confessio, confessio, miserere mei Deus!"*

With that, he was gunned down by a man named Lorenzo de Salduendo, as the mob cheered "Liberty, liberty! Long live the king, the tyrant is dead!"

Alerted by the commotion, Juan de Vargas arrived on the scene, only to be cut down by the mutineers.

As for the young and beautiful Inez de Atienza, she became the lover of the assassin Salduendo. He may have seized her as a prize, but according to Francisco Vásquez, Padre Simon's eyewitness source, she fell willingly into his arms, and into his tent. Perhaps she did so just to survive, or perhaps she imagined that El Dorado would soon be found, and that she could reign as its new queen.

Juan de Castellanos, in his epic *Elegias de Varones Illustres de Indias*, is quite captivated with Inez. So to is Clements Markham, who wrote the introduction to the 1861 English translation of Padre Simon's book, and who referred to Inez as "the heroine of the Amazon," comparing her to Madame Isabel Godin des Odonais, the wife of the eighteenth-century French naturalist Jean Godin des Odonais who survived a 2000-mile odyssey from western Peru to the mouth of the Amazon in order to rejoin her husband.

Bandelier, in *The Gilded Man*, is uncharacteristically indignant about such a depiction, calling her "a concubine in station," and writing that "the comparison is hardly admissible between Ursúa's mistress, who shortly after his death became so readily the mistress of his murderer, and the faithful wife who, to seek her husband toiling in the service of science at Cayenne, bravely made her way through the wilderness of the Amazon shores almost alone."

With Salduendo and Inez standing by, the conspirators proclaimed the popular Fernando de Guzman as the man in charge, while Lope de Aguirre stepped in from the shadows as the new second in command, and as Guzman's future puppet master.

So as to legitimize the insurrection, a document was drawn up stating for the record that the murder of Don Pedro de Ursúa had been an operational necessity.

To this, Aguirre is said to have mocked the signatories, telling them: "You have killed the representative of the king among us, the bearer of his power; do you think that this writing will exculpate you? Do you suppose that the king and his judges do not know what such papers are worth? We are all traitors and rebels, and even if the new country should be ten times as rich as Peru, more populous than New Spain, and more profitable to the king than the Indies, our heads are at the order of the first licentiate or pettifogger [deceitful attorney] who comes among us with royal authority."

With that, El Loco signed his name, "Lope de Aguirre, the traitor."

As Bandelier later summarized, this speech was "shrewdly calculated, and was based on known facts which were extremely unpleasant to most of the men. . . . His unexampled audacity dazzled many and also made him many enemies, but he carried his point."

One point that Aguirre was not able to carry in January 1561 was his opinion that they should abandon their pursuit of El Dorado and go back to seize gold where it was *known* to exist—Peru. However, most of the men were unwilling to retrace their steps for several months only to enter into a war with the viceroy. With Guzman lured to support their position, the majority declared that they should not forsake the quest for the city of gold. They had come so far and it seemed so close.

Aguirre and his henchman Salduendo would bide their time.

Soon, the explorers found that they were not as close as they had imagined. The team that Ursúa had sent to follow the broad path into the interior returned. They had hiked for miles, and had found only a few abandoned houses before the trail disappeared, swallowed by impenetrable rain forest.

It was then decided that the *entrada* should put into the river again and continue, though it is unclear from the eyewitness accounts exactly where next they traveled.

One school of thought is that they traveled downstream to the mouth of the Amazon, but it seems more likely that they began exploring various of the Amazon's parallel channels, as well as some of its tributaries.

Based on what he learned from Vásquez, his primary source, Padre Simon writes that they traveled "through a bend into an arm of the river on the left side. . . . Aguirre determined to turn out of the direct way; and after they had gone three days and one night in a westerly direction, they came to some vacant huts."

This, both Bandelier and Markham interpret as having taken place above the mouth of the Río Negro, and believe it indicates that "the band left the continuous course of the

Amazon and went through one of the numerous bayous that form a network of channels between the Japurá and the Río Negro, into the latter river."

In any case, Padre Simon notes that they traveled through the central Amazon basin for weeks without seeing a soul on the shore. By now, they had run short of food and were eating their horses. Finally, even the people from the Atlantic coast, upon whom the expedition depended for guidance, admitted that they had no idea where next to look.

The more demoralized the men had become, the more powerful Aguirre had become. As Bandelier points out, Guzman had gradually fallen under his spell, and was "only a tool" in the hands of the dark and brooding madman. Bandelier adds that the *entrada*'s nominal leader had become "so infatuated as to call the monster 'father.'"

In turn, the "monster" decreed to the captain that it was time to give up on El Dorado, and to audaciously declare war on Peru and on the Spanish dominion over all its territories in the New World. Guzman timidly agreed, and the expedition put ashore somewhere above the mouth of the Japurá. Here, they would devote around three months to the construction of two ocean-going ships.

Rather than going back through the green hell of the Amazon basin, Aguirre hatched a plan to go the long way around. They would follow the river to the Atlantic Ocean, and then sail northwest to seize Isla Margarita, off the coast of Venezuela. Next, the ambitious scheme called for capturing Panama before moving south into Peru. Here, Guzman would be proclaimed as the "Prince and King of the mainland and of Peru." How Aguirre imagined this could be done with fewer than two hundred undisciplined thugs is a mystery. Of course, they didn't call him El Loco without reason.

Aguirre had continued to permit his puppet to retain the post as the titular head of the *entrada* because of Guzman's popularity with the expedition members, but the idea of being crowned as the King of Peru went to the young fellow's head. The disposition of "the simple minded youth" turned from amiable to arrogant. As Padre Simon writes, it was during Easter week in 1561 that Fernando de Guzman's luck ran the way of Ursúa's.

So too did that of both Lorenzo de Salduendo—the only man powerful enough for Aguirre to consider a worthy rival—and Inez de Atienza. Late one night, the madman slaughtered Salduendo in front of Guzman, while two of his men went to the tent where Inez was sleeping. Bandelier says only that they "took the life of the young woman in the most revolting manner," and we will leave it at that.

Having witnessed Salduendo's death, Guzman joined the roster of about a half dozen officers who were murdered that night.

The following day, the men declared Aguirre as the "General of the Marañón [Amazon]," and themselves as the "Marañónes."

Aguirre himself is said to have declared that "I am the Wrath of God, the Prince of Freedom, Lord of Tierra Firme and the Provinces of Chile."

By the first of July 1561, Lope de Aguirre, his nearly two hundred scoundrels, and their pair of ocean-going brigantines were in the Atlantic. If the ships built in Peru the previous year were pitiful hulks, these vessels were just the opposite, for they successfully carried the Wrath of God, his horde, and his daughter Elvira around the coast of South America, bucking ocean currents, all the way to the shores of Venezuela in less than three weeks.

The Marañónes captured the Spanish fort on Isla Margarita in a violent surprise attack, and began a brief reign of terror against the people of the island. It was as though Aguirre was taking out his entire rage against the Spanish government on the hapless citizenry here. This unfolded in the form of a spree of murder and wanton violence on a scale that would put the Caribbean pirates and buccaneers of later centuries to shame.

The horrified coastal outposts across the channel on mainland Venezuela feared that they would be next, and they were right. Ironically, it had been the many long years of the rulers of the erstwhile Klein Venedig pouring resources into the search for El Dorado that left the colony virtually helpless.

El Loco's obsession with rape and pillage on Isla Margarita delayed his making a swift move against Panama. This bought the defenders time, and eliminated the possibility that Aguirre could reprise his successful surprise attack there.

This led him to change his plans to launch the feared assault on Venezuela rather than going west toward Panama.

Sailing in a vessel flying a flag marked with crossed, blood-red swords, Aguirre and his cutthroats made landfall once again on the South American continent on the last Sunday of August 1561. They came ashore at the small coastal town of Bourburata, about 130 miles east of the city of Coro. The Marañónes bypassed the town, which had been abandoned by its population. From the coast, they marched inland, cutting a swath of terror and destruction all the way to the recently established village of Valencia—now Venezuela's third largest city.

Aguirre had imagined in his twisted mind that he would be greeted as a liberator, with the populace running to join him in his mad crusade against the Spanish monarchy.

Instead, they were running to get away from him, and his own troops were starting to desert him. On top of this, he was sick, having contracted one or more of a myriad of tropical diseases that ran rampant in the South American rain forest. However, according to the accounts of the witnesses, he was more inconvenienced than incapacitated, and this made him much angrier than usual.

Fortunately for all in his path, the clock was now running out for El Loco. He had abandoned his plan of reaching Peru by sea, and was thrashing through a jungle that had chewed up and spit out numerous explorers, and which had simply swallowed up many more. Only a madman would think that he could lead an army through this jungle and be in any kind of shape to conquer Peru on the other end.

Finally, the Wrath of God reached a deserted Barquisimeto, the same town which had been the final crossroads for the German conquistadors von Hutten and Welser the Younger fifteen years earlier. By this time, an emergency force loyal to King Philip, which had been assembled in New Granada under the command of Diego de Paredes, was in a position to intercept Aguirre.

Rather that attacking the Marañónes directly, Paredes cut them off and blocked their progress, his cavalry riding circles around them, all the time shouting amnesty offers. Gradually, the seepage of deserters turned into a flood, and

Paredes decided to launch his final attack on El Loco's position in Barquisimeto.

On or about October 27, 1561, the end came, not as a bang, but as a whimper, with the majority of the surviving Marañónes throwing down their arms to welcome the loyalist troops with shouts of "long live the king!" The "king" whose life they celebrated was that of Philip II, not Lope de Aguirre.

Finally, it was down to just two. With the Wrath of God in the building which he had commandeered in Barquisimeto was his daughter, Elvira, whom Bandelier describes as "a grownup maiden," making her probably in her early twenties. As Paredes and his troops closed in, El Loco stepped into Elvira's bedroom. What he said to her is not known for certain. We have only the dialogue contrived by Padre Simon and later translated by Clements Markham. The phrasing is probably unrealistically florid, but it makes the point.

"My child, God have mercy on your soul, for I am going to kill you, so that you shall not live in misery and shame, the child of a traitor," Aguirre is said to have said.

When the troops crashed into the bedroom, Elvira lay on the floor in a growing pool of blood, an enormous knife wound in the vicinity of her heart.

Diego de Paredes took Lope de Aguirre into custody. As the story goes, he planned to spare him for a life in prison, but Paredes's men shouted for the Wrath of God to be put to death.

Paredes assembled a firing squad, and the job was complete.

His body was drawn and quartered and the quarters taken to various places far apart. His head was taken to Tocuyo, where it was on display inside an iron cage for some time. As late as the nineteenth century, jack-o-lanterns were considered in Venezuela to be a representation of this head.

The great naturalist Alexander von Humboldt, who visited the region at the dawn of the nineteenth century, tells us how his name still sent chills up the spines of the people. Indeed, Humboldt discovered that the people around Cumana, Venezuela, associated his name with the disastrous volcanic eruption, earthquake, and tsunami which devastated the region on December 14, 1797. It was as though the earth opened up, and the sulfurous stench of hell brought forth that sixteenth-century madman. Writes Humboldt in his memoir of his voyage:

> At Cumana, half an hour before the catastrophe a strong smell of sulfur was perceived near the hill of the convent of San Francisco; and on the same spot the subterraneous noise, which seemed to proceed from southeast to northwest, was loudest. At the same time flames appeared on the banks of the Manzanares . . . flakes of fire rising to a considerable height, are seen for hours together. . . . This fire, which resembles the springs of hydrogen . . . what is called the will-o'-the-wisp of our marshes, does not burn the grass; because, no doubt, the column of gas, which develops itself, is mixed with azote [noxious gases] and carbonic acid, and does not burn at its basis. The people, although less superstitious here than in Spain, call these reddish flames by the singular name of "the soul of the tyrant Aguirre"; imagining that the spectre of López [*sic*] Aguirre, harassed by remorse, wanders over these countries sullied by his crimes.

In Venezuela even today, his ghost is regarded as an evil spirit of the highest order.

His epitaph was written by himself just a short time before his death. When he was camped in Valencia, he had penned a letter to Philip II and had entrusted it to a priest whom he had taken as a prisoner on Margarita. The document still survives, and was published in 1961 by the Central University of Caracas in *Documentos para la Historia Economic de Venezuela* (*Documents Related to the Economic History of Venezuela*), edited by Arellano Moreno.

He begins his rambling manifesto with a meandering retrospective of his life in the New World, and the seven years of pain in his right leg from the arquebus wounds. However, he returns repeatedly to a central theme of anger with the king and his agents.

The man who once fought with loyalist royalist forces in the Peruvian civil wars hurls a scathing, mocking indictment of the sovereign, writing: "I firmly believe, most excellent

King and lord, that to me and my companions you have been nothing but cruel and ungrateful. . . . while your father and you stayed in Spain without the slightest bother, your vassals, at the price of their blood and fortune, have given you all the kingdoms and holding you have in these parts."

He goes on to tell Philip that the judges and viceroys who run his New World domains are not being entirely honest with him: "I also believe that those who write to you from this land deceive you, because of the great distance."

In his own recollection of the El Dorado *entrada*, he describes having traveled "a good hundred days" on the "large and fearsome" Amazon, adding that for 800 leagues (roughly 2,000 miles) "along its banks it is deserted, with no towns."

In his concluding paragraph, the madman betrays his own belief that the river itself, and the quest for the mythical city of gold, has driven him to madness. He, of all people, has figured out that El Dorado is not so much a place, as it is a sweet narcotic that has driven a whole generation of conquistadors insane. There is a touch of dread, almost panic, in the tone of his voice as he writes: "I advise you, King and lord, not to attempt nor allow a fleet to be sent to this ill-fated river, because in Christian faith I swear, King and lord, that if a hundred thousand men come none will escape, because the stories are false and in this river there is nothing but despair, especially for those newly arrived from Spain."

El Loco then signs off, not as the "Wrath of God" as he had earlier described himself, but as "Lope de Aguirre, the Wanderer."

The maniacal conquistador briefly considered to be the most feared man in the New World ended his bloody wanderings obsessed not with the riches of the golden city, but haunted by a mortal dread of El Dorado, and what its siren call had done to so many men.

8

Riches That Far Exceedeth Any of the World

I have been assured by such of the Spaniards as have seen Manoa, the imperial city of Guiana, which the Spaniards call El Dorado, that for the greatness, for the riches, and for the excellent seat, it far exceedeth any of the world, at least of so much of the world as is known to the Spanish nation.

—Sir Walter Raleigh, *The Discoverie of the Large, Rich, and Beautiful Empire of Guiana* (1595)

IN DEVONSHIRE, ENGLAND, young Walter Raleigh was nine years old in the year that Lope de Aguirre's body parts were pieced out in an erstwhile German colony in South America. Raleigh was to grow up to be many things. He was a sea captain, a warrior, a tobacco entrepreneur, and the founder of a colony in Virginia called Roanoke that vanished mysteriously. He would be an intimate of Queen Elizabeth I, and an inmate under her successor. He was both a knight and a knave, but mostly, he lived the life which Aguirre lastly described as his own—as a wanderer.

One of the more unique of English history's colorful characters, Raleigh also joined the ranks of that long list of men who abandoned common sense in a mad quest for that place which he described as "the great and golden city which the Spaniards call El Dorado, and the naturals [the natives] Manoa."

Raleigh grew up Protestant during the violent religious strife in England between them and the Catholics. Indeed, his own father narrowly missed being executed during the reign of Queen Mary I, the Catholic eldest daughter of King Henry VIII known to history as "Bloody Mary."

Sharing his family's loathing of Catholics, Raleigh fought against them on the side of French Huguenots in the Battle of Jarnac in 1569 while he was still a teenager. After Mary's Protestant half-sister, Elizabeth I, ascended to the English throne in 1558, Raleigh sided with the crown against Catholics as the conflict continued in his native land. He subsequently fought in the repression of Catholic rebels in Ireland during the Desmond Rebellions, and wound up owning land on the Emerald Isle as a result. This was not an uncommon reward for Englishmen who did battle in Ireland to suppress the Irish.

Through one of his neighbor landholders, the poet Edmund Spenser, Raleigh was introduced to Queen Elizabeth. She took a liking to the young soldier of fortune, and was to be an important, if intermittent supporter in his professional career. She knighted him in 1585 and showered him with favors, including an appointment as vice admiral of Devonshire in 1588.

Whether their relationship evolved into more than merely the warm cordiality of a monarch and favored subject continues to be a topic of innuendo. Elizabeth was famously known as the "Virgin Queen" because she never married, but whether or not she actually remained a virgin all her life will never be known. Nevertheless, the English considered the symbolism of an unmarried female monarch quite significant in the sixteenth century.

For Elizabeth professionally, her "virginity" meant that she shared no power with a consort and remained as England's sole sovereign throughout her reign. There was also a cult of sorts that surrounded Elizabeth and the way she was majestically portrayed in art and literature. The cultists went so far as to suggest that as the Catholics had their Virgin Mary, English Protestants had their Virgin Elizabeth.

In the meantime, Sir Walter's attention was also on events that were unfolding in the New World. Indeed, he was intrigued by tales of Hernán Cortés, Francisco Pizarro, and all those who had later searched the jungles of the New World for El Dorado.

By the 1580s, the Spanish had been campaigning and colonizing in Mexico and South America for two generations, but North America remained relatively untouched by the continent's eventual principal colonizer, England. Feeling his oats as an entrepreneur, Raleigh and some like-minded colleagues cooked up a scheme to change this.

Raleigh headed a venture to establish the first permanent English colony in North America in a place which they dubbed "Virginia," after their Virgin Queen. After two attempts, the experiment ended disastrously as the entire population of the settlement on Roanoke Island disappeared without a trace. An expedition that came looking for them in 1590 after three years of their having had no contact with England discovered their settlement site abandoned. The word "Croatoan" carved on a tree trunk was the only evidence as to what may have happened, but this never-explained clue merely became an enduring part of the unresolved mystery.

Shortly thereafter, Elizabeth became infuriated with her favorite knave when he impregnated and secretly married one of her ladies-in-waiting, Elizabeth Throckmorton.

In 1594, however, Raleigh was handed an opportunity to get back in Her Majesty's good graces. He presented it to her as more than merely another scheme involving the New World. It was also an opportunity to exploit the riches of the New World while taking a jab at the despised (and Catholic) Spaniards.

England had asserted its naval dominance by the resounding and history-altering defeat of the Spanish Armada in 1588, and Raleigh's proposal would give Elizabeth a renewed opportunity to flex English geopolitical muscle. In this case it would be in South America, within what was still a Spanish sphere of influence.

The catalyst came in the form of a letter pilfered on Raleigh's behalf by Captain George Popham. Not to be confused with the later George Popham who was a prominent colonist in Maine, this Popham was an English sea captain who had worked for Raleigh essentially as a hired pirate in the lucrative trade of plundering lone Spanish galleons on the high seas. Aboard one such vessel, which he intercepted early in 1594, Popham took possession of, along with the usual booty, a mail sack. In that sack, there was a letter to Spain's King Philip II from his governor in Trinidad, Don Antonio de Berrío (Raleigh spells his name Berreo).

The memo discussed Berrío's own efforts to find a mysterious city of gold in the headwaters of the Orinoco River. This area, in which Spaniard after Spaniard had sought cities of gold for decades, and where Diego de Ordaz had once quested for the mythical land of Meta—was in the land then called Guiana, a swath of land containing much of the watershed of the Orinoco that is now part of Venezuela, as well as the adjacent area to the south which became British Guiana in the nineteenth century, and which is now the nation of Guyana.

According to Edmund Gosse of Trinity College, Cambridge, in his 1886 biography *Raleigh*, Berrío had annexed Guiana to the dominions of the Spanish crown under the name of El Nuevo Dorado (The *New* Golden One), suggesting some fresh evidence of a golden city that was distinct from all the earlier golden cities.

In the letter handed to Raleigh by Popham, Berrío told a tale with elements matching the earlier El Dorado and Meta stories, but with some new twists. For example, in Guiana, the city of gold was inhabited by not one, but *many*, gold-dust-encrusted chiefs. As Berrío related: "various reports of the country and its inhabitants were repeated, that the chiefs danced with their naked bodies gleaming with gold dust, and with golden eagles dangling from their breasts and great pearls from their ears, that there were rich mines of diamonds and of gold, that the innocent people were longing to exchange their jewels for jews-harps."

Now bitten by the notorious gold bug, Sir Walter pitched the idea of an English expedition to search for the golden city of El Nuevo Dorado to Queen Elizabeth. She apparently liked and encouraged the scheme as it furthered her goals of projecting English power in Spanish territory, though she offered no financial support from the royal treasury. Raleigh would have to do it on his own.

Having sent a fellow Devonshire seaman, Captain Jacob Whiddon, to conduct an initial reconnaissance in late 1594, Raleigh began assembling a flotilla of privateers to cross the Atlantic early in the new year. These included ships captained by Whiddon and Henry Thyn, as well as Captain George Gifford, Raleigh's vice admiral, and a Captain Caulfield. The master of Raleigh's own ship was John Douglas.

Sir Walter's fleet set sail in February 1595, traveling westward in the wake of those two generations of Spanish treasure-seekers.

Anchoring off Trinidad on March 22, Raleigh made his initial contact with the Spanish colonials. He writes that he entertained the Spaniards "kindly" aboard his ship, offering them feasting and drinking "by means whereof I learned of one and another as much of the estate of Guiana as I could, or as they knew; for those poor soldiers having been many years without wine, a few draughts made them merry, in which mood they vaunted of Guiana and the riches thereof, and all what they knew of the ways and passages."

As a cover story, Raleigh "bred in them an opinion that I was bound only for the relief of those English which I had planted in Virginia, whereof the bruit was come among them; which I had performed in my return, if extremity of weather had not forced me from the said coast."

In the meanwhile, Raleigh was approached secretly by some Arawak Indians whose chiefs were being held prisoner in San Juan de Oruña, Berrío's capital. Wishing to create a good impression on the Arawak, who lived in Guiana as well as in Trinidad, Raleigh generously offered to come to their aid. He told them that his "Virgin Queen" had sent him to deliver them from the cruel Spaniards.

"By my Indian interpreter, which I carried out of England," the duplicitous Raleigh wrote, "I made them understand that I was the servant of a queen who was the great cacique [commander] of the north, and a virgin, and had more caciqui under her than there were trees in that island; that she was an enemy to the Castellani in respect of their tyranny and oppression, and that she delivered all such nations about her, as were by them oppressed; and having freed all the coast of the northern world from their servitude, had sent me to free them also, and withal to defend the country of Guiana from their invasion and conquest."

In an ensuing firefight, Raleigh's troops overwhelmed the Spanish, took possession of their city, and captured Berrío himself. As was often the case in that era, when victorious commanders handled the defeated ones with magnanimity, Raleigh treated the Spaniard as a gentleman, and the two seemed to have gotten along cordially.

Raleigh learned that Berrío was married to Doña Maria de Oruña, whom Raleigh writes was the daughter of the notorious conquistador Gonzalo Jiménez de Quesada, the master of New Granada, and of the Cundinamarca Plateau, the source of the early El Dorado legends. Other accounts have it that she was Quesada's niece, but in any case, when Quesada had died in 1579, he had left cash and property in Trinidad to Doña Maria and her husband. The couple and their eight children had arrived in the New World in 1581, only to discover that one of the strings attached to their inheritance was that Berrío had to use part of the gold to pursue a search in the Orinoco headwaters for El Dorado.

As they sat around in San Juan (today's Port of Spain, Trinidad), a city which Berrío himself had founded, drinking wine and getting to know one another, Berrío filled Raleigh in on his findings. He explained that he had been upriver on the Orinoco personally, and from there, up the Río Meta. He told Raleigh that he had seen evidence leading him to believe in the existence of a city of gold which the "naturals" called Manoa.

He also repeated the story often told by Diego de Ordaz and other Spanish explorers of Laguna Parima (Lake Parime), the great lake that was said to be the source of the Orinoco. In his own accounts, Raleigh relates having heard often about this body of water being the size of the Caspian Sea. In addition to its being called Laguna Parima, it was at various times referred to as Lake Manoa, Mar Blanco, or even Mar El Dorado (the Sea of El Dorado). Adolph Bandelier interprets the Laguna Parima element as having been derived from the

Manoa and El Dorado legends being intertwined, as the presence of a lake is a key element in the latter mythology.

Sir Walter Raleigh.
(*Bill Yenne*)

The presence of a major body of water in the interior of Guiana was long assumed to be a geographical fact. This lake was included on many maps, including those of the Flemish engraver and cartographer Jodocus Hondius, by the late sixteenth century. The lake still appeared as a matter of course on maps published into the eighteenth century. Even the meticulous cartographer Jean-Baptiste Bourguignon d'Anville featured Laguna Parima on *L'Amérique Meridionale*, his 1748 map of the Americas. Such an inclusion was considered an endorsement, as he was one of the enlightened cartographers who was so meticulous with his mapmaking that he deliberately left unknown regions blank rather than filling them with the imaginary or mythical.

If fact, Laguna Parima never existed. There would be no lake of any great size in the interior of northeastern South America until the Río Caroni, a major Orinoco tributary, was dammed in the twentieth century.

As Gosse explains, Berrío seems to have "insinuated himself into Raleigh's confidence, and, like the familiar poet in Shakespeare's sonnet, 'nightly gulled him with intelligence.' His original idea probably was that by inflaming Raleigh's imagination with the wonders of Guiana, he would be the more likely to plunge to his own destruction into the fatal swamps of the Orinoco."

In retrospect, it seems almost certain that Berrío was buttering Raleigh up with kindness and sharing tall tales clothed as secrets in order to send the Englishman to his death. In their conversations, they discussed the Spanish and German expeditions that had taken place in the Orinoco watershed early in the sixteenth century, including those of Gonzalo Jiménez de Quesada, marching eastward from Cundinamarca.

Raleigh would have related that, as part of his interest in the Spanish adventures in South America, he had also read, reread, and later quoted the historian and champion of conquistadors Francisco López de Gomora. In his *General History of the Indies*, López wrote of having visited the court of Guyana Capac, whom Raleigh imagined as the "ancestor to the Emperor of Guiana," if such an office still existed in 1595.

Raleigh recalled that López had spoken of the emperor having "in his wardrobe, hollow statues of gold which seemed giants, and the figures in proportion and bigness of all the beasts, birds, trees, and herbs, that the earth bringeth forth; and of all the fishes that the sea or waters of his kingdom breedeth. He had also ropes, budgets, chests, and troughs of gold and silver, heaps of billets of gold, that seemed wood marked out (split into logs) to burn."

Berrío and Raleigh would have agreed that there was great significance in the fact that Guiana was due east of Peru. By this, one might extrapolate a direct connection between the riches of the Inca Empire and those of the notional golden city of the Orinoco, whether it was called Meta, Manoa, or El Dorado. As Raleigh later wrote, perhaps based on a theory that Berrío had learned from Quesada, that Guiana "is directly east from Peru towards the sea, and lieth under the equinoctial line; and it hath more abundance of gold than any part of Peru, and as many or more great cities than ever Peru had when it flourished most."

All this theorizing and reminiscing about familiar legends was one thing, but Berrío had something even more enticing up his sleeve.

The prize artifact which Berrío showed Raleigh was the journal of a man named Juan Martínez, who was said to have been a "master of munition" on the Diego de Ordaz expedition in 1531, and the sole survivor of another *entrada* in the early 1580s. According to the account in Raleigh's memoirs, Martínez claimed in the journal to have traveled inland on his own, and to have spent seven months as a guest of its king, or Inca, to use the Tahuantinsuyo term. Raleigh uses the word "Inga" in his narrative.

It is easy to picture Raleigh's growing excitement in reading this story. He would have reused Martínez's account of being discovered wandering alone by indigenous people, and of being brought blindfolded into this golden city that was called Manoa by its citizens. As Raleigh tells it, Martínez "entered the city at noon, and then they uncovered his face; and that he traveled all that day till night through the city, and the next day from sun rising to sun setting, ere he came to the palace of Inca."

This much walking suggests that the distance from the city gates to the palace was well over 50 miles.

Berrío then described, in detail, the tale of the gold-dusted kings and courtiers. Raleigh later related this, writing that the golden king's courtiers were "stripped naked and their bodies anointed all over with a kind of white balsamum (by them called curca), of which there is great plenty, and yet very dear amongst them, and it is of all other the most precious, whereof we have had good experience. When they are anointed all over, certain servants of the emperor, having prepared gold made into fine powder, blow it through hollow canes upon their naked bodies, until they be all shining from the foot to the head; and in this sort they sit drinking by twenties and hundreds, and continue in drunkenness sometimes six or seven days together."

As Martínez told it, after his seven months in Manoa, the Inca gave him a choice of remaining there or going home. When he chose the latter, the king sent him on his way with as much gold and jewelry as he could carry. Apparently this is where the journal ended, because there are various secondhand accounts of how he lost his loot. Some tell of Martínez having had all his treasure stolen by thieves as he was making his way back to the coast, while others say that he made it out with some jewels hidden in his pipe.

Martínez had died of the fever in Puerto Rico before he could be taken to Spain for a full debriefing, and Berrío had never met him, but his story offered gold-seekers a fresh sighting of an old legend. Raleigh held in his hands the words written by a man who had actually seen Manoa, the place that Raleigh describes as possessing riches that "far exceedeth any of the world, at least of so much of the world as is known to the Spanish nation."

With the unveiling of the Martínez journal, Berrío could tell that Raleigh was hooked.

Now it was time to seal the deal by seasoning the glittering tale with dashes of reality. In order for his tale to be believable, it couldn't be entirely too good to be true. There had to be some bad parts to make it seem real. There was gold, Berrío insisted, but he also cautioned Raleigh with sobering tales of suffering, of difficulties, of "poisonful worms and serpents," and of losing many of his men to the unforgiving hardships of the jungle.

The Spaniard also distressed Raleigh with the horrors of the poison darts used by the indigenous people of the rain forests. As Raleigh was told in Trinidad, and would later lament from personal observation, "besides the mortality of the wound they make, the party shot endureth the most insufferable torment in the world, and abideth a most ugly and lamentable death, sometimes dying stark mad, sometimes their bowels breaking out of their bellies; which are presently discoloured as black as pitch, and so unsavory as no man can endure to cure or to attend them."

From Berrío, Raleigh was learning now of the downside of the glorious quest, the factors which had driven many treasure hunting conquistadors, from Gonzalo Pizarro to Lope de Aguirre, to the brink of madness. As Raleigh put it, the wily Berrío "was stricken into a great melancholy and sadness, using all the arguments he could to dissuade me, and also assuring the gentlemen of my company that it would be labour lost." Naturally, his purpose was just the opposite, but Raleigh took the bait.

He sailed his ships across the Serpent's Mouth, the narrow band of water separating Trinidad from mainland South America and began nosing along the Orinoco Delta. Six decades after Ordaz first ventured upriver in this place, Sir Walter Raleigh was here, and on the hunt.

Sailing separately to cover as much territory as possible, Raleigh's captains searched the many mouths of the Orinoco looking for a main channel that would take them into the interior. As they did so, they learned of the power of the great rivers of South America. In his own description, Raleigh writes of the Orinoco that "it was impossible either to ford it, or to swim it, both by reason of the swiftness, and also for that the borders were so pestered with fast woods, as neither boat nor man could find place either to land or to embark."

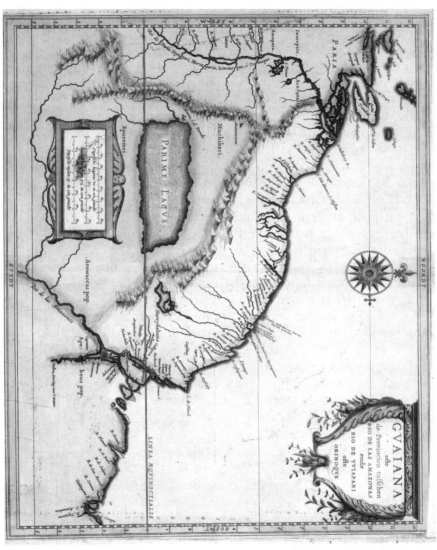

Laguna Parima (Lake Parime), the mythical body of water in the interior of Guiana as seen in a 1625 map by Hessel Gerritsz. For many years before and after Raleigh's expedition it was assumed as a matter of course that this inland sea existed, but this supposition was based on rumors not yet proven false.

He also found that he must delay his expedition until later in the year, "for in June, July, August, and September it is impossible to navigate any of [the mouths of] those rivers; for such is the fury of the current, and there are so many trees and woods overflown, as if any boat but touch upon any tree or stake it is impossible to save any one person therein."

By waiting until the high water and fast current subsided, Raleigh now found the river too shallow because of the sand-bars and submerged driftwood. Therefore, he anchored his ships at sea and proceeded in smaller vessels. These he cate-gorized as "no other than wherries, one little barge, a small cock-boat, and a bad galiota which we framed in haste for that purpose at Trinidad; and those little boats had nine or ten men apiece, with all their victuals and arms."

Concerning the breadth of the Orinoco Delta, Raleigh adds that "we had as much sea to cross over in our wherries, as between Dover and [Calais], and in a great hollow, the wind and current being both very strong."

Guided by an Arawak river pilot known as Ferdinando, they traveled for about a month, making what Raleigh esti-mates as 400 miles, though half that mileage probably involved to-and-fro investigations of side channels. The chan-nel that they took, which they called the "Red Cross" after England's flag, was not the main channel of the Orinoco. Raleigh observes in his account that they did not merge into this for at least six weeks.

Raleigh describes the expedition as being "driven to lie in the rain and weather in the open air, in the burning sun, and upon the hard boards, and to dress our meat, and to carry all manner of furniture . . . so pestered and unsavoury, that what with victuals being most fish, with the wet clothes of so many men thrust together, and the heat of the sun, I will undertake there was never any prison in England that could be found more unsavoury and loathsome." Raleigh also men-tions witnessing the spectacle of a man being consumed by a crocodile.

Nevertheless, they persisted, and farther upriver, condi-tions began to improve. As Raleigh writes: "On both sides of this river we passed the most beautiful country that ever mine eyes beheld; and whereas all that we had seen before was nothing but woods, prickles, bushes, and thorns, here we beheld plains of twenty miles in length, the grass short and green, and in divers[e] parts groves of trees by themselves, as if they had been by all the art and labour in the world so made of purpose; and still as we rowed, the deer came down feeding by the water's side as if they had been used to a keeper's call."

In this passage, he makes mention of what appeared to be deliberately planted fruit orchards, repeating an observation that crops up occasionally in Spanish accounts of the South American interior in the sixteenth century. This would have confirmed the existence of a civilization in the region that had evolved beyond merely that of hunter-gatherers. During the nineteenth and early twentieth centuries, mainstream archaeology dismissed this as pure fantasy, insisting that no such civilization could then have existed there in the sixteenth century. However, by the end of the twentieth century, evidence of fairly advanced agriculture in the sixteenth century was being discovered, suggesting that Raleigh indeed could have seen orchards. Archaeologists such as Clark Erickson of the University of Pennsylvania and Anna Roosevelt of the Field Museum of Natural History in Chicago have interpreted recent findings as sustaining the theory that South American rain forests supported agriculture on a much larger scale than previously imagined.

As they traveled, the Englishmen did eventually find themselves being entertained favorably in a riverside village of friendly Arawak people. Raleigh also encountered a number of indigenous commercial traders, and even a few Spaniards. He writes that Captain Gifford "espied" four Arawak canoes coming down the river, and when their crews spotted the Englishmen, two turned into a side channel and disappeared, while the others "gave over and ran themselves ashore, every man betaking himself to the fastness of the woods."

Inspecting the abandoned canoes on the shore, Raleigh discovered that they were "loaded with bread, and were bound for [Isla] Margarita in the West Indies" to trade with the Spanish. With these Arawak, the Englishmen had also spotted three Spaniards. "Nothing on the earth could have been more welcome to us, next unto gold," effused Raleigh, "than the great store of very excellent bread which we found in these [canoes]."

He adds that upon their finding bread and other food, his men cried out, "Let us go on, we care not how far." This certainly would have encouraged him, given that his expedition was nearing that point when previous expeditions into this jungle had been on the precipice of mutiny.

Also extremely encouraging was what Raleigh found next. He writes that "as I was creeping through the bushes, I saw an Indian basket hidden, which was [a] refiner's basket; for I found in it his quicksilver, saltpetre, and divers[e] things for the trial of metals, and also the dust of such ore as he had refined; but in those [canoes] which escaped there was a good quantity of ore and gold."

Assuming that the refiner's gear belonged to one of the Spaniards, and that he obviously knew of a source of gold upriver, Raleigh announced a £500 reward to whomever of his men could bring back one of the Spaniards who had escaped into the woods with the Arawak.

Though the Spaniards were never caught, Raleigh's men did catch up with several Arawak men and women. They found these people fearing that the Englishmen would eat them, because the Spanish had "persuaded all the nations that [the English] were men-eaters and cannibals."

In his own account, the insulted Raleigh portrays his crew as consummate Protestant gentlemen, distinguishing them from the barbarian and Catholic Spaniards, whom he identifies as rapists. He recalls that "when the poor men and women had seen us, and that we gave them meat, and to every one something or other which was rare and strange to them, they began to conceive the deceit and purpose of the Spaniards, who indeed, as they confessed took from them both their wives and daughters daily."

He goes on to say that *his* men couldn't possibly conceive of raping Arawak women, insisting that: "I protest before the Majesty of the living God, that I neither know nor believe, that any of our company, one or other, did offer insult to any of their women, and yet we saw many hundreds, and had many in our power, and of those very young and excellently favoured, which came among us without deceit, stark naked. Nothing got us more love amongst them than this usage; for I suffered not any man to take from any of the nations so much as a pina [pineapple] or a potato root without giving them contentment, nor any man so much as to offer to touch any of their wives or daughters."

However, Raleigh was apparently not above kidnapping, if that served his purpose. Discovering that one of the Arawak men, who was called Martín by the Spanish, seemed to know where the gold mines might be, Raleigh took him aboard his own expedition as a "pilot."

With this, Raleigh sent a detachment of men, guided by Ferdinando, his previous pilot, back downstream to the ocean, where the ships were anchored, to brief the rest of the expedition on the progress so far. Then, with their purloined provisions, Raleigh's men put into the river and continued their quest for Manoa.

Fifteen days later, by Raleigh's reckoning, they merged into the broad main channel of the Orinoco, and were treated to their first fleeting view of the distant Guiana Highlands. Nearby they went ashore on a sandy beach which turned out to be a turtle nesting area, and enjoyed feasting on the eggs which they found to be "very wholesome meat, and greatly restoring."

They also encountered a group of local people, whose leader was a man named Toparimaca. The people shared food with the Englishmen, who traded Spanish wine to them for their local "clean and sweet" black beer, which Raleigh described as being "very strong with pepper, and the juice of divers[e] herbs and fruits digested and purged." The latter phrase is a reference to the use of the enzymes in human saliva to initiate fermentation, which was not uncommon in the ancient world. In 1987, citing written records dating back to 1557, anthropologist Alan Eames reconstructed the pre-Columbian brewing methods used in the South American rain forest in Raleigh's time, in which a black beer was produced using corn and manioc with natural fermentation. Subsequently, a contemporary black beer based on this process was produced using the original ingredients—minus the human saliva. Named "Xingu," after the Amazon tributary of the same name, this beer is today brewed by Cervejaria Sul Brasileira in Santa Maria, Brazil, and is marketed in the United States.

Raleigh and his crew apparently enjoyed the black beer, and observed that the local people consumed copious amounts of it from earthenware jugs. There were between thirty and forty indigenous people among the drinking companions of the English at this stop, including a visiting chief from farther into the interior and his wife.

As much as Raleigh had to say in praise of the beer, he was more taken with the chief's wife.

"In all my life I have seldom seen a better favoured woman," he practically swoons in his description. "She was of good stature, with black eyes, fat of body, of an excellent countenance, her hair almost as long as herself, tied up again in pretty knots; and it seemed she stood not in that awe of her husband as the rest, for she spake and discoursed, and drank among the gentlemen and captains, and was very pleasant, knowing her own comeliness, and taking great pride therein. I have seen a lady in England so like to her, as but for the difference of colour, I would have sworn might have been the same."

Raleigh eventually bade farewell to his hosts and continued up the Orinoco and into the Río Caroni (which Raleigh calls Caroli). This time he was accompanied by a couple of men whom Toparimaca sent along to introduce the English to people upstream.

At each stop, the Englishmen were met by a different tribe of people who treated them well, if for no other reason than the people they met shared their animosity toward the Spanish. Raleigh played on their feelings by claiming through his interpreters that his virgin sovereign had sent him to deliver the people of Guiana from the Spanish scourge.

Raleigh also eagerly sought information about the city of gold that he was sure existed upriver. The people whom he met spoke of such a place, and of a tribe called Epuremei who wrought large plates of the yellow metal, but they offered no hard evidence.

With growing impatience, Raleigh even started sending men ashore to search for indications of gold ore. Raleigh himself hiked a short distance inland, but left most of the exploring to others, describing himself as "a very ill footman." Numerous rocks were examined in detail, but he despairs in his accounts that no gold was discovered. In fact, traces of gold can be found in quartz specimens from Guiana, but in quantities far below the threshold for commercial extraction.

Among those fascinating characters with whom the Englishmen crossed paths on this part of the river was an old sage named Topiawari, whom Raleigh called the King of Aromaia, claiming him to be as old as 110 years. His people treated the Englishmen to "venison, pork, hens, chickens, fowl, fish, with divers[e] sorts of excellent fruits and roots, and great abundance of [pineapples], the princess of fruits that grow under the sun, especially those of Guiana." The king also gave Raleigh an armadillo, which fascinated him greatly.

Topiawari knew about the Epuremei and he told Raleigh that he was only four days' journey from the Macureguarai, who were

> the next and nearest of the subjects of Inga, and of the Epuremei, and the first town of apparelled and rich people; and that all those plates of gold which were scattered among the borderers and carried to other nations far and near, came from the said Macureguarai and were there made, but that those of the land within were far finer, and were fashioned after the images of men, beasts, birds, and fishes. . . . He told me that the most of the gold which they made in plates and images was not severed from the stone, but that on the lake of Manoa, and in a multitude of other rivers, they gathered it in grains of perfect gold and in pieces as big as small stones, and they put it to a part of copper, otherwise they could not work it; and that they used a great earthen pot with holes round about it, and when they had mingled the gold and copper together they fastened canes to the holes, and so with the breath of men they increased the fire till the metal ran, and then they cast it into moulds of stone and clay, and so make those plates and images.

However, Topiawari also warned Raleigh about the military strength of the Epuremei and their allies, and reminded him of all the Spaniards who had died searching for this city of gold. He told Raleigh that "he could not perceive that I meant to go onward towards the city of Manoa, for neither the time of the year served [for it was now flood season], neither could he perceive any sufficient numbers for such an enterprise. And if I did, I was sure with all my company to be buried there, for the emperor was of that strength, as that many times so many men more were too few."

Nevertheless, Raleigh apparently decided that he had come too far to give up, and asked Topiawari whether he could supply guides to show the English the way. Some of Topiawari's subjects, apparently impressed by the potent firepower of English muskets, relished the proposal, believing that coalition warfare against the Epuremei was a good idea. They told the Englishmen that they would divide the spoils, "their women for us, and their gold for you."

However, the old man added that he would support the venture only if Raleigh could leave fifty armed men behind to protect his village, explaining that he feared an Epuremei massacre if he aided the English. He further feared reprisals from the Spanish for helping Raleigh. Excluding his rowers and laborers, Raleigh had barely fifty soldiers in all, so he could not oblige.

For Sir Walter Raleigh, this marked the end of the road. As he wrote, "I was contented to forbear the enterprise against the Epuremei till the next year." He and Topiawari parted on good terms.

Confidently believing that he really would return early in 1596, Raleigh left two men behind for the stated purposes of learning the language of Topiawari's people, and reconnoitering the golden city of Manoa in advance of the "enterprise against the Epuremei." The two were his cabin boy, Hugh Goodwin, and Francis Sparrow (Raleigh's biographer Edmund Gosse calls him "Sparrey"), who was a servant to Captain Gifford. Raleigh describes Sparrow as being "desirous to tarry," and lauds his usefulness as a chronicler, adding that he "could describe a country with his pen."

Traveling with the current at the end of the season, their trip downstream went considerably more quickly. Reunited with their ocean-going fleet, the English explorers set sail for home.

Berrío's dream of the ruddy Englishman dying a painful death as a pincushion for poison darts, or lunch for a crocodile, never was fulfilled, but he could take satisfaction in having sent Raleigh on a wild goose chase with respect to Manoa.

The old Spaniard died in 1597 without again laying eyes on Sir Walter, but he had to have gone to his grave with the last laugh, when his pivotal piece of "evidence" was shown to be a hoax. As Edmund Gosse writes, the Juan Martínez journal was "afterwards exposed as an invention of the fat friars of Puerto Rico, but Raleigh believed it."

In all probability, Raleigh continued believing in Manoa even after the exposure of Martínez as a deception. After all, he did have the word of his friend, Topiawari.

9

THE ENEMY OF
SPAIN TRIES AGAIN

I am resolved that if there were but a small army afoot
in Guiana, marching towards Manoa . . . [the city]
would yield to Her Majesty by composition so many
hundred thousand pounds yearly as should both
defend [against] all enemies abroad, and defray all
expenses at home. . . . I trust in God, this being true,
will suffice, and that he which is King of all Kings,
and Lord of Lords, will put it into her heart which is
Lady of Ladies to possess it.
—Sir Walter Raleigh, *The Discovery of Guiana* (1596)

BY OCTOBER 1595, Sir Walter Raleigh was back in
Devonshire, where he immersed himself in the task of shaping his notes and journal entries into the book from which
the passages in the previous chapter are quoted. For a work
with such lasting significance, it was finished quickly. Dated
1596, it was actually published by Christmas 1595 with the
long-winded title *The Discoverie of the Large, Rich, and
Beautiful Empire of Guiana, with a Relation of the Great and
Golden City of Manoa, which the Spaniards call El Dorado, and
the Provinces of Emeria, Arromaia, Amapaia, and other Countries,
with their Rivers, Adjoining.* Later editions of this book, which
is still in print, have been published simply as the *Discovery of
Guiana.*

Reprinted in England within a year and soon translated into languages from German to Latin, the book made Raleigh a best-selling international author. Naturally, copies found their way into Spain, where his opinions and commentaries made him, if he was not already, a leading figure on the "enemies list" of Philip II and the Spanish ruling class.

In this role, he took part, later in 1596, in the English capture of the Spanish port city of Cadiz, which was spearheaded by an English fleet under the Earl of Essex and Sir Charles Howard. While the English and their Dutch allies occupied the city for less than a month, the attack decimated the city, and humiliated Spain, which was only then beginning to recover from the embarrassing defeat of the Armada in 1588. Spanish civic and religious leaders who were taken hostage in the sacking of Cadiz would not be released until 1603.

When he should have been planning his return to the Orinoco in the autumn of 1596, Sir Walter Raleigh was nursing a serious leg wound that he suffered during the fighting at Cadiz. In lieu of going back himself, he did as he had done two years earlier when he sent Captain Jacob Whiddon to scout the Orinoco Delta. This time, his surrogate was Captain Leonard Berrie, who reached Guiana, but apparently did little more than lend an ear to the tall tales of Manoa and El Dorado being spun for strangers in the port cities. He returned to England the following year without actually having penetrated the Orinoco watershed any further than Raleigh had.

Raleigh postponed his own return, and postponed it again and again. He remained fairly close to home through the turn of the century. His farthest voyage afield during these years came in 1597, when he served as second in command when Elizabeth I ordered an attack on the Portuguese in the Azores. The commander of this venture was another of Her Majesty's favorites, Robert Devereux, the Second Earl of Essex.

Even as they sailed on this relatively short voyage, the greed for gold clouded the judgment of Raleigh and Devereux. The so-called "Islands Voyage" was bungled when the two captains decided to divert from the planned attack on the Portuguese battle fleet, to instead go after Spanish treasure ships sailing from the New World.

As a result of this shenanigan, both the Earl and Raleigh fell out of favor with Elizabeth. Devereux was jailed two years later after botching another campaign, this time in Ireland, and executed in 1601 for plotting against Elizabeth.

However, time was also running out for Elizabeth. Drained by the political intrigues whirling about her court and the economic downturn then plaguing England, she sickened and died in March 1603. Because the Virgin Queen had no children, and had named no heir, the succession dilemma was settled by the power brokers. They went beyond the borders to pick James VI of Scotland (the son of Mary, Queen of Scots, and the great-great-grandson of England's Henry VII) to rule simultaneously as James I of England.

Unfortunately for Raleigh at this juncture, he would be implicated in a plot to overthrow James later in 1603. He may or may not have actually been involved, but despite his protesting his innocence, he was convicted. He managed to sidestep the death penalty—it was suspended, not over-turned—but the once footloose soldier of fortune found himself imprisoned in the Tower of London for the next thirteen years.

During this time, his supporters on the outside repeatedly petitioned the king for his release. Even James's wife, Anne of Denmark, who had befriended Raleigh, supported the liberation of the old sea dog. While he was in the Tower, though, Sir Walter was not idle. He managed to write a history of the world, and thanks to conjugal visits with his wife, Elizabeth, to father his son, Carew.

In January 1616, James finally issued an order for Raleigh's release, but not so much out of sympathy. Tantalized by the tales of Manoa and El Dorado that were part of the lore wherever the riches of Spanish America were mentioned, the king himself had been bitten by the gold bug. Raleigh's release was conditional on his returning to Guiana.

With the king signing the checks, something Elizabeth had refused to do last time, Raleigh went to work. He assembled a fleet of ships, including a newly built 440-ton flagship that was christened *Destiny*. Having a high-profile inmate such as Sir Walter Raleigh back on the street after more than a decade certainly attracted a lot of attention, but the fact that he was fitting out more than a half dozen vessels certainly turned the rumor mill.

Among those raising an eyebrow at the news of Raleigh outfitting a fleet was Don Diego Sarmiento de Acuña, Count of Gondomar, who had been appointed as Spanish ambassador to England in 1613. Things had changed in the years since Raleigh had last been a free man. One of James I's first diplomatic initiatives when he took the throne had been to end England's three-decade state of war with Spain through the Treaty of London in 1604.

Now, Spain not only had an ambassador in London, but Gondomar communicated regularly with the English king, and they got along as cordially as Raleigh and Berrío had in Trinidad. People spoke of Machiavellian intrigues and even of a "Spanish faction" within James's court, while grumbling about the Scottish king's undue friendliness with England's longtime antagonist.

To Gondomar, it looked as though Raleigh was preparing to set sail for a bit of that favorite pastime of pre-treaty English sea captains—anti-Spanish piracy. When he raised his concerns to James, he was assured that Raleigh was not going to sea to intercept Spanish treasure ships lugging home pilfered Mexican gold and silver. James was very up front with Gondomar, explaining that Raleigh was merely going back to resume his expeditions into Guiana.

Whereas Queen Elizabeth had no qualms about Raleigh's sacking Spanish possessions back in 1595, James asserted to the ambassador that the Englishman would tread lightly in 1616. He even gave him a copy of Raleigh's itinerary, which was dutifully forwarded to Madrid.

With his son Walter, called "Wat," at his side, Raleigh set sail in June 1617. Now in his twenties, Wat was apparently itching for the kind of adventure that his father had once experienced.

After being mauled by bad weather and making several stops, the English were in South America by October. It is ironic to note that one of Raleigh's stated concerns on this voyage was dodging the Barbary pirates who harassed shipping from Gibraltar to the Canaries. The former commerce raider whom Gondomar had suspected of intended piracy had made his run south past Africa while worrying about being attacked himself.

The *Destiny* made landfall at the recently established French port of Cayenne, now the capital of French Guiana. Raleigh was apparently well received—or at least remembered—by the indigenous locals. In a letter home to his wife, he boasted that "I might [as well] be here King of the Indians were a vanity; but my name hath still lived among them. Here they feed me with fresh meat and all that the country yields; all offer to obey me."

While making his port call, Raleigh chanced to find himself—against all odds—face to face with his old cabin boy, Hugh Goodwin, whom he had left behind in the Orinoco headwaters twenty-two years before. It can be said without doubt that each of them had long since given up on any notion of ever seeing the other again. By now, Goodwin, whom Raleigh had once instructed to learn the indigenous dialects in anticipation of his return, had not only done so, but he had almost forgotten how to speak English. It was probably for the best, as he was destined never to see England again. He met his end some time later, killed by a jaguar in the jungles of the homeland imposed upon him by Raleigh.

Meanwhile, Francis Sparrow, who had also been left behind by Raleigh in 1595, had been captured by the Spanish and imprisoned in Spain. He had finally escaped to England in 1602, where he wrote his account of Guiana which Raleigh had anticipated when he said that Sparrow "could describe a country with his pen." It was the part in his narrative about his having traded a half-penny knife for eight teenaged Indian girls which Raleigh probably did not anticipate.

Raleigh was back in Trinidad by December 1617, but as the accounts go, he was not the same brawny swashbuckler who had taken the island by storm a generation earlier—and he finally realized as much. His health had been on the downward slide. His war wounds and his years in the Tower of London had overtaken him. He realized as he stared up the Orinoco that he was a spent man. Thinking back to the "unsavoury and loathsome" experience of before, the old knight decided that he was no longer up to the task.

The mission would go forward, but it would be under the command of Raleigh's lieutenant, Lawrence Kemys (also seen written as Keymis). Young Wat Raleigh would also join the expedition while his father remained behind in Trinidad. As mistakes go, Raleigh had just made the biggest of his life in putting Kemys in charge.

The long-awaited second Raleigh search for Manoa lasted about a week. Kemys had reached the new Spanish settlement of San Tomé and, ignoring the admonition not to provoke the Spaniards, he wound up in a gunfight. Whether there had been a serious disagreement, or it was simply that the English adventurers had gotten drunk and impetuously decided to sack the place, is not known for certain. The essential facts were that when the dust settled, San Tomé was in ruins and young Wat Raleigh was dead.

Having gotten a letter from Kemys in mid-February, Wat's father was already in mourning when the failed expedition straggled out of the jungle in early March. Raleigh angrily blasted his subordinate, not only for the death of his namesake, but for deliberately disobeying the overarching mandate not to mix it up with the Spaniards. The fact that this had all happened only a week into the voyage had to have been especially aggravating.

The rebuked Kemys then retired to his cabin and fired his pistol into his chest. The last, and perhaps only, brave thing that he ever did was to finish himself off with a knife after the lead ball lodged innocuously in a rib.

Raleigh entertained thoughts of sailing up the Orinoco himself, wishing now that he had done so in January. However, his men were on the verge of mutiny after Kemys's fiasco. Even Raleigh knew that it was foolhardy to undertake an expedition with the Spanish up in arms like a disturbed hornets' nest.

News of the San Tomé debacle had been circulating in the halls of power in both London and Madrid for weeks by the time that a sick and wasted Raleigh dropped the *Destiny's* anchor in Plymouth harbor in late June.

Under pressure from Gondomar, and despite the protests of the king's wife, James I rearrested Raleigh on the grounds that he had disobeyed orders to avoid conflict with the

Spanish, and that his actions could potentially reignite the war that James himself had ended. Raleigh had, of course, also failed to find a gold mine or a golden city for his king.

After a trial, Sir Walter Raleigh, now in his early 60s, had his old death sentence reinstated by a Scottish monarch on an English throne. The head of Spain's sworn and mortal enemy was chopped from his body by an ax-wielding English executioner on October 29, 1618. The blood spatters which congealed on the cobblestones of Whitehall that October day were merely the last few drops of an enormous volume spilled over decades in the course of the mad obsession.

Nearly eighty years after Gonzalo Pizarro and Francisco Orellana had crossed the Andes in search of cinnamon and gold, the quest for El Dorado entered a three-century hiatus. The lone soldiers of fortune would never give up, but the century of large government-sponsored expeditions had come to an end. It closed a violent and momentous chapter, but was far from the end of the story.

Many of the documents and manuscripts describing golden cities lay forgotten and undisturbed until the nineteenth century, when they were finally rediscovered, dusted off, and translated.

10

CIUDAD DE
LOS CÉSARES

The true life of the myth has its source in a living word.
—Marcel Detienne, *The Invention of Mythology* (1992)

AT THE OPPOSITE END of the continent from the supposed site of El Dorado, the Spanish were meanwhile hearing stories of a distant southern mountaintop city, in a still-remote area that was yet to be explored, which was piled high with gold, silver, and even diamonds. Some stories, like those of the elusive Paititi, insisted that the city was ruled by exiled Incan royalty. For this reason, the place came to be called Ciudad de los Césares, or City of the Caesars.

While Paititi was notionally farther north in Peru or Bolivia, the Ciudad de los Césares was said to be high in the rugged Patagonian highlands that straddle the border between southern Argentina and southern Chile. Some accounts place it in El Bolsón on the Argentine side, others in the Chilean province of Aysén, which was once called Trapananda.

As with El Dorado, there were variations upon variations on the Ciudad de los Césares story. In the taverns of the cities and of the remote seaport towns across the continent, sailors told and retold these diverse yarns of this city of gold being inhabited by descendants of earlier Spaniards who had been shipwrecked sailing through the perilous Straits of Magellan, while others—seeming to be straight from a modern fantasy film—whisper of a city ruled by ghosts.

Another thread of the legend connects the Ciudad de los Césares with the Patagones, or Patagonian giants, who were said to have been visited by Ferdinand Magellan when he coasted past Tierra del Fuego in 1520.

The "race of giants" story, however, was an embellished rumor. The account by the Venetian scribe Antonio Pigafetta, who was actually there to chronicle the voyage, states only that the *entrada*, or expedition, encountered one man who was so tall that the explorers reached only to his waist. Of course, through the years, the inevitable exaggeration evolved. If one giant is good, then a story featuring a whole crowd of them is better. Soon, there were tales of an entire race of people who were as tall as 15 feet. There may well have been a tribe of especially tall people, as other explorers also mention them, but it is improbable that they were 15 feet tall.

Though these stories often connect the so-called Patagonian giants with the Ciudad de los Césares, the latter was said to be high in the mountains, and the accounts of sailors meeting the giants took place along the coast.

Yet other threads of the story suggest that the inhabitants of the Ciudad de los Césares were descendants of the survivors of a famous battle between Spanish conquistadors and indigenous Mapuche people at a place called Curalaba. However, this event occurred in December 1598, and stories of a mythical Ciudad de los Césares had been around for decades by this time.

These stories, which had originated independently, were probably blended over time, with borrowed elements from tales of golden Paititi, the long-rumored "last refuge" of the Inca.

Both stories may have been fed by accounts of yet another mysterious Inca city, whose existence has been confirmed, albeit not until the twentieth century—Machu Picchu. Though it may have been seen by an occasional European as early as the sixteenth century, and it is known to have been visited by outsiders in the late nineteenth century, the world was almost entirely unaware of Machu Picchu until after 1911. Nor were the gold-hungry sixteenth-century conquistadors aware of the Moche civilization of northwestern Peru, which had boasted a tradition of extraordinary goldsmiths a thousand years earlier.

One of the best known of the early explorers who went looking for the Ciudad de los Césares was Juan de Garay, a Spanish conquistador who came to the New World in 1543 with Blasco Núñez Vela, whom Emperor Charles V had named as the first Viceroy of Peru. Having been named as the governor of Asunción (now the capital of Paraguay) in 1576, Garay four years later succeeded in establishing the permanent Spanish settlement downstream at the mouth of the Río de la Plata (River of Silver). This would grow into the Argentine capital of Buenos Aires.

It was here that the Indians told Garay about that city of gold in the mountains. The old conquistador decided that this had to be the famous Ciudad de los Césares about which he had heard many tales. He went south in 1581, and spent the better part of two years looking for the place, and probably would have continued had he not been ambushed and killed by Indians north of Buenos Aires on an unrelated trip in 1583.

In later years, many others would hike the mountains of Patagonia in search of cities of gold. Captain Juan Fernández came here in 1620 looking for the Ciudad de los Césares, and in the 1760s the Jesuit priest Padre José García Alsue is known to have sought the city in what is now Chile's Queulat National Park.

Though the mountains of Patagonia were home to the indigenous Tehuelche people for centuries, permanent settlement of the rugged area by people of European descent did not occur until the second half of the nineteenth century. Shortly thereafter, the area welcomed a pair of settlers whose names are well connected with treasure tales on another continent—the notorious outlaws Butch Cassidy and the Sundance Kid.

Butch, whose real name was Harry Alonzo Longabaugh, and Sundance, who was really Robert Leroy Parker, arrived there in 1901 along with Butch's girlfriend, Etta Place.

According to the local tourism authority, the cabin they built is still preserved. While there is no evidence that Butch and Sundance ever took an interest in the Ciudad de los Césares, their covetous interest in a certain Bolivian silver mine payroll led to their being gunned down by lawmen in 1908.

Perhaps the most intriguing, and dare we say far-fetched, theory regarding the Ciudad de los Césares is that which connects this city of gold with the Knights Templar, the military brotherhood formed in the twelfth century by crusaders to protect Christian holy sites in and around Jerusalem. The Knights became one of the most powerful military and religious orders in Europe, branching into banking and finance before being persecuted and banned by the Vatican in the fourteenth century. The Knights Templar had possession of the Shroud of Turin, and it has long been rumored that they also had custody of the long-lost Ark of the Covenant.

As the improbable hypothesis holds, the Knights had made numerous trips to South America by the fourteenth century. Here, they established several cities, and they brought the Ark of the Covenant to the New World several centuries before Columbus.

A fort-shaped mesa near the shore of the Gulf of San Matías in Argentina's Río Negro Province has been suggested as the possible location of a coastal Knights Templar Ciudad de los Césares. In an 1865 atlas it is listed as an "ancient abandoned fort" by cartographer Juan Antonio Victor Martín de Moussy, who worked for Argentine president Justo José de Urquiza y García. A Buenos Aires-based organization called the Delphos Foundation made several *entradas* to the location between 1997 and 2006, uncovering artifacts which they link to the Knights Templar. Delphos also postulates that one or more Templar Ciudads de los Césares may have also existed in the mountains of Patagonia.

It would not only be a city of gold or of the Césares that attracted treasure seekers to the continent's southern mountains, but another story that ended up being true.

11

Potosí,
Mountain of Silver

> "If, Sancho," replied Don Quixote, "I were to requite thee as the importance and nature of the cure deserves, the treasures of Venice, the mines of Potosí, would be insufficient to pay thee."
>
> —Miguel de Cervantes, *Don Quixote* (*The Ingenious Gentleman Don Quixote of La Mancha*) (Part 2, 1615)

As the Spanish conquistadors and English knaves coasted the shoreline of South America, probing the mouths of its rivers, their ears were open to the sweet whispered tales of the wily old prospectors and of the indigenous people who could—and did—tell them where to look. While the story-tellers with tales of El Dorado and the Ciudad de los Césares promised gold, there was also mention of silver. Though not as precious as gold, silver also glitters in the eyes of treasure seekers. It was, after all, the lust for a South American silver mine payroll that was the downfall of Butch Cassidy and the Sundance Kid.

Just as heads turned to the references to cities of gold, how could heads not turn when they heard the phrase *sierra del plata*, or "mountain of silver"?

By the sixteenth century, such stories were being told around the fringes of the great bay on South America's south-east shore, which some geographers now classify as the broadest river mouth in the world. This river was named even as the old sea captains were listening to the stories of a wealth in silver that lay in a distant *sierra del plata* somewhere upstream. The Spanish began calling it "Río de la Plata" (River of Silver). In English, it is the River Plate, with "plate" being a word for goods wrought from precious metals, a term which was widely used from the twelfth through the nineteenth century.

The country south of the River Plate meanwhile took its name from *argentum*, the Latin word for silver. We now call this place Argentina.

The first European sea captain to sail a ship into the yawning mouth of the Río de la Plata was probably Juan Díaz de Solís, who came this way in 1516, and who explored the river in the hope that it might be a shortcut across South America. Ferdinand Magellan also nosed around its shoreline four years later on his way around the world. Solís was also probably the first European to sail upriver, from the Río de la Plata into its main channel, the Río Paraná. Indeed, the Paraná is the *real* "river of silver," as some geographers reckon the 180-mile Río de la Plata (nearly as wide as it is long) to be merely the estuary for the 3,000-mile Paraná.

When Solís was killed, reportedly by cannibals, his expedition turned tail and headed for home. However, they made it only as far as Santa Catarina Island, near the southern tip of what is now Brazil, before being shipwrecked in a storm. Among those few who made it ashore alive was a Portuguese soldier of fortune named Alejo García. Having reached dry land, he traveled inland, where he was taken in by the Guaraní people.

Over the course of the next decade, as he made his home among the Guaraní, García heard repeatedly of "El Rey Blanco," a "White King," who lived off to the west, deep in the interior of the continent. He was in García's mind, a New World incarnation of the Old World Prester John. It was still too early on the treasure time line for García to connect the White King with the Golden King, El Dorado.

Like the elusive Presbyter of European legend, El Rey Blanco possessed great wealth in both gold and silver, and García decided that he should get some of this for himself. He eventually organized an army of more than 1,000 Guaraní and marched across the Paraná rain forest and high desert of the Gran Chaco toward the kingdom of El Rey Blanco.

As near as can be pieced together from various accounts, García and his band managed to reach the outer defenses of Tahuantinsuyo, the empire of the Inca. He arrived there from the east in 1525, well ahead of Francisco Pizarro's arrival from the west in 1532. It is generally believed that El Rey Blanco was actually the great Inca, Huayna Capac, the father of Atahualpa and Huáscar, who were fighting their war of succession when Pizarro showed up.

The conquest of Tahuantinsuyo would be left to Pizarro, though. García plundered the empire's perimeter settlements, but was forced to retreat back into the interior. Though he did return with a fortune in silver, he was killed by his Guaraní friends after they reached the vicinity of the Río de la Plata.

The first European to make a detailed exploration of the mouth of the Río de la Plata was neither Spanish nor Portuguese, but a Venetian in the service of the English. Sebastian Cabot was the son of the famous sea captain Giovanni Caboto, who had immigrated to England, changed his name to John Cabot, and had "discovered" North America on behalf of England in 1497.

An explorer in his own right, Sebastian came to the Río de la Plata in 1526 on a mission to sail around the world, but he lingered in the area for several years when he started hearing the same precious metal stories which had seduced Alejo García. He sailed upriver on the broad Paraná, and explored its extensive tributary, the Río Paraguay. Upriver on the latter, Cabot began trading with the Guaraní for beautiful goods made of wrought silver. Unlike Solís and García, Cabot managed to leave the area with his life, becoming the first great evangelist for the gospel of the *plata* in the Río de la Plata, and that mysterious *sierra del plata* upstream.

Among the first to answer the call of the silver was Don Pedro de Mendoza, a wealthy Andalusian who was a favorite of Emperor Charles V. In 1529, the same year that Cabot came out of the jungle with his tall tales and glittering silverware, Mendoza offered to spend his family's money to explore South America from Tierra del Fuego to the Río de la

Plata. He was granted the governorship of all that he could conquer, but on the condition that he establish settlements and populate them with colonists. Mendoza spent five years to outfit his *entrada*, finally setting sail with more than a dozen vessels in 1534.

Mendoza's venture was a comedy of errors with a tragic ending. He is perhaps best remembered for founding the first settlement on the site of Buenos Aires, Argentina's capital, in 1536. The history books tell us that the enclave ultimately failed, but don't often go into detail about uncured adobe walls disintegrating in the rain, or colonists resorting to eating rats, snakes, leather goods, and each other. All the while, Mendoza himself was so delirious with syphilis that he was of little use to the undertaking.

The primary source for information about this comedy-turned-tragedy is Ulrich Schmidl, a German soldier of fortune known to the Spaniards as Ulderico Schmidt, who chronicled the adventure in a narrative published in Frankfurt in 1557. Mendoza gave up in 1537 after just three years, but Schmidl stayed for nearly two decades. Mendoza was dead before he saw Spain again, but Schmidl lived to tell the tale.

Normally one avoids the long-winded book titles popular in the sixteenth century, but in Schmidl's case, the title is worth quoting. In English translation, it reads *The true story of a noteworthy trip made by Ulrich Schmidl von Straubingen in America or the New World from 1534 to 1554, where will be found all his troubles of nineteen years and the description of lands and noteworthy peoples he saw, described by himself.* The phrase "all his troubles of nineteen years" is a good summary. In his narrative, Schmidl describes his own travels into the interior of southern South America, and those of others.

Mendoza's successor as governor was one of his lieutenants, Juan de Ayolas, a man more interested in the mythical *sierra del plata* than in governing a rat-infested colonial outpost. A brash and impatient conquistador in the mold of Gonzalo Pizarro, he lost no time in organizing an expedition to follow the trail of Alejo García toward the realm of El Rey Blanco. Before 1537 was out, he headed up the Paraná and then up the Paraguay. He set out across the rain forest and Gran Chaco toward the Andes and faded into the mist.

When the ill-fated Ayolas *entrada* disappeared without a trace, another conquistador named Juan de Salazar y Espinosa led a relief party. He found a few stragglers who had been left behind along the Paraguay, and went inland far enough to find evidence that Ayolas and his men had been killed by the people whom the Spaniards dubbed "Chaco" after their homeland in the Gran Chaco.

In the meantime, Salazar established a small settlement on the Río Paraguay, 600 miles upstream from the Río de la Plata near the place where Sebastian Cabot once traded for silverware. Because the date was August 15, 1537, the feast day of the Assumption of the Virgin Mary, he named the city "Ciudad de Nuestra Señora Santa María de la Asunción." Long known simply as "Asunción," it has been the capital of Paraguay since the country won its independence from Spain in 1811. After its founding in the sixteenth century, Asunción became the jumping off place for later *entradas* into the interior, and it gradually evolved as the oldest continuously populated European city in the region.

If this were an El Dorado story, there would be a series of anguished accounts of desperate, greedy conquistadors thrashing about in the wilderness, chasing phantoms and shadows and returning bitter and disappointed—if they returned at all. But this is not one of those kind of El Dorado stories. There really is a mountain of silver.

In fact, the Inca had many silver mines, just as they and the Aztec had many gold mines. These aside, the long-rumored *mountain* of silver did turn out to be a reality.

The Inca nobility knew about and had been exploiting the area for its mineral resources, but as for this specific mountain, the folklore embraces a captivating and oft-told "discovery" tale involving a poor herder.

Diego Huallpa (also known as Guallca) was the Spanish name of this man, though he is described as being "Quechua." This term is a broad one for a linguistic group which includes the Inca, as well as many other indigenous people, so he may or may not have been among those people whom we describe as "Inca."

In the 1540s, less than a decade after the times of Mendoza and Ayolas, Diego worked for a Spaniard named Juan de Villarroel in or near the town of Porco on the eastern slope of the Andes, about 650 miles northwest of Asunción and about 600 miles southeast of Cusco. Then part of the Spanish viceroyalty of Peru, the area is now located in Bolivia. To describe the area as "high in the Andes" is no exaggeration— it is two and a half miles above sea level. As the generally accepted story goes, Diego was searching for a lost llama one afternoon on a particular mountain, and had decided to spend the night, rather than trying to reach his main camp in the dark. The following morning, there were congealed rivulets of pure silver in the place where his campfire had been burning.

When Diego told his boss what had happened, Villarroel filed a claim on what was soon being called "Cerro Rico" ("Rich Hill"). The area as a whole became known by the name "Potosí," whose origin is uncertain. Many sources state that it is an indigenous word for "thunder" in the Quechua or Aymara languages, and that it may be derived from the thunderstorms which occur in the Andes. The ensuing rush for riches to Cerro Rico led to the establishment of the city of Potosí at the base of Cerro Rico in April 1545, less than a year after the night of the campfire. With an elevation of 13,420 feet, Potosí was and remains one of the highest cities on earth.

As would be the case 303 years later during the early days of the California Gold Rush, the first prospectors on the scene found their fortune so close to the surface that it could be picked up with bare hands. Gradually, though, shafts were sunk, and the prospectors were replaced by hard rock miners. Entrepreneurs and opportunists were replaced by silver barons served by armies of enslaved Indians.

Despite its lung-exhausting elevation and its distance from any other major European settlement, Potosí quickly became one of the largest cities in the New World. By some accounts, it was larger than Mexico City or even Madrid, and may have had close to 200,000 people by the early seventeenth century. It was one of the richest cities in the entire world.

According to Wendell E. Wilson and Alfredo Petrov, writing in *The Mineralogical Record* in 1999, "a local friar, Joséph de Acosta, estimated that a quarter of a billion dollars in silver was removed between 1545 and 1572. Spanish government records show that duty was paid on roughly a billion dollars in silver from 1556 to 1791 [45,000 tons of pure silver], although far less silver was reported as being dutiable than was actually mined."

Wilson and Petrov provide an illuminating anecdote, writing that "in 1690 a miner named Quiroga is on record as having paid $21 million in duty to the crown, then set at 20 percent. Therefore he had removed over $100 million in silver from his one mine, the Cotamitos mine. With some of the profits he built the Cathedral of San Francisco in Potosí, and was eventually buried there."

According to the *Colección de Documentos Relativos a la Historia de Bolivia* (*Collection of Documents Relative to the History of Bolivia*) of the Archives of Bolivia, edited by Vicente de Ballivian y Roxas and published in 1872, the riches touched all who came to this glittering metropolis at the top of the world:

> During the richest days of the Silver Hill of Potosí, wealth flowed down the hill of society from the diamond-bedecked peaks to the hardly less decorated castes. The miner whose wages were lowest was paid every week a "pine cone of forty marks." Later in the century, when the chronicler of Potosí records, with just the barest enthusiasm which his official position binds him to exhibit, how Potosí turned its wealth to worship instead of pleasure, his lamentations for the days of old [i.e., circa 1650] read like a tale of the one thousand and one nights. "Tell me, oh famous Potosí, what became of your old greatness, wealth and enjoyable pastimes? What became of your brilliant festivities, your reed-spear tournaments, your masks, comedies, receptions with prizes so valuable? Where are now your inventions, mottoes and ciphers under which your famous mine owners entered the lists? What has become of the valor of your Creoles, their elegance, horses and harnesses? What of their ability in striking down bulls. . . . The rich attire of your men, their waistbands and their chains of gold on their chests and hats. . . . The costly dresses of your women and girls. . . . The rich costumes of your half-caste women, their slippers

on their feet, tied with strings of silk and gold, stuffed with pearls and rubies, skirts and bodices embroidered in fine silk cloth, chains of gold? What became of the costumes of the Indian women, those coifs with which they covered their head, adorned allover with pearlseed and precious stones, the cloth with which they dressed, strewn all over with rich pearls and gems; the shirts the Indian men wore, of brocade and rich silk, the fillets on their heads, worth each eight thousand pesos owing to the pearls, diamonds, emeralds and rubies which could be seen in them? What became of those silver bars with which in your vanity you covered the floor before your altars and all the space between the Mint and the Royal Treasury on Corpus Christi day?

Writing of the importance of Potosí, the historian Jean Descola says that "from 1560 to 1600, 6,872 metric tons— well over 15 million pounds—of silver crossed the Atlantic. In forty years Spain received double the stock of silver existing in Europe before Columbus. . . . Subsequently the exploitation of the Potosí mines must have multiplied the production of silver tenfold."

Just as the gold of the Aztec and Inca was the catalyst which began Spain's *Siglo de Oro*, its Golden Age, the silver from Potosí kept it going, sustaining it into the seventeenth century, and perpetuating that comfortable milieu in which great art and literature, like that of Miguel de Cervantes, who introduces this chapter, could flourish.

Because of the cost of shipping from such a remote location, the ore was smelted in Potosí. By the last quarter of the sixteenth century, the mint was stamping out Spanish dollars (also called "pieces of eight" because they were equal to eight reals) bearing a mint mark composed of the letters "PTSI" superimposed upon one another. The resemblance of this mark to a dollar sign suggests that it may have been the inspiration for the design of the symbol "$" which is used for United States dollars, as well as for early Spanish dollars and Mexican pesos.

At first, the silver from Potosí's Cerro Rico was extracted by smelting, but in the 1550s, the "patio process" of refining ore was introduced. This process was first developed by

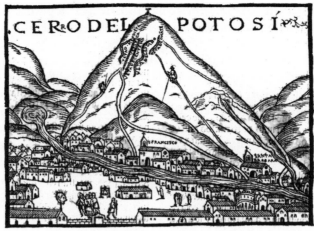

An illustration of the mountain of silver at Potosí, from Pedro Cieza de León's *Cronicas del Perú*, published in 1522.

Bartolomé de Medina in Mexico in 1554 as a means of getting more silver from lesser grade ores that were coming out of the Mexican silver mines. In Peru, and in Mexico, the richest ore was picked over early, so it was desirable to wring more silver out of lesser quality ore. The patio process, which uses mercury as a catalyst in an amalgamation reaction, was further developed in Potosí during the early seventeenth century by Alvaro Alonso Barba. His book, *El Arte de los Metales* (*The Art of Metallurgy*), which was first published in Spain in 1640, became an important source of information on the early mining industry in Potosí. The Spanish government considered the work so important that it was classified as a state secret. Nevertheless, a handful of copies survived and were later translated.

Just as the patio process made extraction of silver from lesser grade ores possible, it made extraction more expensive. Another expense in the exploitation of the Cerro Rico was labor. In 1542, Emperor Charles V had promulgated the Leyes Nuevas (New Laws of the Indies for the Good Treatment and Preservation of the Indians, which curtailed the use of indigenous people as slave laborers). Francisco Alvarez de Toledo, the Viceroy of Peru from 1569 to 1581, got around these by reintroducing the *mit'a* system. This was the pre-Columbian mandatory public service procedure by which Inca royalty used conscripted labor to build the vast infrastructure within Tahuantinsuyo, including the marvelous trails and footpaths that connected the empire. In Potosí, *mit'a* essentially became a new form of slave labor.

Rather than it being a case of wealth flowing down the hill of society from the peaks to the hardly less decorated castes, it was now a case of mercury poisoning flowing into the blood of people enslaved through a loophole. Some have estimated that more than a million people lost their lives in Potosí's mine shafts. Once celebrated as an allegory for wealth itself, the Cerro Rico became known as "the mountain that eats men." Just as El Dorado would become the metaphor for cities of gold, Potosí became a dark allegory for pain and suffering.

By the eighteenth century, as the mines grew less profitable, the erstwhile largest city in the New World withered to near ghost-town status. In the nineteenth century, as Bolivia became independent, the national mint was established there and various British and American mining firms attempted with marginal success to revive the productivity of the Cerro Rico silver mines.

By the twentieth century, however, Potosí evolved into an important source of a metal ignored by the Spaniards—tin. Today, the Corporación Minera de Bolivia (COMIBOL), created in 1952 and controlled by organized labor, is the second largest tin producer in the world. In the twenty-first century, Potosí is sort of its old self again, a rich global center of mineral production on the surface, but still a murky and miserable place for the armies of the rank and file who toil in the dirt and darkness far below.

Beyond the billions in silver which flooded into the world market, Potosí's importance to the imagination of the sixteenth- and seventeenth-century treasure hunters was the fact of its being confirmed as real—and billions of dollars worth of real—unlike the shadowy El Dorado of Gonzalo Pizarro and the elusive Manoa of Sir Walter Raleigh. This would keep endless generations of undaunted adventurers on the road to other Potosís, and other El Dorados.

12

THE SEVEN
CITIES OF CIBOLA

The tradition of the "Seven Cities of Cibola" included a kernel of fact enveloped by a shell of exaggerated fancies and hopes. Much interest has been taken in recent times in inquiries respecting the "where" and the "how" of that kernel.

—Adolph Bandelier, *The Gilded Man* (1893)

IN JULY 1536, ON THE NORTHERN fringe of Spanish colonial rule, near the outpost of Culiacán, in what is now the Mexican state of Sinaloa, a man given up for dead walked out of the Sonoran Desert. On his parched, cracked lips were the ravings of a madman—and stories of cities of gold and emeralds.

The Seven Cities of Cibola were, and remain, the El Dorado of North America, both as a catalyst for sixteenth-century exploration, and as an allegory for fabulous wealth that exists just out of reach in remote and inhospitable places. In the latter form, the Seven Cities of Cibola, like El Dorado, still fire imaginations in the twenty-first century.

Just as the cities of South American gold existed in the vague *terra incognita* of the South American interior, the cities of North American gold existed in the vague *terra incognita* of the unexplored lands north of Mexico which, like Mexico, were part of New Spain, which had been claimed for that country by Cortés in 1521, and designated as a Spanish viceroyalty in 1535.

In both South America (including the viceroyalties of New Granada and Peru) and New Spain, the news of the cities of gold always seemed to come from storytellers who indulged listeners with tales they wanted to hear. The Indians and some wayward travelers, acting as our metaphorical "old prospectors," told of cities of gold because Europeans seemed to like the stories. In some cases the stories were true, while in other cases, the fact that a listener failed to find a city of gold didn't mean that it was not there.

In North America, the first "old prospector" was actually an unfortunate victim of circumstance. He was Álvar Núñez Cabeza de Vaca, the dead man who walked out of the desert in 1536.

Nine years earlier, Cabeza de Vaca had sailed from Spain with the conquistador Pánfilo Naváez, who had been appointed by Charles V as the *adelantado*, or governor, of Florida. No stranger to the New World, Naváez had been involved in the conquest of Jamaica and Cuba earlier in the sixteenth century, and now he was in charge of the ambitious project of adding the jewel of Florida to the monarch's crown. Naturally, it was expected that gold would be found here, just as it had been in Mexico and points south.

Cabeza de Vaca had signed on as one of Naváez's senior officers, and was designated to serve as his treasurer when he set up his administration in Florida and began raking in the riches of his new dominion. What lay ahead for him was far beyond the clerical job he imagined.

Battered by storms in the Atlantic and Caribbean, Naváez wintered in the West Indies, recruiting men and taking on supplies. In April 1528, he finally landed in what is now Tampa Bay on Florida's west coast, and headed inland with a contingent of three hundred men. Rather than finding gold, they got lost in the dense and bewildering swamps, and were harassed by indigenous tribes who reacted unfavorably to the intruders.

After being badly mauled by the Apalachee people of north Florida, Naváez finally abandoned his march and ordered his command back to the coast. Here, he planned to build log rafts and attempt to reach Mexico by heading west along the Gulf Coast. He erroneously thought they were relatively close, when, in fact, they were more than 1,500 miles away.

The Spaniards failed to anticipate the wrath of the Gulf Coast hurricane season, and only a handful of men were still alive when the last of the rafts were wrecked on a barrier island somewhere on the upper Texas coast early in November. Cabeza de Vaca called it the Isla de Malhado, or Isle of Misfortune. Historians suppose that it was either Galveston Island or the Bolivar Peninsula. Pánfilo de Naváez made it this far, but one night he decided to ride out a storm aboard one of the rafts, and was swept out to sea never to be seen again.

Their clothes in tatters, their stomachs aching, the living turned to cannibalism on the dead. Then, they set out to walk to Mexico, taking a circuitous and unnecessarily long route. In his subsequent book entitled *Naufragios* (*Castaways*), Cabeza de Vaca relates the trials and adventures that led him and only three others finally to their goal eight long, hard years later.

Beginning on the first day, ongoing through those eight years, the Spaniards had almost continuous contact with the indigenous peoples of the American Southwest. In his book, Cabeza de Vaca reports many details that have been considered important by ethnographers of later centuries. Indeed, the University of Texas considers him to have been the state's "earliest ethnohistorian."

Some tribes treated them as a curiosity, but others were openly hostile. Cabeza de Vaca was considered to be a shamanistic healer in an early encounter, but he and his companions were later held prisoner for six years as slaves. This had to have seemed particularity ironic to a North African Berber from Morocco who was among them. Known in Spanish as Estevanico el Negro (Steven the Black, or Steven the Moor), he had been a slave of the Spaniards!

Of the original three hundred men, only Cabeza de Vaca, Estevanico, and the would-be conquistadors Alonso del Castillo Maldonado and Andrés Dorantes de Carranza (Estevanico's "owner") survived.

Once they finally escaped from their keepers, the men did not head south, directly toward the Spanish ports on the Mexican east coast, along a coastline frequented by Spanish galleons. Instead, they headed westward toward the "Mar del Sur" or the "South Sea" (the Pacific Ocean).

For two years, they wandered across Texas, northern Mexico, and westward into the present American Southwest, accompanied by Indians whom they met and befriended along the way.

Cabeza de Vaca's accounts of crossing the Plains of Texas tell of hardship and adversity, but by the time they reached the Southwest, things began to get interesting. They found that the people were well clothed, well fed, and that they lived in what he calls "permanent houses."

He writes of coming to "a river that flows between mountains," which seems to be the upper Rio Grande (which the Spaniards called Río del Norte, the River of the North) in New Mexico. Here, they encountered "the first abodes we saw that were like unto real houses."

These houses were probably in one or more of the pueblos that were—and still are—concentrated near the Rio Grande generally between present-day Albuquerque and Taos. There is evidence that the four men also visited the pueblos of the Zuni, which are still located about 120 miles west of where the Rio Grande now passes through Albuquerque.

Many centuries earlier, permanent cities with complex multistoried structures had been constructed in the area by the ancient pueblo-dwelling people who were long known by the Navajo name "Anasazi," meaning "ancient ones" or "ancient enemy." Today, the term is shunned by academia in favor of the more mundane "Ancient Pueblo Peoples." We use the term Anasazi because it has been in use for a century, and because the term in the people's own original language is unknown.

The Anasazi cities were located 80 to 150 miles north of the Zuni pueblos at places such as Canyon de Chelly in Arizona, Chaco Canyon in New Mexico, and Mesa Verde in Colorado. These cities were larger and more complex than those of the Rio Grande Valley and at the Zuni sites, but archaeologists are certain that the entire Anasazi culture col-

The ruin of the multi-story "White House" at the Anasazi city in Canyon de Chelly, Arizona, photographed by Timothy H. O'Sullivan in 1873. It is easy to imagine a visitor being awestruck at the scale and dignity of sites such as this when first encountered. By the time the conquistadors arrived, Canyon de Chelly was abandoned, and they never found it.

lapsed in the fourteenth century. That would have meant that these sites had been abandoned and uninhabited for around two hundred years by the time that Cabeza de Vaca passed through the Southwest. They would remain essentially unknown to nonnative people until the nineteenth century.

Cabeza de Vaca tells that the city-dwelling people whom he met "harvested maize, of which and of its meal they gave us great quantities, also squashes and beans, and blankets of cotton, with all of which we loaded those who had conducted us thither, so that they went home the most contented people upon earth. We gave God our Lord many thanks for having taken us where there was plenty to eat." This is entirely consistent with Pueblo culture.

As they satisfied their hunger, the four men were given other items which only served to arouse a hunger of another kind: "They also gave us plenty of beads made out of the coral found in the South Sea [and] good turquoises, which they get from the north," Cabeza de Vaca writes. "They finally gave us all they had; and Dorantes they presented with five emeralds, shaped as arrow-points, which arrows they use in their feasts and dances. As they appeared to be of very good quality, I asked whence they got them from, and they said it was from some very high mountains toward the north, where they traded for them with feather-bushes and parrot-plumes, and they said also that there were villages with many people and very big houses."

The notion of emeralds coming from somewhere in the land up north where many people lived in "very big houses" was the spark that would later fire the flames of lust for the North American variation on El Dorado. For Cabeza de Vaca and his companions, however, they were apparently more concerned with getting on with their journey to Mexico.

As for treasure tales, however, this was only the beginning. As the wanderers continued westward across what is now Arizona, Cabeza de Vaca notes that "we saw many signs of gold, antimony, iron, copper and other metals. . . . The Indians who live in permanent houses and those in the rear of them pay not attention to gold nor silver, nor have they any use for either of these metals."

The idea that the people had no use for gold is very reminiscent of the original premise of the El Dorado legend, then beginning to flourish in South America, that gold was so plentiful as to be inconsequential.

Technically, the four castaways did not get to the Mar del Sur, but they thought they had. They reached the Gulf of California, which was then assumed to be part of the Pacific Ocean because the long, slender Baja California Peninsula was thought to be an island. Indeed, all of California (including Alta California, which became the United States state of California) appears as an island on European maps published in the sixteenth and seventeenth centuries, and even later.

Following its shoreline, they headed south, then inland. Finally, they were picked up by some Spanish troops, who treated the strangers suspiciously and killed some of the Akimel O'odham (Pima) people who had been traveling with them. Eventually, they were able to convince the Spaniards that they too (except Estevanico) were also Spaniards, and they were taken to Mexico City.

Cabeza de Vaca then traveled onward to Spain, where he asked Charles V to send him to Florida to serve as *adelantado* and resume his exploration of North America. However, the emperor had already tapped Hernándo de Soto for the Florida job. In 1540 Cabeza de Vaca was given the assignment of reestablishing an outpost at the mouth of the Río de la Plata in South America on the site of one started by Pedro de Mendoza several years earlier. Cabeza de Vaca's settlement also failed. He was tried for incompetence in Spain, but

The title page of *La Relación* by Álvar Núñez Cabeza de Vaca, later called *Naufragios* (*Castaways*), his account of his eight years of captivity and wanderings in the interior of North America from 1528 to 1536.

acquitted. It was another four decades before another treasure-hungry conquistador, Juan de Garay, founded the permanent settlement that eventually evolved into Buenos Aires, Argentina.

Álvar Núñez Cabeza de Vaca finally published his memoirs in 1542, but in the six years since he had rejoined the living, the verbal variation on the story, widely told and wildly embellished, had taken on an independent life of its own.

Like a tributary stream, it had flowed into the river of those tall tales and speculation about great riches beyond the horizon which were the lifeblood of conversation in the Spanish coffee shops and cantinas from Culiacán to Mexico City.

The main current of this golden river swirled around the vibrant folklore of the mythical land of Cibola and its Seven Cities. The exact origin of the term "Cibola" is uncertain, though it is almost certainly an indigenous word. Cabeza de

Vaca's place up north where many people lived in several cities with "very big houses" was interpreted as a confirmation that Cibola was not an imaginary place, but real.

How the idea came about that there were *seven* cities of gold at Cibola and not six, eight, or some other number, may be the importance of the numeral in Christian religious practice. "Seven" appears often in the Bible, from the seven days of creation in Genesis to the seven churches in Revelation. In the Catholic dogma familiar to the Spaniards hearing and retelling the "Seven Cities" stories, the number is again used often from the seven acts of mercy, to the seven deadly sins, to the seven sacraments, and so on.

The "seven cities" legend is also often associated with a much earlier Portuguese legend of the Ilha das Cete Cidades (Isle of Seven Cities). These seven were supposedly established about eight hundred years earlier, beyond the Pillars of Hercules (Gibraltar) on an island named Antillia (or Atullia), somewhere in the mysterious *Mare Tenebrosum* of the Atlantic. Indeed, G. R. Crone, writing in the March 1938 issue of the *Geographical Journal*, mentions that a place of this name appears on a fourteenth-century Venetian navigational chart by Franciscus Pizzigano. Of course, one will note the obvious similarity of Antillia's location to that of the wonderful golden city of Atlantis. The conquistadors, especially those with maritime connections, would have been familiar with the Antillia stories.

However the number seven had also been important in indigenous North American mythology in pre-Columbian times. The archaeologist and folklorist Adolph Bandelier looked into the obvious question of whether stories of Seven Cities had existed among the indigenous people of North America before the arrival of the Spanish. In his book *The Gilded Man*, he begins his commentary by pointing out that where ancient legends are passed from generation to generation via verbal traditions: "We are surprised at finding that the legend has been preserved with careful fidelity through centuries, and that any novelty or change which has been introduced into it must always be ascribed to foreign influence. . . . Great care is therefore necessary to extract the real kernel of the Indian traditions, in Mexico for instance, from the investing shell of the legends of the sixteenth century."

Bandelier mentions various pictographic codices that were produced in the sixteenth century under the orders of Don Martín Enríquez de Almanza, who served as the fourth viceroy of New Spain (Mexico) from 1568 to 1580. His idea was to invite indigenous people to pictographically record their narrative traditions so that there could be a written record of these legends before "any novelty or change" was introduced. These pictographic documents were common to many indigenous cultures in North America, such as the Lakota *waniyetu wowapi* (winter counts) in which the events of each year were recorded pictorially. Another example from among the Lakota were the famous "hieroglyphic autobiographies" written by various Lakota, including the great leader Sitting Bull.

Bandelier specifically cites the *Codex Telleriano Ramensis*, which gets its name from Charles-Maurice Le Tellier, archbishop of Reims, who somehow got his hands on it in the late seventeenth century. Later in the collection of the Bibliothèque Nationale de France in Paris, it includes details of the 365-day *xiuhpohualli* solar calendar and the 260-day *tonalpohualli* calendar.

Looking for kernels, Bandelier discovered references to a creation myth among the Nahuatl people who believed that they had originated in seven caves. He notes that subsequent novelties and changes transformed the references to caves into seven mythical cities.

In mid-sixteenth century Mexico, as all the amazing stories seemed to confirm one another, this fueled fires of excitement, and talk naturally turned toward mounting an *entrada*. In his 1615 book, *Los Libros Rituales y Monarchia Indiana* (*Rituals of the Indian Monarchies*) Franciscan missionary and historian Juan de Torquemada mentions that an expedition had headed toward Cibola in 1538, but if so, little is known. They were, perhaps, one of the many *entradas* to head north never to return.

Among those who had acted on the Seven Cities legends before Cabeza de Vaca was the conquistador Nuño Beltrán de Guzmán. In 1530, while he was governor of the New Spain frontier province of Nueva Galicia, he made a tentative expedition into the *terra incognita* to the north, but apparently came home empty handed. Parenthetically, it should be said that Guzmán was one of the most ruthless and sadistic abusers of indigenous people in the history of Spanish rule in America.

The Seven Cities of Cibola tales had also attracted the attention of Antonio de Mendoza, the Marqués de Mondéjar and Conde de Tendilla, who had been named by Charles V as the first viceroy when New Spain became a viceroyalty in 1535. The latter explains Mendoza's interest in Cibola, which lay in the mysterious northern part of his domain.

The first major expedition specifically in search of Cibola on Mendoza's watch was launched in March 1539, three years after Cabeza de Vaca appeared out of the drifting sands of the Sonoran Desert, and two years before Gonzalo Pizarro and Francisco Orellana set out from Quito on their quest for El Dorado.

Though officially sanctioned by Mendoza, this trek was more of a scouting party than an expedition. Whereas the Pizarro-Orellana *entrada* had involved battalions of conquistadors, hundreds of porters, and long pack trains of baggage, the first dedicated Cibola venture involved just a handful of men and was headed by a Franciscan friar.

Padre Marcos de Niza, who was then in his mid-forties, had been born in Nice on what is now the French Riviera, and had first come to the New World in 1531, where he served as a missionary in Peru and Central America before coming to Mexico.

Not wanting to operate blindly in the trackless wilderness to the north, Niza engaged the services of someone who had actually been there—Estevanico el Negro.

They rode out of Culiacán and headed north toward what is now Arizona, accompanied by several Indians, including some of the Akimel O'odham people who had accompanied Cabeza de Vaca on his trip south three years before. People from other tribes, such as the Tohono O'odham (Pagago), joined the company as they traveled north. Also along for a time was a fellow Franciscan friar, Padre Onorato, but he grew ill and parted company with Niza along the way.

The farther north Niza traveled, the more he heard tantalizing stories of the Seven Cities of Cibola. However, despite his apparent eagerness to reach Cibola, Niza sent Estevanico ahead, while he took his time.

At last, an Indian messenger brought word to the friar from his scout, relating that Estevanico had reached Cibola. According to Niza in his account of the *entrada*, *Descubrimiento de las Siete Ciudades* (*Discovery of the Seven Cities*), Estevanico explained that Niza would not believe his eyes. There were "Seven very large cities which were all subject to one lord. In them were large houses of stone and mortar, the smallest of which were one story high with a terrace, and there were besides two- and three-storied buildings. The chief's house was of four stories. There were many decorations at the entrance of the principal houses, and turquoises, which were very plentiful in the country. The people of these cities were very well clothed."

This description, including the part about the people being well clothed, is quite similar to Cabeza de Vaca's observations of the people whom he and Estevanico had met several years earlier. Niza had to see for himself, so he hurried northward.

In fact, Estevanico had returned to a place where he had been with Cabeza de Vaca, the homeland of the Zuni people, who call themselves A:shiwi. This homeland, called Shiwinna, is referred to by modern archaeologists as the Zuni-Cibola Complex, and encompasses several settlements, including those now called Háwikuh, Yellow House, Kechipbowa, and Great Kivas, which could easily have been interpreted by Estevanico and the Spaniards as "Seven Cities." (Declared as a National Historic District in 1974, the complex is adjacent to the present homes of the Zuni people.)

Of all the people of the Southwest who dwelt in what Cabeza de Vaca called "permanent houses" in the sixteenth century, the Zuni are unique in that their language is completely unrelated to any other. This would have made them a people whom others in the Southwest would have considered different. When this distinction was conveyed to outsiders through a translator, it would have made them seem unusual and even mysterious.

In the meantime, there was trouble brewing. According to Bandelier, as he hastened to see the seven cities, Niza was met by other of the Indians who had been traveling with Estevanico. They explained that the Moor had entered one of the Zuni pueblos, probably Háwikuh. He had passed himself off as a healer, then angered the people when "he sought greedily for precious metals and green stones, and abused the superstitious Indians because they had not enough of them to satisfy his avarice. He seems also to have made requisitions upon the highest and most precious possession of the people, their women."

Niza relates that Estevanico was killed by the Zuni, although Juan Francisco Maura, writing in *Revista de Estudios Hispánicos* (*Magazine of Hispanic Studies*) in 2002, theorizes that he may have enlisted the help of the Zuni to fake his death so that he would not have to go back to Mexico and his life as a slave of the Spaniards.

According to Bandelier, the Indians told Niza that the place where Estevanico was killed was

> only one of the Seven Cities of Cibola, and was not the most populous one. The priest concluded from their accounts and expressions that even to go to the place would be attended with great risk to life. . . . Obviously nothing was to be gained by a heroic sacrifice of his life, while everything, the whole object of his journey, might have been defeated by it. . . . He would have to give up his missionary work temporarily, for a martyr's death would under such circumstances be fruitless. Yet it seemed possible to him to steal carefully into the vicinity and cast a glance from some favorable point into the region of his hopes and desires, in order to be satisfied by seeing for himself, even if it were only from a distance, of the truth or untruth of the accounts that had been brought to him.

Without actually setting foot in one, Niza took one last, lingering look at the pueblos, attached a wooden cross to a tree high on a mountain as a marker, and quickly retreated to Mexico.

Viewing the Zuni villages on the mesas from a great distance, Marcos de Niza felt that he had "seen" Cibola. In the late afternoon sun, the golden adobe of the "permanent

This nineteenth-century photograph of Zuni pueblos viewed from the south gives an idea of how Marcos de Niza could relate that he had seen the legendary cities of Cibola.

houses," which contained flecks of mica, shimmered as though sheathed in plates of pure gold. Even today, if you are driving east on New Mexico state route 53 at sunset, it is easy to imagine Niza's excitement.

In his *Descubrimiento de las Siete Ciudades*, he let his imagination run rampant, reporting things that he could not have seen without entering one of the seven cities. He wrote of huge pearls and emeralds, probably borrowing the latter from Cabeza de Vaca. He said that the people ate off of gold and silver plates, perhaps because he had heard about such a thing having been seen in Peru. In fact, the Zuni people have long been noted silversmiths, but they probably were not in the sixteenth century.

He also claimed that the Seven Cities of Cibola were equal in population to Mexico City. Cortés had estimated at 60,000 when he first encountered it as Tenochtitlan two decades earlier, but by the 1530s, the population may have been less. One might be inclined to think it improbable that a population center the size of the former Aztec capital could have existed in isolation without being surrounded by lesser towns and vast expanses of cultivation. However, given the changes undergone since the Spanish takeover, Bandelier believes that "instead of being exaggerated, [Niza's estimate] seems to have been fitting and correct." Because he viewed the Seven Cities from afar, Niza almost certainly could not have accurately estimated the population, so the comparison is a moot point.

Today, about 7,000 Zuni live in the 8.8 square miles of the census-defined area of the Zuni pueblo, about half of the total members of the Zuni tribe.

Nevertheless, Bandelier is disparaging of Niza's other comments about Cibola. Of *Descubrimiento de las Siete Ciudades*, he writes, "few documents of Spanish origin concerning America have been exposed to a sharper and more severe criticism. . . . It has been condemned for defectiveness and superficiality, and charges of exaggeration and untruth have been made against it."

There is even a school of thought that he fabricated the whole story. Bandelier says that his "one-sided and inadequate investigation has also caused doubt to be cast upon the declaration that he saw Cibola." According to a fascinating conspiracy theory advanced by Richard Flint and Shirley Cushing Flint, and noted on the website of the Office of the State Historian of New Mexico, Niza never even saw the Zuni pueblos, and concocted the story so that he could come back with an army and force a religious conversion on the people of the Seven Cities before the end of the world—which Niza thought was imminent.

A century earlier, Adolph Bandelier had written that he too had been inclined to accept the idea of Niza fabricating his Cibola story—until he met Frank Hamilton Cushing and had a chance to review his files. Having worked with the great explorer John Wesley Powell, founding director of the United States Bureau of Ethnology (later part of the Smithsonian Institution), Cushing spent a great deal of time in the Southwest, where he lived with the Zuni continuously between 1879 and 1884. He amassed an invaluable record and understanding of classic Zuni culture and folklore at a time when the Zuni contact with Euro-Americans had been minimal.

"The Zunis definitely informed Mr. Cushing, after he had become an adept by initiation into the esoteric fraternity of warriors, that a 'black Mexican' had once come to O'aquima [Háwikuh] and had been hospitably received there," Bandelier writes, adding that he "very soon incurred mortal hatred by his rude behavior toward the women and girls of the Pueblo, on account of which the men at last killed him."

Bandelier summarizes that this oral history "proves that Cibola represented the present country and tribe of Zuni. It is also of great importance in its bearing upon the truth of the statements of Padre Marcos. The hill from which he, coming from the southwest, looked at Cibola, could have been nowhere but on the southern border of the plain of Zuni; and it is only from that side that the Pueblo of O'aquima can be seen, while it is possible to approach it thence unremarked to within two miles, and to observe everything plainly. There, too, the remains of a wooden cross were visible till a few years ago. It has been supposed that this was the cross which the monk erected; considering the dry atmosphere of the region, the supposition, even if it is not probable, is not to be wholly rejected."

When Marcos de Niza walked out of the *terra incognita* of the northern desert in early November 1539, there was no second-guessing, no revisionism, and no accusations of lying. The Franciscan Order honored him by elevating him to the post of provincial superior, and he basked in the glow of celebrity. Whereas Cabeza de Vaca had been greeted with suspicion and disbelief three years earlier, people gathered around Niza, as eager to hear his tales from the unknown as were the journalists who debriefed the first astronauts who walked on the moon in 1969. As Bandelier writes:

> The return of the priest, his remarkable experiences, and the stories which he brought from the far north attracted the highest degree of attention from the officers and people of Mexico. Nobody doubted the truth of the statements of Padre Marcos. He had not found gold and silver, but he had discovered settled tribes

and a fertile country. The notion of great wealth in metals readily associated itself with these two elements, and it was not difficult to obtain help in men and means for the organization of a campaign on a larger scale into those regions. Don Antonio de Mendoza therefore did not hesitate, after the discovery had been made and the way pointed out, to proceed to conquest. For this he found a ready and willing instrument in Francisco Vásquez de Coronado.

13

Coronado

This account was in a very short time repeated on many tongues, and it shared the usual fate of stories transmitted verbally in being added to, exaggerated, and colored in the imaginations of those through whom it successively passed. . . . The officers. . . . suffered only the most flattering parts of it to be put forward.

—Adolph Bandelier, *The Gilded Man* (1893)

FRANCISCO VÁSQUEZ DE CORONADO was an ambitious young conquistador from a well-heeled family in Salamanca, Spain. He had come to the New World in 1535 when he was about twenty-five, accompanying Don Antonio de Mendoza when he arrived to take up the position of viceroy of New Spain. Coronado then married Beatriz de Estrada, the daughter of Alonzo de Estrada, the royal treasurer in Mexico, a man with a prominent role in the colonial government and a reputation for incorruptibility and integrity. This union would net Coronado a substantial dowry, and eventually, eight children.

From Mendoza, Coronado received the governorship of the province of Nueva Galicia (New Galicia), the post previously held by the notorious Nuño Beltrán de Guzmán. It was located northwest of Mexico City which included the present Mexican states of Jalisco and Nayarit, as well as Sinaloa, in which Culiacán is located. As such, Coronado had been well aware of the stories of the expeditions of Cabeza de Vaca and Marcos de Niza. The rumors of the Seven Cities were on the lips of every Spaniard in Nueva Galicia in those days.

Mendoza had taken a personal interest in Niza, and when he brought the friar to Mexico City so that he could hear the story firsthand, Coronado was present. Coronado was immediately bitten by the gold bug, and offered to outfit an *entrada* at his own (and his wife's) expense to go to Cibola. This offer from one of his favorite young conquistadors delighted Mendoza, not to mention that it would save him at least a portion of the cost of such a venture. Mendoza did chip in to advance part of the salaries for Coronado's officers, as well as to cover other expenses.

Just as Thomas Jefferson would take a layman's interest in "helping" Meriwether Lewis to plan the minute technical details of the 1804–1806 Lewis and Clark expedition, Mendoza got involved, and soon the project mushroomed. Simultaneous with Coronado's overland march, Mendoza arranged for, and paid for, a seagoing fleet commanded by Hernándo de Alarcón to travel northward along the west coast of Mexico, carrying supplies and maintaining contact with Coronado.

In retrospect, we can see how the judgment of Coronado, Mendoza, and indeed everyone in New Spain was clouded by a lust for fantastic wealth. We can wonder how and why they were so sure of what they were doing despite the fact that Niza, the single surviving eyewitness, had only seen Cibola from a distance.

Bandelier's description of how Niza's Cibola story was received was almost identical to any number of the fantastic rumors told of El Dorado and so many other cities of gold: "This account was in a very short time repeated on many tongues. It shared the usual fate of stories transmitted verbally in being added to, exaggerated, and colored in the imaginations of those through whom it successively passed. The original account, by which all these falsifications might have been corrected, was not given to the public, and the officers, using Coronado as their instrument, suffered only the most flattering parts of it to be put forward. What Pray

Marcos said of gold was from hearsay, and was so represented by him."

Nevertheless, Mendoza and Coronado were sure the account was true—or at least they were determined not to take a chance that it might not be true.

Coronado departed from Compostela, the main city of Nueva Galicia, about 250 miles south of Culiacán, in February 1540. He led a contingent which included around three hundred Spaniards and more than a thousand Indians, as well as a long pack train of supplies, hundreds of extra horses, and a herd of cattle to provide beef for the hungry explorers. As his guide, Coronado brought Marcos de Niza.

Chronicling the *entrada* would be Pedro de Castañeda. His account, *Relación de la Jornada de Cíbola 1540*, was published in the 1560s, but was lost, and is known through a 1596 edition translated in 1896 by George Parker Winship of the U.S. Bureau of Ethnology.

Coronado's expedition had been preceded by Mendoza's having sent Melchior Díaz out with a small team less than two weeks after Niza's return. When Coronado and company started out three months later, Díaz had not yet come back. However, when Coronado reached Culiacán on Easter Monday, he met Díaz coming south.

Díaz explained that he had made it only as far as the adobe ruins called Chichilticalli, meaning "Red House" in the native Uto-Aztecan dialect, where he was forced to turn back by a blizzard. Castañeda, who repeatedly describes Chichilticalli as the place "where the wilderness begins," writes that it was "220 leagues," or about 300 miles north of Culiacán, which would have placed it somewhere between the Sierra Madre, in what is now central Chihuahua, and the mountains south or east of present-day Tucson, Arizona. Here, in midwinter, heavy snow on the mountain passes would certainly have been a problem.

Adolph Bandelier supposes that Díaz had made it as far as the present Arizona border, but no farther, and certainly not as far as the Zuni pueblos. Frederick Hodge of the U.S. Bureau of Ethnology, who edited the edition of Castañeda's book published in 1907, insists that Chichilticalli was "doubtless situated on or near the Río Gila, east of the mouth of the San Pedro, probably not far from the present Solomonville [now Solomon, near Safford] in southern Arizona."

The significance of this particular ruin seems to have been little more than as a landmark. The nineteen archaeologists and ethnographers who surveyed the region reported widespread ruins, although none on the scale of the multi-story ruins at the Anasazi sites much farther north, nor of the still-occupied pueblos at Zuni and on the Rio Grande.

At Culiacán, Coronado would still have been reasonably close to the coast, and to continued logistical support from Alarcón's supply vessels. However, from here, he would have had to head inland and north by northeast in order to follow the trail which Estevanico had previously shown to Niza, and which Niza now showed Coronado. In their making the ships a key part of their planning, Mendoza and Coronado had been operating under the erroneous assumption that Cibola was relatively near the coast. In fact, the Zuni pueblos are more than 600 miles inland from the Pacific Ocean or the Gulf of California.

Before commenting that Mendoza and Coronado "should have known better," we should note how little was really understood by Europeans in 1540 of the geography north of the present United States border. Juan Rodríguez Cabrillo did not reach the coast of the present state of California until two years later, and the permanent English settlements on the East Coast of what would become the United States were still three generations in the future.

This ongoing mystery of the land where Cibola lay is perhaps best summarized by Castañeda in the preface to his book. He wrote it was remarkable that some stories told a quarter century later still called Cibola "an uninhabitable country, others have it bordering on Florida, and still others on Greater India, which does not appear to be a slight difference."

After lingering for two weeks in Culiacán, Coronado seemed now to be in a hurry. With Díaz having joined his expedition, Coronado departed Culiacán around the end of April with an advance guard of fifty horsemen, a smaller number of foot soldiers, some of the Indians, and five priests, including Niza. He left orders with Tristan de Arellano to follow him in two weeks with the rest of the troops. They continued north, tackling the Sierra Madre in the spring, rather than the dead of winter.

They passed through the valley of the Sonora River, which flows westward into the distant Gulf of California. Bandelier, who had traveled this route himself, describes riding between the present Sonora towns of Sinoquipe and Arispe: "At Sinoquipe the Spaniards would come upon the series of deep ravines which extend uninterruptedly to Arispe, and thence with slight intermissions to near Bacuachi, and often force the traveler to take to the bed of the river. In the whole distance of 140 miles between Babiacora and the source of the Sonora the traveler leaves the river bank only once for a short time, while he crosses the narrow stream 250 times. It is one of the most charming and at the same time least difficult routes which the North American continent offers to a horseman. A steadily mild climate enhances the traveler's pleasure."

Castañeda writes that fifteen days after passing the Red House of Chichilticalli, they reached what they called the "Red River" because "its waters were muddy and reddish." The expedition now reckoned that they were only eight leagues from Cibola. Based on this description, Frederick Hodge and Adolph Bandelier both surmise that this was the Zuni River, in the vicinity of present-day St. John's, Arizona. A seasonal stream, it does indeed run a muddy red in the spring and early summer.

In early July, they finally reached Háwikuh, the Zuni "city" which Niza identified as the place where Estevanico was killed a year earlier.

Coronado demanded to be admitted to the city, but the people inside refused. With about two hundred warriors, they had the Spaniards outnumbered, and they figured that they had the defensive advantage. Conquistadors being conquistadors, they did what they had come to do and launched their attack.

The city was, according to Castañeda, "taken with not a little difficulty, since they held the narrow and crooked entrance." He adds that Coronado himself was knocked down with a large stone, which would have killed him had it not been for the intervention of Don García López de Cardenas and Hernándo de Alvarado, who saved his life. Within an hour, the battle was over and the Spaniards were in possession of Háwikuh, which they believed to be "Cibola."

Though outnumbered, the Spaniards possessed superior firepower. Arguably more significant, they also had the speed and mobility of their horses, which the Indians did not have. As with the Inca in Peru, when they encountered Francisco Pizarro's men mounted on these strange beasts, the Pueblo people were greatly intimidated by the horses. Within a generation, of course, the Indians across the West had seamlessly adopted horses as part of their way of life, and had become some of the most skilled horsemen on earth.

As the conquerors took stock of what they had captured at Háwikuh, the disappointment was unabashed. It would be an understatement to say that the city was merely a village, and that it did not live up to the grandiose expectations of the members of the expedition.

They immediately took out their anger on Niza for leading them on a wild-goose chase. As Castañeda writes, "such were the curses that some hurled at Friar Marcos that I pray God may protect him from them. It is a little, crowded village, looking as if it had been crumpled all up together. There are haciendas in New Spain which make a better appearance at a distance. It is a village of about two hundred warriors, is three and four stories high, with the houses small and having only a few rooms, and without a courtyard."

Coronado must have felt as though he had gambled and lost. The chagrin and humiliation that Niza must have felt can easily be imagined.

In September, when Coronado dispatched a messenger to take his report about his disappointing discoveries back to Mendoza, he gave Niza the option of going back with him, rather than remaining with the expedition. The friar readily accepted. In his reference to this, written a quarter century later, Castañeda's disgust with the Franciscan for having stretched the imaginations of the conquistadors is still evident. He writes that Niza returned to Mexico City "because he did not think it was safe for him to stay in Cibola, seeing that his report had turned out to be entirely false, because the kingdoms that he had told about had not been found, nor the populous cities, nor the wealth of gold, nor the precious stones which he had reported, nor the fine clothes, nor other things that had been proclaimed from the pulpits."

In Niza's defense, although his deliberate exaggerations make him hard to support, we should say that he did take Coronado back exactly to the place where Estevanico had taken him. Although Niza is at fault for imagining more than he actually saw, Estevanico certainly deserves his share of the blame for exaggerating what he had seen on his trip with Cabeza de Vaca.

Francisco de Coronado.
(*Bill Yenne*)

Coronado set up a temporary headquarters at Háwikuh, where his men could avail themselves of captured food stores while waiting for the troops who had been left behind with Tristan de Arellano to catch up.

Once rested, Coronado set about dispatching his captains to investigate the region. In so doing, he initiated the first systematic European exploration of the American Southwest. For the first time in history, Europeans with the luxury of the time to contemplate it stared upon this spectacular mesa-studded landscape. As the great folklorist and chronicler of the soul of the Southwest, J. Frank Dobie, described it in *Apache Gold and Yaqui Silver* (1939), this vast land is: "A world of little rain wherein races of men no longer extant left hieroglyphic records of thriving population, arts, fierce struggle and then vanishment. It is a world of illimitable vistas, of geological inscrutabilities, and of things both animate and inanimate deeply hidden. Manmade highways and automobiles crisscross this world but hardly penetrate it, enter it but scarcely get into it deeper than the furrow of an ocean liner gets into the waters of the everlasting deeps."

Even today, in the mountains and canyons beyond the few large cities and on the byways beyond Interstates 10, 14, 25, and 40, this landscape the size of France is still much as it was in Dobie's time, when U.S. Route 66 was new. In the Sangre de Christo or the Mogollons, one can still hike for hours and stop to hear no sound but the call of the jay and the wind toying with the piñon pines.

After having defeated the Zuni and stolen their food supplies, Coronado now had a more peaceful objective. As Castañeda writes, he wanted to tell the native people to "tell their friends and neighbors that Christians had come into the country, whose only desire was to be their friends, and to find out about good lands to live in, and for them to come to see the strangers and talk with them."

A twenty-man contingent led by Don Pedro de Tovar headed northwest into what is now northeastern Arizona, becoming the first Europeans to visit the "Three Mesas" of the Hopi (also called Moqui), hilltop settlements that were very similar to the Seven Cities of the Zuni. The Spaniards called the place Tusayan, a name that continued to be widely used until the early twentieth century, and which exists today in several place names within Arizona.

The Hopi people (shortened from Hopituh Shi-nu-mu, meaning "the Peaceful People") remain on the Three Mesas. Among the best known settlements today are Waalpi (Walpi) and Hano (Tewa) on the First Mesa, and Oriabi on the Third Mesa. These all existed when Tovar visited in 1540.

After some initial tension, the two sides regarded one another peaceably, if warily. The Hopi did present the Spaniards with gifts, including some cotton clothing, dressed animal hides, and cornmeal. Castañeda adds that the Hopi also gave them "some turquoises, but not many."

The people whom Tovar encountered told of a large, westward flowing river farther to the north. This was the mighty Colorado, the largest in the region between the Southwest and the Pacific. Coronado correctly deduced that such a river would flow into the same body of water where Hernándo de Alarcón and his flotilla were. (Coronado assumed this to be the "South Sea," or the Pacific Ocean, but it is actually the Gulf of California, which is indeed fed by the Colorado River.)

Eager to locate this river and to thereby gain access to Alarcón, Coronado ordered García López de Cárdenas to

The Hopi city of Waalpi on the First Mesa photographed at the turn of the twentieth century.

check it out it, which he did. Though he was within sight of the Colorado by the end of September, Cárdenas and his dozen men could not reach it. They were standing on the South Rim of the Grand Canyon.

More than a mile deep, the Grand Canyon is 277 miles long and 18 miles across at its widest point. They spent three days looking for a way down, but found it impossible. As Castañeda reports:

> Captain Melgosa and one Juan Galeras and another companion, who were the three lightest and most agile men, made an attempt to go down at the least difficult place, and went down until those who were above were unable to keep sight of them. They returned about four o'clock in the afternoon, not having succeeded in reaching the bottom on account of the great difficulties which they found, because what seemed to be easy from above was not so, but instead very hard and difficult. They said that they had been down about a third of the way and that the river seemed very large from the place which they reached, and that from what they saw they thought the Indians had given the width correctly. Those who stayed above had estimated that

some huge rocks on the sides of the cliffs seemed to be about as tall as a man, but those who went down swore that when they reached these rocks they were bigger than the great tower of Seville.

The Giralda, the famous bell tower in the Cathedral of Seville, stands over 340 feet tall.

Having tried and failed to descend the cliffs, the first Europeans ever to behold the Grand Canyon, gave up and headed back to Háwikuh.

Unbeknownst to Cárdenas or to Coronado, Alarcón was sailing north in the Gulf of California. He had reached the mouth of the Colorado River in late August, and had sailed upstream. He was never close to the Grand Canyon, but may have gotten as far as the vicinity of Needles, California, where old Route 66, and later Interstate 40, have crossed the Colorado since the twentieth century. Commenting on Alarcón, Bandelier writes that "although the main object of this voyage, cooperation with Coronado, was not gained, it contributed much to geographical knowledge, for it determined the form of the Gulf of California and elicited the first information concerning the lower course of the largest river on the western coast of America, the Río Colorado."

Melchior Díaz, whom Coronado had sent back toward Culiacán at the same time as Niza, did turn westward to travel overland across what is now northern Mexico to the Gulf of California. When he arrived, he discovered a message and some gear that had been cached by Alarcón, but the ships had long since sailed south toward Compostela.

As had been the case with Antonio Pigafetta in Tierra del Fuego two decades earlier, Díaz's companions reported discovering a race of giants living in underground houses in the Sonoran Desert. These people may have been the Cocopah, who call themselves Xawi Kwñchawaay (the people who live on the river), although they are normal sized.

While still in the desert, Díaz injured himself in an accident, and died a painful death before he reached Culiacán. As Castañeda relates, "one day a greyhound belonging to one of the soldiers chased some sheep which they were taking along for food. When the captain noticed this, he threw his lance at the dog while his horse was running, so that it stuck up in the ground, and not being able to stop his horse he went over the lance so that it nailed him through the thighs and the iron came out behind, rupturing his bladder. . . . He lived about twenty days."

Meanwhile at Háwikuh, Coronado had received some visitors. They explained that they lived in the pueblo of Cicuye (now called Pecos), about 300 miles to the east, near present-day Santa Fe. Their leader, who the Spaniards called "Bigotes" because of his long mustache, explained that they wanted to be friends, and offered to guide them through their territory. Coronado accepted their invitation, and sent a contingent of troops under Hernándo de Alvarado to go east to reconnoiter Cicuye.

Five days into the journey, they reached the Acoma pueblo, which Castañeda describes as being

> very strong, because it was up on a rock out of reach, having steep sides in every direction, and so high that it was a good musket that could throw a ball as high. There was one entrance by a stairway built by hand, which began at the top of a slope which is around the foot of the rock. There a broad stairway for about 200 steps, then a stretch of about 100 narrower steps, and at the top they had to go up about three times as high as a man by means of holes in the rock, in which they put the points of their feet. . . . There was a wall of large and small stones at the top, which they could roll down without showing themselves, so that no army could possibly be strong enough to capture the village.

Alvarado had the presence of mind to make peace before things spun out of control. Today, the Acoma pueblo claims to be the oldest continuously inhabited town in the United States. The steepness of the stairways which Castañeda described can be confirmed by this author, who has climbed them.

Three days later, the Spaniards were at what Castañeda calls the "Tiguex" pueblos, and five days after that, they finally reached Cicuye. While Acoma is still inhabited, Cicuye has been abandoned since the nineteenth century, and the ruins are now part of the Pecos National Historical Park. Cicuye

The Acoma pueblo appeared much the same in the late nineteenth century as it had when first visited by Europeans more than 400 years earlier.

and other pueblos now unoccupied were located to the east of the Rio Grande Valley.

"Tiguex" is actually an early term for a linguistic group common to several pueblos. It later evolved into the Spanish term "Tigua," which was translated into English by Frederick Hodge as "Tiwa," the term commonly used today. The Rio Grande pueblos where this language is spoken today include Isleta and Sandia near Bernalillo and Albuquerque, and Taos and Picuris north of Santa Fe. Another Tiwa pueblo in the Bernalillo vicinity that is mentioned by the early Spaniards is Puaray. Castañeda indicates that the Tiwa pueblos which he saw included about a dozen villages.

The Rio Grande pueblos in the area roughly between Albuquerque and Santa Fe are grouped as to the language spoken. In addition to Tiwa/Tigua are the Keres (or Keresan), Towa, and Tewa (or Tano). The Keres-speaking pueblos include Acoma, Cochiti (Kotyit), Kewa (formerly Santo Domingo), San Felipe (Katishtya), Laguna, and Zia. The Tewa pueblos are those of Nambe (Oweenge), Ohkay Owingeh (formerly San Juan), Pojoaque (P'osuwaegeh), San

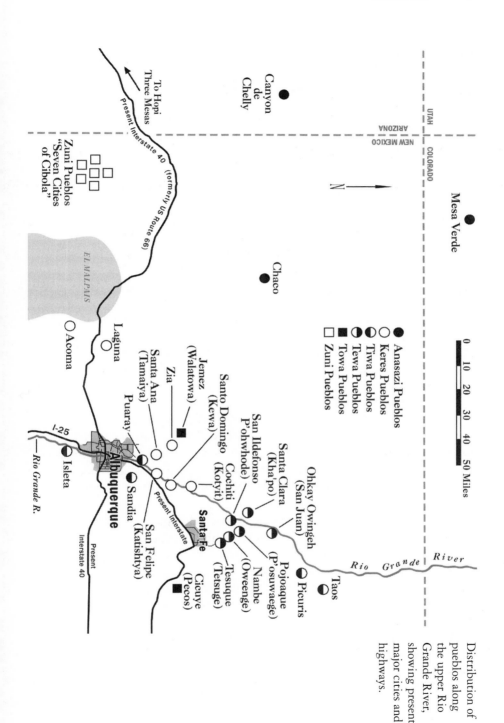

Distribution of pueblos along the upper Rio Grande River, showing present major cities and highways.

Ildefonso (P'ohwhóde), Santa Clara (Kha'po), and Tesuque. Jemez (Walatowa) is the still-extant Towa pueblo.

While Alvarado marched toward Cicuye, Castañeda reports that Coronado ordered García López de Cárdenas to march on the Tiwa pueblos, to "get lodgings ready for the army" for the winter of 1540–1541. This essentially amounted to brutally kicking people out of their homes, or, "as it was necessary that the natives should give the Spaniards lodging places, the people in one village had to abandon it and go to others belonging to their friends, and they took with them nothing but themselves and the clothes they had on."

At Cicuye, Alvarado is recalled as being every bit as amiable and gracious as Tovar had been on the Hopi Three Mesas. As a result, he was well received initially. Castañeda describes this city as "a very strong village four stories high," and writes that "the people came out from the village with signs of joy to welcome Hernándo de Alvarado and [Bigotes], and brought them into the town with drums and pipes something like flutes, of which they have a great many. They made many presents of cloth and turquoises, of which there are quantities in that region."

Furthermore, they told the Spaniards about "many towns up toward the north," implying that they possessed great wealth. However, the Spaniards quickly put the "many towns up toward the north" out of their minds as they came under the spell of a mysterious stranger, who appears to have been an Indian slave whose original home was far to the east, possibly somewhere along the Mississippi River. Castañeda says that he was "a native of the country toward Florida." There is no record of his name. Castañeda says simply that they called him "El Turco," or "the Turk," because "he looked like one."

It was not unusual in pre-Columbian North America for people captured as hostages or slaves to be traded from one tribe to another, and wind up a thousand miles or so from their original home, where they were treated not so much under our traditional idea of slavery, but more as a valued servant. To put this into context, we are reminded of the Shoshone teenager named Sacagawea (Sacajawea), who achieved immortality as a guide for the Lewis and Clark expedition in 1805–1806. When Lewis and Clark met her, she was with the Hidatsa, who had captured her at about the age of twelve and had taken her about 750 miles east of her Shoshone homeland. Although she was reunited with the Shoshone during the expedition, she returned to the Hidatsa.

The Turk, who was apparently quite charismatic and eloquent in his storytelling skills, told Alvarado and his men wonderful anecdotes about the lands to the east. He mentioned a race of large, shaggy wild cattle—which turned out to be American bison, or buffalo. For perhaps the first time, Europeans were shown buffalo hides. However, more captivating to the conquistadors than buffalo were tales of "large settlements in the farther part of that country" with a great wealth of gold and silver.

As soon as Coronado heard about it, this country, which was called Quivira, became the symbolic substitute in his mind and his longings for the recently discredited Seven Cities of Cibola.

According to Castañeda, the Turk said that in Quivira

> There was a river in the level country which was two leagues wide [either the Missouri or the Mississippi], in which there were fishes as big as horses, and large numbers of very big canoes, with more than twenty rowers on a side, and that they carried sails, and that their lords sat on the poop under awnings, and on the prow they had a great golden eagle. He said also that the lord of that country took his afternoon nap under a great tree on which were hung a great number of little gold bells, which put him to sleep as they swung in the air. He said also that everyone had their ordinary dishes made of wrought plate, and the jugs and bowls were of gold. He called gold acochis. For the present he was believed, on account of the ease with which he told it and because they showed him metal ornaments and he recognized them and said they were not gold, and he knew gold and silver very well and did not care anything about other metals.

As Bandelier put it, Coronado "saw that his highly strained anticipations were not fulfilled in Zuni-Cibola, and that his campaign to that place had been a material failure. The force which he commanded was still more bitterly disappointed, for their expectations had been of a more immediate character. . . . The stories told [by the Turk] awakened hopes that there were perhaps better regions and mountains richer in metals in those directions."

Only one question asked of the Turk by the Spaniards mattered—Would he take them to Quivira?

"Of course," smiled the Turk. He would do anything to get away from the pueblos.

Temporarily frustrated by the Seven Cities disappointment, Francisco Vásquez de Coronado now had Quivira to reawaken his conquistador's spirit. He had come in 1540 to conquer, and now he had exciting new horizons to look toward for the coming year.

One is left to ponder whether Coronado, as he had assumed in the summer of 1540, had actually found the real Seven Cities of Cibola, or had missed them entirely. Based on all accounts, it is almost certainly true that Marcos de Niza had taken Coronado to the place where Estevanico had taken him in 1539, but was that place *really* Cibola?

In his various writings, Adolph Bandelier insists emphatically and repeatedly that the Zuni pueblos, including Háwikuh, were one and the same with Cibola, but were they?

As we recall Cabeza de Vaca's account, which was not published for another two years, he had specifically said that the place where wealthy people lived in "very big houses" was to the north. While it is uncertain exactly where in the Southwest that Cabeza de Vaca was when his source pointed to the north, the Zuni pueblos were at the southern edge of the region where people then lived in multistory houses. Therefore, it can be argued that the Zuni pueblos could not have been the great city of which Cabeza de Vaca had heard.

Furthermore, Coronado had just been told by the people of Cicuye and Tiwa that there were multiple cities up north, and he had chosen to ignore this information in deference to the sweet yarns of the honey-tongued Turk who pointed eastward.

Might the great cities at Chaco or Mesa Verde still have been inhabited in the sixteenth century? Modern archaeologists don't think so, but it would be another three centuries before outsiders came across these cities and confirmed that they had been abandoned.

As Castañeda writes with a quarter century of hindsight, "I believe that it would have been much better to follow [the northerly] direction than that of the Turk, who was the cause of all the misfortunes which followed."

14

A DEVIL
IN THE PITCHER

Gold [found in the New World] is, like another gold-
en calf, worshipped by [the Spanish conquistadors] as
a god; for they come without intermission and without
thought, across the sea, to toil and danger, in order to
get it. May it please God that it be not for their
damnation.

—Padre Toribio of Benevento, Minorite monk,
Historia de los Indios de Nueva España (1540)

THE WINTER OF 1540–1541 was an auspicious time. The
same months that Francisco de Coronado was dreaming of
Quivira, Philipp von Hutten and Gonzalo Pizarro were 2,500
and 3,000 miles to the south, respectively, each preparing
excitedly for separate *entradas* which each was sure would take
him to the gates of El Dorado.

However, as electric as the atmosphere in Quito and Coro
probably was, the mood on the 5,000-foot plateau of the
upper Rio Grande was deeply gloomy. This was in part
because the weather consisted of relentless snowstorms alter-
nating with leaden, low-hanging clouds. The Rio Grande
itself was frozen over, and the snow was far too deep for
Coronado to even contemplate getting on with his quest for
cities of gold.

The gloom was also in part because the relations between the Spaniards and the local people, which had been strained to begin with, were going from bad to worse. Even at Cicuye, where Hernándo de Alvarado's entrance in the previous autumn had been greeted by flute players, things had gone sour.

The Turk, who was by now the favorite muse of the conquistadors, had complained that the people at Cicuye had stolen some gold bracelets from him at the time he was captured. When Alvarado stormed over to Cicuye to demand the bracelets, his friend, Bigotes, said that he knew nothing about them, and said the Turk was lying. Alvarado promptly put Bigotes and the Cicuye head man into chains and took them as prisoners.

At the Tiwa settlements, things were even more precarious. As temperatures plummeted, the Spanish demand on the locals for supplies was unreasonable. As Adolph Bandelier writes in *The Gilded Man*, "the manner in which the articles were demanded and obtained deserves the severest reprobation. The Pueblos on both sides of the river were ravaged and plundered, and outrages were committed against the women."

Pedro de Castañeda, who was there during that winter, goes into detail on the latter in his firsthand *Relación de la Jornada de Cíbola 1540*. He writes of a particular conquistador, who, seeing

> a pretty woman . . . called her husband down to hold his horse by the bridle while he went up [into their house]; and as the village was entered by the upper story, the Indian supposed he was going to some other part of it. While he was there the Indian heard some slight noise, and then the Spaniard came down, took his horse, and went away. The Indian went up and learned that he had violated, or tried to violate, his wife, and so he came with the important men of the town to complain that a man had violated his wife, and he told how it happened. When the general [Coronado] made all the soldiers and the persons who were with him come together, the Indian did not recognize

the man, either because he had changed his clothes or for whatever other reason there may have been, but he said that he could tell the horse, because he had held his bridle, and so he was taken to the stables, and found the horse, and said that the master of the horse must be the man. He denied doing it, seeing that he had not been recognized, and it may be that the Indian was mistaken in the horse; anyway, he went off without getting any satisfaction.

A series of events such as this, coming on top of the confiscation of property, touched off a general uprising among the pueblos, which was answered by conquistadors wielding superior firepower, including crossbows and muskets.

Coronado responded to the insurrection with a firm hand, and that firm hand was García López de Cárdenas. He found that the people had sealed themselves inside their cities and could not be dislodged. Coronado ordered Cárdenas to surround the one where the incident with the woman had occurred, and make it an example. They took the Indians by surprise and managed to capture the upper story, but suffered many wounded in the process. The defenders holed up inside lower stories of the pueblo and in the subterranean ceremonial room, which is known as a kiva.

As Castañeda writes, the Spaniards' "Indian allies from New Spain smoked them out from the cellars [the kiva] into which they had broken, so that they begged for peace. Pablo de Melgosa and Diego López, the alderman from Seville, were left on the roof and answered the Indians with the same signs they were making for peace, which was to make a cross. They then put down their arms and received pardon."

However, when the people who had surrendered were taken to Cárdenas at his tent, he acted under Coronado's orders that they were not to have been taken alive; Castañeda believes that he reacted not knowing that they had given themselves up of their own accord. He goes on to tell the story of what happened, writing that Cárdenas then

ordered 200 stakes to be prepared at once to burn them alive. Nobody told him about the peace that had been granted them, for the soldiers knew as little as he, and those who should have told him about it remained silent, not thinking that it was any of their business. Then when the enemies saw that the Spaniards were binding them and beginning to roast them, about 100 men who were in the tent began to struggle and defend themselves with what there was there and with the stakes they could seize. Our men who were on foot attacked the tent on all sides, so that there was great confusion around it, and then the horsemen chased those who escaped. As the country was level, not a man of them remained alive, unless it was some who remained hidden in the village.

As those who were hidden escaped into the night, it began to snow. Castañeda adds that when the news spread "that the strangers did not respect the peace they had made, [it] proved a great misfortune."

The "example" that Cárdenas attempted to set had certainly backfired. When the Spaniards later tried to tell the people that they "would be pardoned and might consider themselves safe," they naturally "replied that they did not trust those who did not know how to keep good faith after they had once given it."

Castañeda writes of a fifty-day siege of another village, in which the Spaniards were thwarted in an effort to use scaling ladders against the walls, and in which the "enemy threw down such quantities of rocks upon our men that many of them were laid out, and they wounded nearly 100 with arrows, several of whom afterward died on account of the bad treatment by an unskillful surgeon who was with the army."

Nevertheless, when the besieged Indians asked to surrender their children in safety, Cárdenas "rode up in front of the town without his helmet and received the boys and girls in his arms." He then "begged them to make peace, giving them the strongest promises for their safety," and they responded by beginning "to shoot arrows in showers, with loud yells and cries."

At last, the besieged people, both men and women, tried to escape by sneaking out at night to cross the Rio Grande. The following morning, the Spanish found most of them on the opposite shore, either dead or suffering from hypothermia.

Additional cities were besieged and taken down, and by the end of March 1541, the last of the surviving Tiwa people had been captured.

In analyzing the revolt and its repression, Bandelier writes that "Coronado and his company behaved on this occasion with a cruelty that fixes an indelible stain on their memory. . . . This was the only instance during the whole continuance of the expedition in New Mexico in which the Spaniards behaved barbarously and cruelly, but their treatment of the [Tiwa people] is not easier to explain on that account. I can find no ground of excuse for it; and the behavior of Coronado is in so complete contradiction with his previous and subsequent course that I cannot easily understand it, unless it be that necessity drove him to the first summary measures, and the severe cold and the scarcity of provisions then provoked his soldiers to wild excesses."

Even before the regrettable "Tiguex War" had finally ground to a halt, Coronado decided to mend fences with the people of Cicuye. Their chief, who had been in Spanish custody for months, was released and Coronado promised that he would release Bigotes as well—as soon as the Spanish left the area and headed east toward the mysterious Quivira, the land of the Turk.

Throughout the winter, the Turk had been a continuous presence at Coronado's camp. As enthralled as the general and his officers seemed to be with him, the infatuation was by no means universal. For many, there was a distrust of the man, and a sense of foreboding about his intentions.

Castañeda later related a strange incident involving the Turk, writing that "there were already some in the army who suspected the Turk because a Spaniard named Cervantes, who had charge of him during the siege, solemnly swore that he had seen the Turk talking with the devil in a pitcher of water, and also that while he had him under lock so that no one could speak to him, the Turk had asked him what Christians had been killed by the people at Tiwa. He told him 'nobody,' and then the Turk answered: 'You lie; five Christians are dead, including a captain.'"

Cervantes knew that this was correct, and he asked the Turk who told him. The Turk replied that he knew it without anyone telling him, and turned back to "speaking to the devil in the pitcher."

After spending the cold winter months besieging the pueblos or languishing in the drafty, smoky, commandeered pueblos, Francisco Vásquez de Coronado and his conquistadors were more than anxious to strike out for the golden land which the Turk had described. As Bandelier writes, both Coronado and the men "awaited with impatience the mild weather, when they could go forward into the great unknown region on the edge of which they were."

The Spaniards were eager to get going.

15

QUIVIRA

What men believe or fancy to be true, what they have faith in, whether phantom or fact, propels their actions. The hunter of precious metals is always a fatalist, no matter how civilized above superstition he may be. Deep in his heart he believes that somewhere out in the sierras, the magic scales are awaiting him.

—J. Frank Dobie, *Apache Gold and Yaqui Silver* (1928)

ACCORDING TO A LETTER written by Francisco Vásquez de Coronado to Emperor Charles V, and referenced by George Park Winship in the *Fourteenth Report of the Bureau of Ethnology* (1896), Coronado and his Spaniards departed the land of the blood-stained Tiwa pueblos on April 23, 1541.

One is left to wonder why they waited until so late in the season, given the distances they had ahead of them. The snow had probably melted by that time in the area around the Rio Grande, but perhaps there was continued concern about the amount of snow that might still clog the mountain passes, and about rivers swollen by runoff.

Coronado's first stop was Cicuye, where he released his former friend and present hostage, Bigotes, into the arms of his own people. Pedro de Castañeda writes that "the village was very glad to see him, and the people were peaceful and offered food [to the Spaniards]."

They were happy to see Coronado and company, if only because they knew that they were merely passing through, and that they were about to cross the horizon and disappear forever in the direction of Quivira.

As a parting gift, the people of Cicuye gave Coronado a slave, a young man named Xabe, who was a native of Quivira, or some nearby place in the distant east, and who could help direct them there. Naturally, the Turk took umbrage to the notion of sharing the role of Coronado's native guide, especially when Xabe started spinning yarns which were at variance with those of the Turk. Xabe told Coronado that, yes there *was* gold in Quivira, but not nearly as much as the Turk claimed. The Turk told Coronado that Xabe didn't know what he was talking about.

It is uncertain whether Coronado took Xabe with him or not. Castañeda later mentions another Quiviran named Ysopete who did accompany the Spaniards, and who also disagreed with the Turk.

The Coronado *entrada* finally departed from the land of the pueblos. Castañeda gives the date as May 5, 1541. The people at the pueblos no doubt breathed a sigh of relief, but their respite was to be short-lived. Before the coming summer was over, Coronado would send back a substantial part of his army so that he would have a smaller and more mobile force, and could therefore move more quickly in his search for Quivira.

Before turning eastward, Coronado is generally believed to have traveled to the southeast, crossing the Pecos River in the vicinity of present-day Puerto de Luna in Guadalupe County, New Mexico. Castañeda tells that they found the river so high that they had to build a bridge to get across. He gives no details other than to say that it took four days to construct, and that they got all the men and horses across without a mishap.

About a week after crossing the Pecos, they began to encounter buffalo herds for the first time. This suggests that they were on the fringes of the Great Plains in or near the Texas panhandle. As Adolph Bandelier colorfully explains, until this point, "the Spaniards had to endure only the dangers and hindrances offered by mountains. Now they encountered difficulties of another kind such as they had not before met [by Europeans] on the American continent. They were to enter upon the boundless plains, the endless uniformity of which, fatiguing to body and mind alike, slowly and surely unnerved and finally crushed them. For, uncertain as was their aim, still more uncertain was the end."

They were also beginning to see people whom Castañeda described as living in "tents made of the tanned skins of the cows," probably meaning Plains Indian tipis. He also writes that "they travel like the Arabs, with their tents and troops of dogs loaded with poles," which was the typical means of transporting tipis until the Plains people adopted the horse.

Castañeda tells that they "did nothing unusual when they saw our army, except to come out of their tents to look at us." He adds that the fact that "they were very intelligent is evident from the fact that although they conversed by means of signs they made themselves understood so well that there was no need of an interpreter." Indeed, the use of sign language was widespread on the Plains, where the nomadic tribes roamed far and wide, frequently encountering many other tribes with different spoken languages.

These people, whom Castañeda refers to as "Querechos," are generally believed by ethnographers to have been the Na'isha, or Naishan Dene, also called Plains Apache. They are also called the Kiowa Apache, because, while they speak an Athapaskan language similar to the Apache of the desert Southwest, they were then culturally similar to the Plains tribes, especially the Tanoan-speaking Kiowa, who ranged from the Texas panhandle to Montana.

Among the other people whom they met as they moved eastward were those whom Castañeda calls the Tejas (or Teyas), who are thought to have been the Wichita or people related to them. The name Tejas is the root word for the eventual place-name Texas. Though the Wichita speak a Caddoan dialect, they were able to communicate with other tribes and with the Spaniards by the universally understood sign language of the Plains.

Of the contrasts and differences between the Southwest and Plains lifestyles, Castañeda writes, "they do not make gourds, nor sow corn, nor eat bread, but instead raw meat— or only half cooked—and fruit." The latter would have included the berries, chokecherries, and crabapples which often grow along streams in the Plains.

The Spaniards saw many people as they traveled, but none who lived in permanent settlements. They were obviously nomadic, and there was nothing to indicate that there would be multistoried buildings such as they had seen in the Southwest. The Plains tribes all told of many settlements in distant places, and of great rivers, but they had no knowledge of cities of gold. The Tejas, some of whom traveled with the Spaniards as guides, said that there was a major population center, but it lay more to the northeast than to the east as the Turk insisted.

The Turk now said that they were just two days ride from a place which he called Haxa (or Haya). Castañeda reports that Coronado "sent Captain Diego López with ten companions lightly equipped and a guide to go at full speed toward the sunrise for two days and discover Haxa, and then return to meet the army."

When López returned, he told the general that he had seen nothing "but cows and the sky," adding that he had seen a lot of both. At least, with the vast profusion of buffalo, the expedition never wanted for fresh meat. Castañeda mentions that they killed five hundred bulls in a fortnight.

Meanwhile, another scouting party, led by Don Rodrigo Maldonado, traveled four days and did find a large settlement. According to Castañeda, these people remembered meeting Álvar Núñez Cabeza de Vaca and Andrés Dorantes de Carranza when they passed through six or seven years earlier. He also mentions that they met an "Indian girl here who was as white as a Castilian lady, except that she had her chin painted [possibly tattooed, as was the custom] like a Moorish woman."

Castañeda adds that the people at this settlement were very generous with Don Rodrigo, giving him "a pile of tanned skins and other things, and a tent as big as a house, which he directed them to keep until the army came up."

Sadly, when Coronado did catch up, there was a free-for-all at the camp in which the Spaniards seized a number of buffalo hides that had not been given as gifts. Whether from coincidence or heavenly retribution, the Spaniards shortly thereafter endured a punishing rebuke from out of the sky. Hailstorms are common on the Plains in the summer, and can be quite severe. As Castañeda recalls, the storm which Coronado's *entrada* endured in 1541 was one for the record books. He writes that hailstones

> as big as bowls, or bigger, fell as thick as raindrops, so that in places they covered the ground two or three spans or more deep. And one hit the horse—or I should say, there was not a horse that did not break away, except two or three which the [slaves] protected by holding large sea nets over them, with the helmets and shields which all the rest wore; and some of them dashed up on to the sides of the ravine so that they got them down with great difficulty. If this had struck them while they were upon the plain, the army would have been in great danger of being left without its horses, as there were many which they were not able to cover. The hail broke many tents, and battered many helmets, and wounded many of the horses, and broke all the crockery of the army.

Just as the sky possessed its wrath for the Spaniards, so too did the boundless, endless uniformity of the land. Castañeda says that "many fellows were lost at this time who went out hunting and did not get back to the army for two or three days, wandering about the country as if they were crazy, in one direction or another, not knowing how to get back where they started from."

By now, Coronado's patience was wearing thin with the Turk. Ysopete had long insisted that the Turk was outright lying, and Coronado was growing angry. At last, the Turk made an admission. While he had not exactly lied, he had stretched the truth. There were great population centers, but Ysopete and the Tejas were right, they were actually more to the northeast than due east. The people did not exactly live in great stone houses, but they did have a lot of gold.

Coronado had reached a decision point. Even if the Turk had not been truthful, the other evidence did indicate that Quivira, at least in some form, did in fact exist.

Should he continue? He had come this far. To turn back would have been to admit failure.

"Coronado sets out to the North," Frederic Remington's iconic illustration of the optimistic beginning of the conquistador's search across the plains of North America for an elusive city of gold.

But could he continue? Provisions were running short, most of all their water. In May, they had started out from New Mexico worried about rivers too swollen to cross. Two months later, the streams on which they depended for fresh water were shriveling up in the heat of the summer. More often than not, spotting what looked like a stream yielded only the disappointment of a dry wash. The corn they had brought from New Mexico was almost gone, and so too was the supply of meat that had once seemed endless. The buffalo, upon which they had depended for a fresh supply of meat, had also reacted to the heat and the lack of water. The great herds had migrated away from the southern Plains. Where once there was nothing "but cows and the sky," there was now nothing but the wrathful, hailstorm sky.

The distances were seemingly infinite, and progress was slow, especially when they were compelled to search for way-laid hunters from the group, who lost their way searching for game. If he was to find any sort of resolution to the question of Quivira, Coronado knew that he had to speed up the pace.

The only way to do that, he decided, was to separate the fastest parts of the expedition from the slowest.

Joining his officers for a council, they all agreed. Coronado would press on with thirty horsemen, half a dozen foot soldiers, and some Tejas guides, and head northeast. Meanwhile, Tristan de Arellano would turn back to Tiwa with the remainder of the army. The place where the two contingents of conquistadors parted is unknown, but it was probably somewhere in the Texas panhandle east of present-day Amarillo.

Castañeda reports that "when the men in the army learned of this decision, they begged their general not to leave them to conduct the further search, but declared that they all wanted to die with him and did not want to go back." This had to have warmed the old conquistador's heart, but the decision had been made.

Both Ysopete and the Turk would accompany Coronado, but Castañeda notes that from this point, the discredited Turk was "taken along in chains."

Heading north, Coronado and his men crossed an endless undulation of canyons, ravines, and dry creek beds. They marveled at the vast profusion of prairie dog towns, something they could never have imagined. They passed the occasional river, flowing with the water they now greatly prized. They crossed the Canadian River (which appears on early Spanish maps as the Magdalena), passed through what is now the Oklahoma panhandle, and rode into modern Kansas.

On the Feast Day of Saints Peter and Paul (June 29) the expedition reached the "river below Quivira," which is thought to have been the Arkansas River, at a place somewhere east of present-day Dodge City. The date is according to Castañeda. Others have calculated different dates; Adolph Bandelier mentions August 21. From here, their Tejas guides took them in a northeasterly direction, following the river for about a week.

Coincidentally, at this same moment, Coronado's countryman, Hernándo de Soto, had crossed the Mississippi River near present-day Memphis, Tennessee, and was headed westward across Arkansas on a direct line toward Coronado's position. He would explore the downstream portion of the

Arkansas River before the year was out, but the two conquistadors remained several hundred miles apart.

Beneath the towering cumulus that glows a brilliant white against the deep blue skies on a Kansas summer day, Francisco Vásquez de Coronado first saw Quivira. It was during the first week of July, by Castañeda's reckoning, that his conquistadors reached the first of a series of settlements that they believed to be Quivira. The city that Coronado had once imagined as having architecture rivaling that of the Aztec in Mexico was more humble than that of the pueblos of New Mexico.

Instead of multistoried houses plated with gold, the people lived in modest, rectangular, thatched houses clustered into many groups of a dozen or two, located a mile or so apart along the banks of the Arkansas and its tributaries.

In all probability, the Tejas who had guided Coronado to this place had done so in good faith. Coronado had said he wanted to go to a place where there were many fixed houses—not portable tipis—and they took him there. This was a clear illustration of the shortcomings of their method of communication. The sign language of the Plains may have been universally understood, but it lacked the nuance that would have saved Coronado a great deal of disappointment. Of course, Coronado probably would have gone to see for himself regardless.

The location where Coronado first saw the thatched homes was probably at the place in central Kansas where the Arkansas River alters its northeasterly trend and turns southeasterly toward the present state of Arkansas and the Mississippi River.

Archaeological evidence and radiocarbon dating have indicated that roughly between 1450 and 1700 there was a substantial population center here in the vicinity of the present town of Great Bend, Kansas. The remains of several such settlements have been found near Lyons, Kansas, which is about 30 miles east of Great Bend on Cow Creek. The town is now home to the modest Coronado-Quivira Museum. The total number of people in all of the villages may have been as many as 10,000. The present, and declining, population of surrounding Barton County is less than a third of this today.

Based on their thatched homes, unique in this part of the Plains, archaeologists believe that the people were the Wichita, who would have probably been closely related to the people whom the Spaniards called Tejas. An adjacent population center, which Coronado called Harahey, may have been a concentration of linguistically similar Pawnee people which was to the northeast on the Smoky Hill River near the present city of Salina, Kansas.

As Coronado himself wrote in a letter to Charles V: "I had been told that the houses were made of stone and were several storied; they are only of straw, and the inhabitants are as savage as any that I have seen. They have no clothes, nor cotton to make them out of; they simply tan the hides of the cows which they hunt, and which pasture around their village and in the neighborhood of a large river. They eat their meat raw, like the Querechos and the Tejas, and are enemies to one another and war among one another."

Castañeda writes that they "reached Quivira, which took 48 days' marching, on account of the great detour they had made toward Florida," though he does not say forty-eight days from when. It was not from their original May 5 departure, because that would have been closer to sixty days. Perhaps it was from when they crossed the Pecos or from when they reached the Plains.

As for the notation about the "detour toward Florida," Castañeda means their traveling due east under the directions given by the Turk. It was still not understood how far west they were, and at that time "Florida" was a term not only for what we know as Florida, but for most of eastern North America.

For conquistadors dreaming of gold, finding this place, which they assumed to be Quivira, was as profound a disappointment as they had experienced a year earlier at the "Seven Cities of Cibola." Castañeda writes that "neither gold nor silver nor any trace of either was found among these people. Their lord wore a copper plate on his neck and prized it highly!"

Coronado writes in one of his letters to the emperor that "there were no signs of gold or silver; some iron pyrites and a few pieces of copper were all the metal that was found."

However, he did add that "the soil is the best that can be found for all the crops of Spain; besides being strong and black, it is well watered with brooks, springs, and rivers. I found plums like those in Spain, nuts, very fine grapes, and mulberries."

Juan de Padilla, one of the Franciscan missionaries traveling with Coronado, tried to do some planting of his own. After having made an effort to bring Christianity to Quivira's citizens, he erected a wooden cross on the Kansas prairie.

It was now the time of reckoning for the Turk.

As a thunderstorm shimmering with lightning bolts loomed on a late Kansas summer afternoon, Coronado had the Turk brought before him. The man who had walked from Texas to central Kansas in chains may have hung his head, though he was a proud and arrogant man. He was also shrewd and clever, but his days of being shrewd and clever had run out weeks before.

Why, Coronado demanded, had the Turk lied?

Why, Coronado demanded, had he guided them so far out of their way?

The once arrogant Turk became a river of remorse, though probably not without some "inducements" from the hands of angry conquistadors.

Castañeda, who was probably present at this interrogation, reports that the Turk acknowledged having done so because his own country was toward the east, and he wanted to go there. He added that he had also lied in part because "The people at Cicuye had asked him to lead them off on to the plains and lose them, so that the horses would die when their provisions gave out, and they would be so weak if they ever returned that they could be killed without any trouble, and thus they could take revenge for what had been done to them. This was the reason why he had led them astray, supposing that they did not know how to hunt or to live without corn, while as for the gold, he did not know where there was any of it."

With this, the life was brutally strangled from the man who had once been seen talking to the devil in a pitcher of water. A clap of thunder boomed from the closing, steel gray thunderheads.

Castañeda writes that "they garroted him, which pleased Ysopete very much, because [the Turk] had always said that Ysopete was a rascal and that he did not know what he was talking about."

It was early August when Coronado departed the manifestation of disillusion which was Quivira. He reached the Rio Grande pueblos as the autumn rains began to fall. Castañeda writes that the return, by lightly equipped men taking a more direct route, took forty days. Of course, if he had chosen to travel downstream on the Arkansas instead, he would have run into De Soto in fewer than forty days.

Castañeda mentions that young Xabe, the slave given to Coronado in the spring, was with Tristan de Arellano at Tiwa when he heard that Coronado was on his way back. Castañeda is unclear as to whether he had been with Arellano in Texas or whether he had remained behind in New Mexico all summer. In any case, Castañeda writes that "when he learned that the general was coming he acted as if he was greatly pleased."

"Now when the general comes, you will see that there are gold and silver in Quivira," Xabe told the Spaniards, "although not so much as the Turk said."

When Coronado did arrive, and he was empty handed, Xabe "was sad and silent, and kept declaring that there was some."

Though a gold-plated civilization eluded Coronado's grasp, the expedition itself was a gold-plated adventure, as Europeans first gazed upon the magical landscape of the Southwest. Observing that Coronado had spent the summer traveling in a circle, Adolph Bandelier crafts a summary metaphor around this symbolism:

> It is a well-known fact that lost travelers involuntarily walk circuitously, generally toward the right, and so gradually return to the place whence they started. This phenomenon is especially frequent in wide, treeless plains, where prominent objects by which the wanderer can direct himself are wanting. It has an extremely dangerous effect upon the mind, and may, if it occurs repeatedly, easily [drive him] to despair and frenzy. What happens to individuals may also occur to a larger

number. This was the fate of Coronado and his company when they sought and found Quivira. They returned in a wide bend to their starting point, after they had wandered for months on the desolate plains, led around in a circle as if by some evil spirit.

16

GOD AND GOLD

It was the same old, old story that had urged on every Spaniard since the discovery of the New World; the old, old story that had excited their cupidity, urged them on in their cruelty, and driven them to their death.

—Mara Louise Pratt-Chadwick, historian (1890)

FRANCISCO VÁSQUEZ DE CORONADO had ridden north into the *terra incognita* of North America in the spring of 1540, a proud and energetic conquistador. He returned to New Spain twenty-four months later, an exhausted and broken man.

He was broken emotionally and spiritually by his failure to find cities of gold in the Seven Cities of Cibola, compounded by his disappointment in having expended great effort to find no treasure at Quivira.

He was broken physically by a fall from his horse while he was still in the Tiwa pueblo country in December 1541.

He was broken financially by his having gambled his bank account only to come up with nothing.

He was broken politically by having squandered the friendship and patronage of the most powerful man in New Spain. When Coronado had arrived in North America, Viceroy Antonio de Mendoza had regarded him as his favorite fair-haired boy. Two years later, Mendoza regarded him as a

traitor. The fact that Coronado had written a number of letters directly to Emperor Charles V while he was in the field
was the cause of great irritation for Mendoza, who interpreted
this as a subordinate going over his head. Adolph Bandelier
writes that Mendoza regarded this "as bordering on treason."

Furthermore, Mendoza and his political cronies were also
furious at Coronado for his decision to pull his exhausted
Spanish army out of the north entirely. It had been Mendoza's
intention that Coronado should be the harbinger of a permanent Spanish presence in what is now the American
Southwest. Instead, Coronado abandoned it to its indigenous
people. Bandelier observes that "his evacuation of New
Mexico and return seemed at least a gross violation of duty, for
it was ascribed to disobedience, incapacity, and cowardice."

Coming to Coronado's defense, Bandelier writes that "no
one is disposed to write long letters in the pueblo houses;
moreover, in winter and on the road to Quivira the ink may
have failed. Don Antonio de Mendoza understood none of
these conditions, and did not realize the great difference
between the situations of the seaman and of the officer in the
heart of the continent. With all the traits for which he was
distinguished, the viceroy was first of all things a European
officer, who, however ably he could direct from his desk, had
no comprehension of American camplife."

The permanent Spanish presence in the Southwest would
not come to pass for more than half a century, long after
Mendoza had passed from the scene.

Coronado retained his office as governor of Nueva Galicia
until 1544, after which he was called up on charges for his
failings in the north. Eventually cleared of wrongdoing, he
retired to Mexico City, where he lived with the constant recollection of his enormous gamble, and his disappointment,
until his death on July 21, 1554.

If Francisco Vásquez de Coronado believed that the reason
for his failure to find great treasure in either the Seven Cities
of Cibola or Quivira was because it did not exist, he was in a
minority. Numerous people from the impetuous young Xabe
to members of his own army believed that he did not find it
because he failed to look for it in the right place.

Many of the men who wintered with him at Tiwa had
murmured about returning to Quivira in the summer of

1542. In fact, Padre Juan de Padilla did leave for Quivira as the rest of the men went home.

Taking his role as a missionary priest to heart, another Franciscan friar, the elderly Padre Luis de Úbeda, chose to remain in Cicuye to minister to its people. They took him in, provided him with a room, and agreed to supply his temporal needs as he cared for what he interpreted as their spiritual needs. He was never again seen by European eyes. Of course, more than a generation would pass before European eyes saw Cicuye again.

Accompanied by a Portuguese interpreter named Andrés do Campo, a couple of North African slaves, and several Indians, Padilla did make it all the way to Quivira. The cross he erected the year before was still standing. The small group set out after the "real" Quivira, but somewhere out in the Kansas prairies north of Quivira, they were attacked by people who were probably not Quivirans. Padilla was killed and the others captured. In 1543, do Campo managed to escape and make his back to New Spain to tell his tale.

In New Spain, the notion that Quivira existed beyond the settlements Coronado had found had taken on a life of its own. As Bandelier writes, "Quivira continued to exercise an unperceived influence on the imaginations of men. Notwithstanding, or perhaps because, Coronado had told the unadorned truth concerning the situation and conditions of the place, the world presumed that he was mistaken, and insisted on continuing the search for it."

However, for all the talk of the "true" Seven Cities or for the "real" Quivira, there were very few who were willing to put their money onto the same trail as their imaginations. During the later sixteenth century, in the years which followed Coronado's *entrada*, barely a trickle of adventurers followed his trail, and these set their limited horizons on the pueblo country of the American Southwest, and the still-flickering dream of the Seven Cities.

Part of the reason that so few tried was the ambitious nature of such a quest. It was easy for the coffeehouse conquistadors back in Mexico City to blame Coronado for failing to find cities of gold through negligence or short-sightedness. It was another thing to saddle up and head out into the smoldering deserts of *terra incognita*.

Another reason that so few sought this phantom treasure so far away was that very real treasure cropped up closer to home. In the fall of 1546, great quantities of silver ore were discovered in Nueva Galicia, and the town of Zacatecas (originally called Minas de los Zacatecas or "Mines of the Zacatecas") became an overnight boomtown. Zacatecas joined Potosí as one of Spain's most lucrative colonial profit centers.

With this, as settlement within New Spain crept northward, especially into the parts of the later Mexican state of Chihuahua east of the Sierra Madre, a new concept of the geography of the route to North America had emerged. Coronado had launched his *entrada* from Culiacán in Nueva Galicia on the west side of the mountains, which required crossing the Sierra Madre in order to go north into the American Southwest.

On the east side of the Sierra Madre, though it would not soon be utilized, a potential direct line went from Mexico City to present-day New Mexico through the province of Nueva Vizcaya without crossing the mountains.

Indeed, in 1562, Francisco de Ibarra, later the governor of Nueva Vizcaya, had been one of the men who made a tentative search for cities of gold in the north. He probably never made it as far north as the American Southwest, but he did make some silver discoveries in what is now the Mexican state of Durango. As a result, his family would remain powerful in the Nueva Vizcaya ruling elite for many years.

Among the settlements that were established in northern Nueva Vizcaya, within what is now eastern Chihuahua, were a proliferation of little hardscrabble mining towns that took advantage of silver ore discoveries on the periphery of the Zacatecas mother lode. These included San Bartolomé and Santa Bárbara, the latter founded in 1567 by the conquistador Rodrigo del Río de Losa.

About a dozen years later, a friar named Augustin Rodríquez was posted to this area. He began to hear stories repeated by the Indians about people way up north who lived in big houses and wove cotton cloth. Though he knew about the Coronado *entrada* only by way of fragmentary hearsay, he had devoured Álvar Núñez Cabeza de Vaca's *Naufragios* (*Castaways*) with great interest.

Gradually, the idea of going to see these places began to come alive within Padre Rodríquez's imagination. He shared his thoughts with a soldier of fortune named Francisco Sánchez. Better known as "El Chamuscado" ("the singed") because of his "fiery" beard, Sánchez admitted that he had heard the same stories and that he had been thinking the same thing. Between them, they decided to mount an expedition.

Like the expeditions of Coronado and Marcos de Niza before him, the party would be composed both of priests and laymen. In addition to Rodríquez, the priests included an Andalusian, Padre Francisco López, the senior cleric on the trip, and Juan de Santa Maria. Herbert Eugene Bolton of the University of California, an important twentieth-century scholar of early Spanish exploration in the Western United States, mentions in his book *Spanish Exploration in the Southwest* that Padre Santa Maria was also a Catalonian astrologer.

In 1580, while El Chamuscado was rounding up a crew of men, Rodríquez traveled to Mexico City to secure an official permit for the venture from Viceroy Lorenzo Suárez de Mendoza, the successor and second cousin of the Coronado-era viceroy Antonio de Mendoza. According to a memo which the viceroy sent to Madrid two years later, the purpose of the expedition, as outlined by the priest, was "to preach the holy gospel in the region beyond the Santa Bárbara mines."

If the friars were undertaking this venture with the goal of bringing an acquaintance with their faith to the Indians, the laymen were going for the gold. They were tired of merely listening to the stories of the cities of gold being told and retold in the cantinas of Nueva Vizcaya.

Along with El Chamuscado, the nine lay adventurers included Pedro de Bustamante and Hernándo Gallegos, whom Bolton calls "typical of that far northern frontier and significant of the interests in whose behalf the frontier was being extended. [Gallegos] was a native of Spain, had spent eight years in Mexico as a prospector and soldier, and was among those who had made expeditions beyond the mines against the Indians."

It was clearly a symbiotic relationship. Neither party really wanted the other, but sometimes you must accept what you need in order to get what you want. The priests needed the protection of the gunslingers, who needed the official permission for the *entrada* that the viceroy had granted to Rodríquez. In the *New Mexico Historical Review* in 1948, Angelico Chavez suggested a slightly alternative theory. Though it is clear that Padre Rodríquez was willing, even eager, to risk life and limb to take his Gospel message to the pueblos, Chavez interprets Gallegos's later accounts of the expedition to conclude that the priests had merely been conned by the others into providing a front for a treasure hunt.

Departing from Santa Bárbara in June 1581, El Chamuscado and the priests traveled north along the Río Conchos to the point where it flows into the Rio Grande, across from present-day Presidio, Texas. From here, they followed the Rio Grande all the way north to near present-day Albuquerque, where they were probably the first European *entrada* to arrive on the doorstep of the Tiwa pueblos in more than forty years. They were greeted at Puaray, probably warily, by the "people in cotton clothing" whose historic memory almost certainly recalled the bloodshed of their previous interaction with Europeans.

This new batch of Europeans also "discovered" Cicuye, probably not realizing that Cicuye was a place where Coronado had spent so much time those many years before. Wanting to impress those back home, Gallegos exaggerated for dramatic effect in his subsequent report, noting that it was comprised of "five hundred houses of from one to seven stories."

Also in an effort to butter up to the lords of New Spain and Old, El Chamuscado and Rodríquez named this town Nueva Tlaxcala after the capital city of the pre-Columbian kingdom which had allied itself with Hernán Cortés against the Aztec. Meanwhile, they started calling the surrounding country "Nuevo México" (New Mexico), a name which continues as that of the present state.

The priests and conquistadors spent August and September visiting Acoma and the Zuni pueblos, perhaps still imagining the latter as the mysterious and magnificent Seven Cities of Cibola. They even traveled eastward to the

One of the few visible changes at the Zuni pueblos between the sixteenth and the twentieth century was the addition of a Christian cross.

Plains to catch a glimpse of those shaggy, humped cattle, the American bison. El Chamuscado had planned to visit the Three Mesas of the Hopi, but the snowflakes had begun to fly and he decided to return to Puaray, where the priests had set up shop.

Meanwhile, though his companions tried to dissuade him, Padre Santa Maria had decided to head back down the Rio Grande to New Spain before the heavy snows made travel impossible. He intended to give the coffeehouse conquistadors back home their first fresh report on the amazing pueblos in four decades.

He didn't make it very far. According to the *Oroz Codex*, a second-hand account penned by historian Padre Pedro Oroz in 1584–1586, he was killed in his sleep less than a week later when someone dropped a large rock on him. Oroz adds that this was the method used by the Indians living south of the pueblos to kill witches and sorcerers. In relating this story, one must resist the temptation to add that as an astrologer, he should have seen it coming.

In late January 1582, having found no gold, the soldiers of fortune themselves decided to return to New Spain, and parted company with the two surviving Franciscans, who remained as missionaries to the people of the pueblos.

On the way home, El Chamuscado grew ill and his friends ministered to him as best they could. This being the sixteenth century, the treatment involved bleeding the patient, which naturally had a tendency to do more harm than good. Added to this was the fact that their instrument of choice was a rusty horseshoe nail, so the prognosis was not good. A bad cold complicated by loss of blood and an infection from a nail contaminated by being where horses walk would not always be fatal, but it is no surprise that in this case it was. The man with the fiery beard never saw Santa Bárbara again, but Bustamante and Gallegos were back by Easter.

Gallegos returned to Mexico City and filed his report with the viceroy. This document, *Relación y Conducta del Viaje que Francisco Sánchez Chamuscado con Ocho Soldados sus Companeros Hizo en el Descubrimiento del Nuevo México en Junio de 1581* (*Relation and Conduct of the Voyage that Francisco Sánchez the Singed with Eight Soldiers, his Companions Did in the Discovery of New Mexico in June 1581*) was deposited in the Archivo General de Indias (General Archive of the Indies) in Seville, along with a similar *relación* by Bustamante.

17

WITH MY OWN HANDS
I EXTRACTED ORE

The opportunity that Coronado thus opened has never since his time been neglected; the dream he dreamed has never died. For thousands of happy folk the mirage that lured him on has never faded, and today all over the wide, wide lands where conquistadors trailed and padres built their simple missions and in yet more places never glimpsed by Spanish eyes—tradition has marked rock and river and ruin with illimitable treasure.

—J. Frank Dobie, *Coronado's Children* (1930)

UPON LEARNING OF THE PRIESTS having remained behind—and feared abandoned—in this place now being called "Nuevo México," there was concern within the Franciscan community for their welfare. Padre Bernardino Beltrán, who was based at a monastery in Durango, the capital of Nueva Vizcaya, decided that he should go check on them. As had been the case with Padre Rodríquez, he needed to ally himself with someone who could provide security for his venture.

In Padre Bernardino's case, the soldier of fortune was Antonio de Espejo, a man who had come north to the frontier to dodge a fine that he owed as a result of having been complicit in a homicide committed by his brother. Naturally, he had heard the Cibola and Quivira stories, and it was not easy to avoid being clipped by the gold bug. However, according to Espejo's own account, or *relación*, on file in the Archivo General de Indias in Seville, he saw a priest in need and generously offered his services.

"As I was in that area at the time and had heard about the just and compassionate wishes of said friar and the entire Order," Espejo relates. "I made an offer—in the belief that by so doing I was serving Our Lord and His Majesty—to accompany the friar and spend a portion of my wealth in defraying his costs and in supplying a few soldiers both for his protection and for that of the friars he meant to succor and bring back."

As with El Chamuscado and his fellow frontiersmen two years earlier, Espejo was spending a portion of his wealth not so much as a charitable contribution to the Franciscans, but an investment in a more worldly quest for the elusive Seven Cities. For all his rough edges and his conquistador's greed, Espejo had been raised as a literate, cultured man from a noble class, and his recollections of the quest were seen as fitting to be included in the Archivo General de Indias, and have since been the primary source of information about the Nuevo México trip.

The makeup of the Espejo-Beltrán group paralleled that of the Chamuscado-Rodríquez party which had left Santa Bárbara a year and a half earlier—a priest and a gunslinger balanced in symbiosis. Both men needed, but neither wanted, the other.

They were accompanied by more than a dozen armed conquistadors, including Miguel Sánchez Valenciano, who brought his wife, Casilda de Amaya. Rounding out the contingent were a number of servants and interpreters, many of whom could be described as slaves, as well as 115 head of horses and mules, some sheep for food, and an expedition permit signed by Juan de Ibarra, the governor of Nueva Vizcaya, who made no secret of the fact that he cared more about cities of gold than rescuing Franciscans.

As for Espejo, he was not so much one to follow the fleeting rumors of cities of gold, as he was in determining the source of the gold. All around him back in Nueva Vizcaya, he was very aware of the great fortunes that had been made, not out of the discovery of silver-plated cities, but out of the ground, from which silver could be extracted. He theorized that behind every folklore of golden anything, there were gold *mines*.

The party departed San Bartolomé on November 10, 1582, despite the fact that such a late start guaranteed traveling through deeper and deeper snow as they went north. Nevertheless, they managed to get through, generally following the route of the previous year's venture, down the Río Conchos and up the Rio Grande.

Of the people whom they encountered along the way, Espejo writes that "all of them fondled us and our horses, touching us and the horses with their hands, and with great friendliness giving us some of their food. . . . We gave some things to the caciques [leaders], and through interpreters gave them to understand that we had not come to capture them or to injure them in any manner. Thereupon they were reassured, and we erected crosses for them in their rancherias and explained to them something about God our Lord. They appeared pleased."

Along the lower Rio Grande, they met another group, who Espejo calls "Jumanos," but whose exact identity has not been confirmed with certainty by modern ethnographers. He writes that their "nation appeared to be very numerous, and had large permanent Pueblos. In it we saw five Pueblos with more than 10,000 Indians, and flat-roofed houses, low and well arranged into Pueblos."

In his *relación*, he makes no mention of gold mines—yet.

The people did tell him that long before, "three Christians and a negro had passed through." Espejo took this to mean Cabeza de Vaca and company, although it may have been a remnant of Coronado's army. The recollection does illustrate that the institutional memory among the people of New Mexico was a long one.

By late December, Espejo and Beltrán had reached the snow-covered Tiwa pueblos near the Rio Grande around present-day Albuquerque. Though the institutional memory did recall the bloody war with Coronado in the winter of 1541–1542, the people apparently greeted the outsiders cordially.

The Spaniards were on hand to witness the sacred rituals involving the elaborately masked and costumed kachina dancers, but they thought that their hosts were trying to entertain them. Espejo mentions the people "coming out in fine array [performing] many juggling feats, some of them very clever, with live snakes." The latter is a reference to the annual Snake Dance ritual which is common to many Southwest ceremonial calendars even to this day.

During January and February, the Spaniards visited the pueblos, both Keres and Tiwa, throughout the region. Espejo mentions the Keres, calling them "Quires," and writes that their "province has five Pueblos, containing a great number of people, it appearing to us that there were 15,000 souls." Today, including Acoma, there are still five Keres-speaking pueblos.

Impressed with the Zia pueblo, which is still-extant, he effuses that it had "eight plazas, and better houses than those previously mentioned, most of them being whitewashed and painted with colors and pictures."

Espejo goes on to say that the Keres people "received us very well, and gave us some cotton mantas, many turkeys, maize, and portions of all else which they had." However, at Acoma, they got into a brief altercation with the locals, who sheltered a couple of slave girls who had escaped from Espejo.

Inquiring after the two Franciscans, Padres Francisco López and Augustin Rodríquez, they finally learned that they were dead. They had been killed at the Tiwa pueblo of Puaray, which Espejo calls Puala, along with four Indians, possibly local converts, three of them just boys. Remembering Coronado and fearing that the Spaniards meant to massacre them, the people of Puaray abandoned their pueblo and ran to the hills.

To Beltrán, it was a case closed, and mission accomplished. They had come to find out what happened to López and Rodríquez. They had, and now it was time to go home. Espejo naturally disagreed. He had come for gold mines, which he had not yet found.

In his later recollections, he phrased it more diplomatically, writing that "it seemed to me that all that country was well peopled, and that the farther we penetrated into the region the larger the settlements we found, and as they received us peacefully, I deemed this a good opportunity for me to serve his Majesty by visiting and discovering those lands so new and so remote, in order to give a report of them to his Majesty, with no expense to him in their discovery."

Not only Padre Beltrán, but a number of the conquistadors, including Miguel Sánchez Valenciano and his wife, were ready to bail out of the *entrada* and return to Nueva Vizcaya because, as Espejo complained, "they had learned that Francisco Vásquez Coronado had found neither gold nor silver and had returned, and that they desired to do likewise."

Though they had parted company, Beltrán's contingent remained in the area for some time, and actually crossed paths with Espejo and his men during the summer.

With the first order of business about the missing Franciscans having been concluded, Espejo could now turn his attention to his real reason for coming to Nueva México, although with fewer soldiers, so he had to be careful where he stepped. He writes that "The mountains thereabout apparently give promise of mines and other riches, but we did not go to see them as the people from there were many and warlike. The mountain people come to aid those of the settlements, who call the mountain people Querechos [Apache]. They carry on trade with those of the settlements."

With his horses and arqubuses, Espejo could intimidate Pueblo people living in fixed settlements, but he knew better than to tangle with the Apache in the mountains with his nine remaining soldiers.

Knowing this, he turned away from a general search through the mountains and headed out to learn what he could from the cities he knew existed. They might not be the cities of gold that Coronado had imagined, but they could be cities populated by people who could tell him where to look for gold mines.

South and west of Acoma, they rode through a vast wasteland of black lava they called "El Malpaís," or "the badlands." The razor-sharp volcanic rock could easily damage the feet of horses and men alike. Especially when covered with a few inches of snow, the potential danger can go unnoticed until it is too late. For Espejo, as for Coronado, avoiding El Malpaís would have involved a detour, rather than a straight route to the Zuni pueblos.

The people here at the place which the Spaniards still called the Seven Cities of Cibola received them nervously, admitting that they still remembered Coronado, and not fondly.

In an obvious effort to keep the foreigners moving along, they eagerly nudged the Spaniards toward the Three Mesas of the Hopi, telling them that the real gold was not here, but just over the horizon.

Antonio de Espejo.
(*Bill Yenne*)

They told him that "Francisco Vásquez Coronado and his captains had been there, and that Don Pedro de Tovar had gone in from there having heard of a large lake where these natives said there were many settlements [the Three Mesas]. They told us that there was gold in that country, and that the people were clothed and wore bracelets and earrings of gold; that these people were six days' march from [the Zuni pueblos]."

Departing "Cibola" in mid-April, Espejo and his nine companions rode on to the land of the Three Mesas. In his account, he calls the place "Mohoce," a precursor to the term "Mohoqui," coined a generation later by Juan de Oñate, which evolved into "Moqui," which was still widely used for the Hopi well into the twentieth century.

"Before reaching Mohoce they sent us messengers to warn us not to go there, lest they should kill us," Espejo writes. "A league before we reached the province over 2,000 Indians, loaded down with provisions, came forth to meet us. We gave them some presents of little value, which we carried, thereby assuring them that we would not harm them, but told them that the horses which we had with us might kill them because they were very bad."

Apparently, this turned the tide, for Espejo was welcomed among the Hopi, who even constructed a corral for the Spanish horses. Of particular note is his very substantial population estimate of 50,000, which compares to around 5,000 Hopi living on the Three Mesas in 1900 and 7,000 (roughly 60 percent of all tribal members) today.

Espejo goes on to say that "a great multitude of Indians came out to receive us, accompanied by the chiefs of [the now abandoned] Awatobi pueblo. . . . A chief and some other Indians told us here that they had heard of the lake where the gold treasure is and declared that it was neither greater nor less than what those of the preceding provinces had said."

Again, one is inclined to observe that this was yet another case of people telling Espejo only what he wanted to hear in order to have the Spaniards move along as soon as possible. However, this time, the Indians were not kidding.

With several guides whom the Hopi sent with him, Espejo and four of his men rode west for 45 leagues and found a gold mine.

There have been many guesses through the years as to the location of this mine, most of them in northwestern Arizona. However, using the value of the Spanish legua in use at the time, one would have placed Espejo in the Black Mountains of what is now Mohave County, Arizona, in the place where old U.S. Route 66 crosses the steep and hair-raising Sitgreaves Pass. This author has been in the Black Mountains and has seen several operating, or recently operating, gold mines.

Others have calculated that Espejo was south and east of the Black Mountains in an area west of Prescott, either along the Bill Williams Fork of the Colorado (also called the Bill Williams River) or in the Verde Valley near Clarksdale. There is a history of mining activity in these regions as well.

On or about May 8, 1583, wherever exactly Espejo was, he was able to write excitedly, "I found them, and with my own hands I extracted ore from them, said by those who know to be very rich. . . . The [region] where these mines are is for the most part mountainous. . . . The Indians of that region plant fields of maize, and have good houses. They told us by signs that behind those mountains, at a distance we were unable to understand clearly, flowed a very large river." The Black Mountains are within 20 miles of the Colorado River.

Espejo apparently did not continue west as far as the Colorado, but returned in the direction of the Three Mesas.

Exploring the country as he went, he reports finding more deposits of shiny metals, especially silver, encouraging him to believe that he was discovering the source of the legendary treasure of the American Southwest. If he had joined Coronado on the long roster of those who had failed to find the Seven Cities of Cibola, he had at least found what could be construed as the source of their riches.

Having crossed the Rio Grande, the expedition continued eastward through the Gallisteo basin south of present-day Santa Fe, toward the river which they named Río de las Vacas (River of the Cows) because they were now starting to see large herds of buffalo. This was probably the Pecos River, which Coronado's expedition had bridged in the spring of 1541. Because it was now late summer, the water was low and Espejo was able to cross the river more easily than Coronado.

He writes that they visited a pueblo on the river which he called Ciquique. This was probably the now long-abandoned Pecos pueblo, which his predecessors had called Cicuye. Espejo then followed the Pecos River as far as the site of the present town of Pecos, Texas, before turning south to the intersection of the Rio Grande and Río Concho. From here, his men retraced their route back to Nueva Vizcaya, where they arrived on September 20.

Espejo had brought back several Indians, including a Hopi girl and a boy from Cicuye. They had either volunteered out of curiosity, or were kidnapped as souvenirs. The boy wound up in Mexico City in the care of the Franciscan historian Pedro de Oroz, who learned a great deal about native culture from him.

Once back in Santa Bárbara, Antonio de Espejo sat down to write his *relación*. Finished in less than a month, it is written in the form of a glowing report to Philip II, the son of the late Emperor Charles V, and now the king of Spain, Portugal, Naples, and Sicily.

"Everything narrated herein I saw with my own eyes, and is true, for I was present at everything," Espejo insisted. "Sometimes I set out from the camp with a number of companions, sometimes with but one, to observe the nature of that country, in order to report everything to his Majesty, that he may order what is best for the exploration and pacification of those provinces. . . . There are very good pastures for cattle, lands suitable for fields and gardens, with or without irrigation, and many rich mines, from which I brought ores to assay."

What Antonio de Espejo was leading up to was that he wanted Philip to name him to establish a permanent Spanish colony—with him in charge. He outlined a plan by which the Nueva México province should answer directly to Philip, rather than being beneath the viceroy of New Spain in the colonial chain of command.

Using the phrase "your servant kisses the hands of your most Illustrious Lordship," Espejo literally begged for the king to name him to run a colony in Nueva México.

He implores the king that if he were

> to favor me by entrusting to me the exploration and settlement of these lands and of the others which I may discover, for I shall not be satisfied until I reach the coasts of the North and South seas. Although they have attached part of my estate, I shall not lack the necessary means to accomplish the journey with a sufficient number of men, provisions, arms and ammunition, should his Majesty grant me the favor, as one has a right to expect from his most Christian and generous hand. I would not dare to write to your Lordship if this undertaking were not of such importance to God and his Majesty, in whose name your Lordship acts. May our Lord guard and preserve the illustrious person and state of your Lordship many years, as we all, your humble servants.

It was not to happen.

The man who looked for mines instead of cities and found them, died in Cuba two years later on his way to Madrid to make his case to the king personally.

When Espejo had returned from the *terra incognita* of Nueva México in the autumn of 1583, it had not taken long for the stories to circulate among the coffeehouse conquistadors of Mexico City and the barflies of the Nueva Vizcaya cantinas that he had touched the treasure with his own hands, and he had returned with samples.

The excitement thus fueled a flurry of talk about treasure hunts. The ink was hardly dry on Espejo's *relación* when one Cristobal Martín proudly declared that he would lead a force of two to three hundred men to colonize Nueva México 4,000 miles beyond the pueblos, and establish ocean ports on the Atlantic and Pacific to supply such a dominion. As history is our witness, this geographically impossible scheme never came to fruition.

In 1589, four years after Espejo died en route to Spain to beg Philip for an appointment as ruler of Nueva México, a wealthy Nueva Galician named Juan Bautista de Lomas cut a deal with Alvaro Manrique de Zúñiga, the new viceroy of New Spain for an incursion into Nueva México.

When the king did not sign off on this arrangement, Francisco de Urdiñola stepped in. He was one of the wealthiest silver barons in Nueva Galicia, who also added to his fortune with woolen mills and wine warehouses. However, this transaction fell through when Urdiñola was arrested for murdering his wife, who was having an affair with a servant. Lomas resubmitted his own petition to pacify Nueva México in 1592, and again in 1595, but it was never granted.

It now seemed to be harder than ever to cut through the red tape within the viceroy's growing Mexico City bureaucracy to get the necessary permits.

Finally, someone did go north with a large *entrada*. Gaspar Castaño de Sosa, the lieutenant governor of Nuevo León and a mine owner in his own right, set out in 1590, leading a contingent of 170 men. They followed Espejo's return route, ascending the Pecos River as far as the pueblo which Espejo had named Ciquique, capturing it by force. From there, he marched westward to the Kewa pueblo on the Rio Grande, naming it Santo Domingo, the name by which it would be known through the end of the twentieth century. Indeed, Sosa assigned the Spanish names to many of the pueblos by which they would be known for five hundred years. In his book, *Documentary History of the Rio Grande Pueblos of New Mexico*, Adolph Bandelier is charitable to Sosa, calling his later *relación* of his *entrada* "explicit and sober." To this, one can add the adjective "incomplete," as the narrative ends abruptly at Kewa without any mention of that lifeblood of treasure hunters, substantial findings of gold.

Given the complexities of applying for permits to explore the northern lands, it is probably safe to say that there were far more undocumented and unauthorized expeditions than there were ones for which we have any information. Among the latter was an effort by Francisco Leyva Bonilla (also called Leyba) and Antonio Gutiérrez de Humana (also called Umana). In 1594, they set out not merely to visit Nueva México, but to follow the trail of Francisco Vásquez de Coronado all the way to the mythic Quivira.

The Leyva-Humana *entrada* is an example of how fragile the records of early exploration are. All we know is what was gleaned from the expedition's sole survivor, an illiterate Indian porter from Culiacán named Jusepe Gutiérrez, who was probably a man whom Leyva and Humana knew by sight but never really got to know.

According to Gutiérrez's recollections when he was finally debriefed early in 1599, the expedition reached the area of the Rio Grande pueblos by way of the Pecos River, following the same route as Sosa. They spent about a year in the area around the Tewa pueblo of P'ohwhóde (named San Ildefonso by the Spanish, and still known by that name), roughly in the area between the present cities of Santa Fe and Los Alamos, before starting off across the Plains.

Gutiérrez spoke at length about the buffalo, and the immense sizes of the herds. His descriptions of a large settlement with thatched houses on a great river coincide with the Coronado and Castañeda descriptions of Quivira—and what was almost certainly the vast settlement of the Wichita along the Arkansas River in central Kansas.

Gutiérrez goes on to describe their continuing onward for ten days to an even larger river, which has been interpreted as their having observed the Missouri River in the vicinity of Kansas City. If so, they would have been the first Europeans, and probably the first Mexican Indians, to see the river, at least upstream from its mouth at St. Louis.

Somewhere between the Arkansas and the Missouri, Leyva and Humana got into an argument, and Gutiérrez witnessed Humana hacking his partner to death with a butcher knife.

After having seen the Missouri, five of the Indians, including Gutiérrez, deserted the expedition and tried to reach New Spain. Only Gutiérrez made it, but he was captured and held by the Apache for about a year in the process.

Nobody south of the Rio Grande ever saw Humana again.

18

JUST ACROSS
THE HORIZON

The great wealth which the mines have begun to
reveal and the great number of them in this land,
whence proceed the royal fifths [taxes levied by the
crown on minerals] and profits. Second, the certainty
of the proximity of the South Sea, whose trade with
Peru, New Spain, and China is not to be depreciated,
for it will give birth in time to advantageous and continuous duties.

—Don Juan de Oñate, letter to Alvaro Manrique de
Zúñiga, viceroy of New Spain (March 2, 1599)

AT THE TURN OF THE NEW, seventeenth century, the illiterate wanderer and massacre survivor Jusepe Gutiérrez met a
man named Don Juan de Oñate y Salazar.

In his 1991 biography of Oñate, Marc Simmons uses the
title "The Last Conquistador," a description which certainly
summarizes the life of the man, and the times when he was
active in the arena of heavy-handed Spanish exploration and
exploitation of what would become the American Southwest.

The rise of Oñate uniquely coincided with the transition
from the era of exploration to the era of colonialism. When
King Philip II of Spain made Nueva México an officially designated province of New Spain, he made Oñate its governor.

When he had begun his career, Nueva México was a mysterious and dangerous *terra incognita* which often swallowed explorers without a trace. The route into this wilderness was followed at one's peril. During Oñate's career, this route became a Spanish highway, and the permanent Spanish presence in what is now the Southwest became a reality.

Juan de Oñate was part of a new generation, a conquistador born not in Madrid or Seville, but in Zacatecas, Mexico. He was a citizen of New Spain, who had never *seen* the "Old" Spain. He was born in the New World in 1550, a decade after Coronado went north. His father was Cristóbal de Oñate, himself an example of the evolving Spanish presence in the New World. He had come from Spain as a soldier of fortune, but stayed on to become a man of wealth and position, and one of New Spain's first great silver barons.

Juan de Oñate's wife, meanwhile, was herself a child of sixteenth-century Spanish history in the New World. Also born in New Spain, she was the daughter of another silver baron. Senora Oñate, born Isabel de Tolosa Cortés de Moctezuma, was the granddaughter of Hernán Cortés and the great-granddaughter of his rival, the Aztec emperor Moctezuma.

Oñate's era also coincided with a conceptual transition in how the Spanish viewed the New World and their official perspective of their role in it. King Philip II had promulgated a kinder, gentler approach to Spanish dominions. Anyone who feels that "political correctness" is a phenomenon of our own age, will be fascinated to discover that the king ordered those who wrote official *relacións*, diaries and journal entries about their *entradas* to no longer use the term *conquista* (conquest), but rather the gentler word *pacificación* (pacification). In 1595, he also decided that Nueva México was ready to be pacified and colonized. His chosen instrument to make this happen was Juan de Oñate.

As is still often the case, when the political correctness of the king's directive reached the frontiers of New Spain, it was just as thin as the paper on which his calligraphers had inscribed it. Whether it was *conquista* or *pacificación*, conquistadors like Oñate saw all official paperwork merely as a pretext for plunder. The documents may change over time, but the motives did not. In the early 1580s, *entradas* used the fiction of a Franciscan front man, and since Espejo, they were veiled with proposals to create a permanent Spanish colonial presence in the north. Oñate was no less interested in cities of gold than Coronado had been.

Indeed, as his actions over the coming years proved, he was *very* interested in cities of gold—both in rediscovering the mines of Antonio de Espejo in western Arizona, and in seeing for himself the elusive city of gold which lay beyond the Quivira of Francisco Vásquez de Coronado.

It took Oñate nearly three years to organize his venture, which was not just an expedition, but the transplanting of Spanish civilization. Whereas earlier *entradas* had consisted mainly of armed men, hardy friars, and their servants and slaves, Oñate headed north early in 1598 leading a train of eighty-three wagons and oxcarts. Of the 400 men, 130 brought their families.

Oñate was also accompanied by a number of priests, who added the air of legitimacy to the project through their plans to establish permanent missions in Nueva México, and by his nephews, Juan and Vicente de Zaldívar. Juan was Oñate's *maestro de campo*, or chief of staff, while Vicente, whose rank was that of a *sargento mayor* (sergeant major), had earlier played an important role in organizing the expedition.

On April 30, they began crossing the Rio Grande near the site of present-day Ciudad Juárez. The place where they forded the river became known as El Paso (the Pass). This name was later adopted for a city founded on the north side—El Paso, Texas.

Oñate formally claimed all of the land to the north of El Paso for Spain. Back in 1583, the audacious Cristobal Martín had the notion to claim everything from the Rio Grande to the Atlantic and Pacific without ever venturing much farther than his own hacienda. Oñate had now done much the same, but he had brought the colonists to make it stick.

The Spaniards called the Rio Grande, especially that part of it which flows west to east between El Paso and the Gulf of Mexico, the Río del Norte (River of the North). Part of the reason for this was that it was a tangible dividing line between colonized New Spain and the mysterious lands stretching into the unknown from its northern shore.

By mid-July, Oñate had traveled over 250 miles due north in present northern New Mexico, and had set up a temporary camp at the Tewa pueblo of Ohkay Owingeh. As soon as the friars dedicated a mission church to St. John the Baptist in September 1598, Ohkay Owingeh became the San Juan pueblo, a name by which it would be known until the original name was finally restored in 2005.

Oñate officially named his province Santa Fé de Nuevo México (Holy Faith of New Mexico). The Spanish provincial capital city, would later be located about 25 miles south of the church of San Juan. Named Santa Fe (originally named La Villa Real de la Santa Fé de San Francisco de Asís, the Royal Town of the Holy Faith of Saint Francis of Assisi), it was founded several years later, in the winter of 1607–1608, but it did not become the capital until 1610, two years after Oñate's departure.

In a subsequent letter to Viceroy Acevedo in Mexico City, dated March 2, 1599, and one of several preserved in the Archivo de Indias (Archive of the Indies) in Seville, Oñate wrote in minute detail of his province. He estimated the combined population of the Keres, Tewa, and Tiwa pueblos at 70,000, more than Cortés had estimated for the population of Tenochtitlan (Mexico City) when he first saw it. This compares to 15,000 estimated by Espejo for the five Keres pueblos alone. The current United States Census reckoning of the combined pueblo population is virtually the same as that of Oñate.

Of these extremely compact cities, Oñate writes of "house adjoining house, with square plazas. They have no streets, and in the pueblos, which contain many plazas or wards, one goes from one plaza to the other through alleys. They are of two and three stories, of an *estado* [the height of a man] and a half or an *estado* and a third, which latter is not so common; and some houses are four, five, six, and seven stories."

He vividly describes people wearing "very good clothes [made of] colored cotton . . . most excellent wool [and] buffalo hides, of which there is a great abundance." Acting almost like a travel promoter, he adds that "it is a land abounding in flesh of buffalo, goats with hideous horns, and turkeys . . . bees and very white honey, of which I am sending a sample. . . . There are vegetables, a great abundance of the best and greatest *salines* [salt deposits] in the world, very fine grape vines, rivers, forests of many oaks, and some cork trees, fruits, melons, grapes, watermelons, Castilian plums, pine-nuts, acorns, ground-nuts . . . and other wild fruits. There are many and very good fish in this Río del Norte, and in others."

With the province formally established, and the missionaries busy installing their missions, Oñate was able to turn his attention to his real interest in being in Nueva México, to follow the route of Antonio de Espejo in 1582, all the way to the gold mines of Arizona.

Oñate had even entertained thoughts of riding as far as the "South Sea," that is, the Gulf of California at the mouth of the Colorado River, which the Spaniards still had yet to understand was not the Pacific Ocean. Since the first *entrada* of Coronado, the Spaniards longed in vain for an ocean-going port on the Gulf of California that could be used to support expeditions into the Southwest.

As Oñate prepared to head west, he dispatched his trusted nephew, Vicente de Zaldívar, to go east of the Pecos with sixty men. Oñate was certainly interested in Quivira, but it is unclear whether he planned to send Zaldívar all the way to Quivira on a preliminary reconnaissance. Though it seems more likely that he just sent him to the Plains on a buffalo hunt, one member of Zaldívar's team suggested that there was more to it than that: Jusepe Gutiérrez, the erstwhile porter on the ill-fated Leyva-Humana *entrada*.

By now, Oñate had gotten his hands on Gutiérrez, who was the only man alive from New Spain who had actually been to Quivira. In an expedition to that mystical place, Gutiérrez would be useful, both because he sort of knew the way, and because he had learned to speak Apache during his year in captivity.

In any case, even though Gutiérrez was along, a buffalo hunt was all that was accomplished in 1598. The venture is best remembered mainly for having involved the first European attempt to capture and domesticate the buffalo. The Spaniards went as far as building a corral for this purpose, but the dangerous and ill-considered experiment failed.

In a report to Oñate preserved in the Archivo de Indias, Zaldívar recalls that:

> The cattle started very nicely towards the corral, but soon they turned back in a stampede towards the men, and, rushing through them in a mass, it was impossible to stop them, because they are cattle terribly obstinate, courageous beyond exaggeration, and so cunning that if pursued they run, and that if their pursuers stop or slacken their speed they stop and roll, just like mules, and with this respite renew their run. For several days [Zaldívar and his men] tried a thousand ways of shutting them in or of surrounding them, but in no manner was it possible to do so. This was not due to fear, for they are remarkably savage and ferocious, so much so that they killed three of our horses and badly wounded forty, for their horns are very sharp and fairly long."

Zaldívar returned with plenty of hides and dried meat, but no live buffalo.

While this was going on, Oñate was retracing Espejo's steps. On the Feast Day of All Saints, November 1, 1598, he arrived at the Zuni pueblos, or that which popular folklore now understood to be the Seven Cities of Cibola, which were not so golden after all.

In a report dictated on January 16, 1599, and now in the Archivo de Indias, he described the place as the "Province of Zuni," noting correctly that it consisted of six pueblos, of which the "last" was the one called "Cibola." This would have been the pueblo which Coronado, and Marcos de Niza before him, had encountered first, as they were approaching from the south. It would have been the same one which Coronado had called Háwikuh.

As Oñate wrote, "they received us very well with maize, tortillas, gourds, beans, and quantities of rabbits and hares, of which there are a great many. They are a very amiable people and all rendered obedience to his Majesty."

As always, the natives were telling the Spaniards what they wanted to hear, always in an effort to keep them moving on toward the horizon.

And move on they did. On November 8, as the snow began to fall, they headed out to the Hopi Three Mesas, which Espejo had called "Mohoce," and which Oñate calls "Mohoqui," or "Mohoje."

Visiting the Three Mesas, the Spaniards were well received at each. In his later report, Oñate described the fascinating Hopi kachina dolls, writing that "their religion consists in worshipping idols, of which they have many; and in their temples, after their own manner, they worship them with fire, painted reeds, feathers, and universal offering of almost everything they get, such as small animals, birds, vegetables, etc."

Of course, Oñate's reason for being here was not to marvel at crafts or study religious rituals, but to follow Espejo's trail, and confirm the stories of ore deposits. When, sitting around a Hopi campfire, he began to hear tales of glittering metal off in the direction of the sunset—from the same people who told the same stories to Espejo—it got his attention and warmed his conquistador's heart.

On November 17, as Oñate returned to Cibola, he sent Captain Marcos Farfán de los Gados, his "captain of the guard and of the horses," to follow the directions provided by the Hopi, and to find the mines of Antonio de Espejo. Taking eight Spaniards and some Indian guides, he traveled westward across Arizona.

In his research in the early twentieth century, Herbert Bolton followed Farfán's route by correlating actual Arizona places, such as the San Francisco Peaks north of Flagstaff and Bill Williams Mountain near Williams, with various landmarks mentioned in Farfán's reports to Oñate. When Farfán's own account mentions a "mountain range, which was covered with snow," it is easy to picture the San Francisco Peaks.

Somewhere near the present location of Flagstaff, the Spaniards encountered the "rancheria" of some local people who approached them with drawn bows. Between sign language and the intervention of his Indian guides, Farfán was able to reassure them that he meant no harm. Bolton believes that this place was the Rancheria de los Gandules, near the present town of Moenkopi, Arizona. The people who Farfán met were probably the Yavapai, who lived throughout what is now northwestern Arizona. In contrast to all the pueblo-dwelling people, who practiced agriculture on a substantial scale, the Yavapai were primarily hunter-gatherers.

The Spanish camped away from the Yavapai village, but the following day, Farfán went back to the rancheria, finding it deserted except for "two chiefs and a woman." In his report to Oñate, he explains that "as a token of peace [the Indians] gave [the Spaniards] pulverized ore and a great quantity of ground dates, which is their food, and a few pieces of veni-

Juan de Oñate.
(*Bill Yenne*)

son." When Farfán "begged them to go with him to show him where they got that ore . . . one of the Indian chiefs complied willingly."

Traveling through deep snow, they passed several other rancherias, at which Farfán tells of receiving "powdered ores of different colors" in exchange for trade beads. Bolton calculates that the route took them past Bill Williams Mountain, which is about 100 miles southwest of Moenkopi. From here, they continued south to the northwestern branch of the Verde River. Farfán reports that at each in this succession of rancheria, people promised to take them to the mine. When instead, they merely took him to yet another village where the promise was repeated, he was probably growing impatient and a bit nervous.

Finally, they reached a stream Bolton interprets as "Big Sandy or the Spenser River. . . . on the eastern slope of the Aquarius Mountains." Here, Farfán found himself staring into a mine shaft, in which "there were many and apparently very good ores. . . . The vein is very wide and rich and of many outcrops, all containing ores. The vein ran along the hill in plain view and crossed over to another hill which was opposite. . . . At one side of the said hill they found another vein of more than two arms' length in width . . . and on the other side, on the hill of the outcrop, they found another vein."

He visited a number of similar mines, noting their locations and naming them after saints. The richest of the deposits was named San Andreas.

Farfán reported finding silver mines 30 leagues west of the Three Mesas, which would agree with the notion that some of the sixteenth-century Spanish mineral finds were in the area west of Prescott, Arizona, in the valleys of the Verde River and the Bill Williams Fork of the Colorado.

In calculating distances using sixteenth-century data, there is some confusion as to what Oñate meant when he gave distances in leagues. Prior to 1568 and a decree on the subject by King Philip II, a Spanish "legua" or league was equal to about 2.6 statute miles. Thereafter, it was the equivalent of 4.2 miles, although it is possible that some people continued using the earlier measurement. When Oñate describes the distance between the Three Mesas and the Zuni pueblos as 20 legua, which is about 80 miles as the crow flies, it is clear that he is using the latter.

To make things even more interesting, Farfán notes that some of the people whom he met near the mines were wearing oyster shells as jewelry. When he asked them where they had gotten these, they indicated a body of salt water that was about thirty days' journey to the south. This would correspond with the Gulf of California, or the "South Sea." The people said that when they had opened these shells, they "found some white and round objects as large as grains of maize."

Not only had Farfán found gold and silver, he had been directed to a place where he could find pearls! The place, as always, was beyond the horizon.

When Farfán reconnected with Oñate at Cibola after three weeks of exploring, he found his leader beginning to doubt whether the stories of Espejo were true. Then Farfán showed up and handed him ore samples, tangible proof of a mission accomplished, as well as tales of much more where that had come from. Oñate was overjoyed.

Oñate recalls that Farfán "brought flattering reports of the good mines . . . and they brought very good ores from which silver was later extracted by many and divers very rich assays, by means of mercury. This infused new life into over a hundred lifeless residents of this camp. They are ores which can be smelted."

Farfán told Oñate that in the past he had been to some of the richest mines in Nueva Vizcaya and Nueva Galicia, and that "these mountains [in western Arizona] were without doubt the richest in all New Spain." Farfán went on to paint a picture of a utopia, adding that "near to the very mines themselves are enormous pines, oaks, mesquites, walnuts, and cottonwoods . . . much game, as deer, hares, and partridges . . . and great pastures and plains and fine lands for cultivation. The maize which the Indians gather gives most excellent evidence of the bounty of the land." Along with the ore, he handed Oñate an ear of dried corn that was as thick as his wrist.

The corn was nice, and the ore fantastic, but when Oñate heard of the pearls, his imagination practically exploded. In a memo to Viceroy Acevedo, Oñate relates excitedly that "I have numberless reports [of] pearls of remarkable size from the [South] sea, and assurance that there is an infinite number of them on the coast of this country."

Before he could indulge fantasies of pearl diving in the warm waters of the South Sea, Oñate had a serious issue to sort out. His happy rendezvous with Farfán was soon eclipsed by bad news. While he was en route back to San Juan to spend the winter, he heard of an event which would cast a dark shadow across the historic memory of Juan de Oñate.

While Vicente de Zaldívar was on his buffalo hunt with Gutiérrez east of the Pecos, his brother, Juan de Zaldívar, had been traveling from San Juan toward Cibola to meet up with Oñate. He made it as far as Acoma when he ran into trouble with the people there. There was apparently a demand made by the Spaniards for provisions which the people needed to get themselves through the winter. The bickering had turned violent and Juan de Zaldívar was killed, along with about a dozen of his men. Oñate later observed tersely that "my maestro de campo was not as cautious as he should have been."

When Juan's brother returned to San Juan with the fruits of the buffalo hunt and heard about what had happened, he needed no additional urging when Oñate sent him to Acoma.

Vicente de Zaldívar went to Acoma with revenge on his mind. According to an entry in his diary, as quoted by

Herbert Bolton, he brutally attacked, and in two days, "most of them were killed and punished by fire and bloodshed, and the pueblo was completely laid waste and burned." By some accounts as many as eight hundred were killed, and the left foot of each man over the age of twenty-five was cut off. Taking credit for these actions himself, Oñate told the viceroy in a memo that "as punishment for [Acoma's] crime and its treason against his Majesty, to whom it had already rendered submission by a public instrument, and as a warning to the rest, I razed and burned it completely." The Spaniards now probably considered Acoma to have been "pacified."

Even as the flames were withering into embers, Oñate returned to San Juan to reflect and report on the progress of his province since his arrival in the summer of 1598. As he composed his March 2, 1599, report to the viceroy on the status of Nueva México, he knew that it would be shared with Spain's new monarch. Philip II had died in September 1598 while Oñate was exploring, and the new king's subjects naturally wished to ingratiate themselves to him. Oñate wrote that Philip III had every reason to be pleased. He tells the viceroy to tell the new king that: "His royal Majesty [had] acquired a possession [of a province] so good that none other of his Majesty in these Indies excels it, judging it solely by what I have seen, by things told of in reliable reports, and by things almost a matter of experience, from having been seen by people in my camp and known by me at present. This does not include the vastness of the settlements or the riches of the West which the natives praise, or the certainty of pearls promised by the South Sea from the many shells containing them possessed by these Indians, or the many settlements called the seven caves."

The latter is a reference to the old stories of "las Siete Cuevas" which had long circulated, and which were woven into the "Seven Cities" lore before Coronado set out in search of Cibola in 1540. This mention indicates that despite Coronado's disappointment with the Zuni pueblos—and the subsequent Spanish acceptance of their being ordinary pueblos—the Seven Cities in their "Seven Caves" incarnation were still alive in the treasure lore in the last year of the sixteenth century. Perhaps Oñate also wanted to justify to both viceroy and king his obsessive urge to explore.

Indeed, the idea of treasure caves and mysterious lands across the horizon was just as alive in the imagination of Juan de Oñate as were the tangible mines of Arizona. As he concentrated on managing his province, he took time to dream about that ultimate of lands across the horizon—Quivira.

19

Return
to Quivira

I should never cease were I to recount individually all
of the many things which occur to me. I can only say
that with God's help I shall see them all, and give new
worlds, new, peaceful, and grand, to his Majesty,
greater than the good Marquis [Hernándo Cortés,
Marquis of the Valley of Oaxaca] gave to him,
although he did so much, if you, Illustrious Sir, will
give to me the aid, the protection, and the help which
I expect from such a hand.

—Don Juan de Oñate, letter to Alvaro Manrique de
Zúñiga, viceroy of New Spain (March 2, 1599)

SEVEN YEARS AFTER he had traveled across the Pecos onto
the Great Plains with Francisco Leyva Bonilla and Antonio
Gutiérrez de Humana, Jusepe Gutiérrez was going back.

In 1594, he had been a lowly servant, probably even a
slave, whom the great captains on their proud horses hardly
noticed. In 1601, he was a minor celebrity. Ever since he had
met Don Juan de Oñate, he had been courted by the governor of Nueva México, for he was a unique man. He had been
to Quivira, and there was nobody else whom the governor
had met who could boast of such valuable experience. The
two had known one another for years before this experience

would be brought into play, but Oñate was now finally ready. He was ready to follow the footsteps of Coronado to these distant lands, and the promise of the cities of gold, which lay across the horizon from the mundane grass huts along the Arkansas River.

On June 23, 1601, Juan de Oñate rode out of the town of San Gabriel, which was then the Spanish administrative center, and located near the mission church at the pueblo of Ohkay Owingeh, which had been renamed San Juan. According to his own *relación* of the *entrada*, he brought with him "more than 70 picked men for the expedition, all very well equipped, more than 700 horses and mules, six mule carts, and two carts drawn by oxen conveying four pieces of artillery, and with servants to carry the necessary baggage."

A few days out, Oñate reached the headwaters of the Canadian River, becoming the one who gave it the long-standing Spanish name, Magdalena. He may or may not have been aware of the Magdalena River in South America which had, six decades earlier, played such an important role in the geography of the quest by Germans and Spaniards for the elusive El Dorado on the Cundinamarca Plateau.

Following the path of the Leyva-Humana *entrada*, because this was the route which Jusepe Gutiérrez knew, they stayed with the river as it crossed the present-day Texas panhandle north of Amarillo. By now, they were well beyond the place where Gutiérrez had guided Vicente de Zaldívar on his buffalo hunt in 1598. They had seen the herds of buffalo, and had met the Apache, whom Oñate describes as "the ones who possess these plains," without incident.

In his account, Oñate is pleased by their having access to the river for a supply of water and "the luxury of an abundance of fish," adding that "the fruits gave no less pleasure, particularly the plums, of a hundred thousand different kinds, as mellow and good as those which grow in the choicest orchards of our land."

At some point, probably east of the Texas panhandle in present-day Oklahoma, they left the river and started north toward the Big Bend of the Arkansas, picking a trail that their wheeled vehicles could negotiate. This was apparently not their biggest problem. Oñate mentions that "the land was so level that daily the men became lost in it by separating themselves for but a short distance from us."

About 80 miles north of the Magdalena, they crossed the Cimarron River, and began meeting people whom Oñate calls the Escanjaque, but whose true identity has not been agreed upon by modern ethnographers. The essential fact was that these people told the Spaniards through sign language that the people who lived in thatched houses were yet farther ahead. This told Oñate and company that they were on the right track.

Oñate deduced that the Escanjaque were aware of the 1594 expedition and its fate:

> Thinking that we were going to avenge the murder of the Spaniards who had entered with Humana, [they] of course took the opportunity to throw the blame upon their enemies and to tell us that it was they who had lolled them. Thinking that we were going for this purpose only, they were much pleased, and offered to accompany us, and as we were unable to prevent it, lest we should cause them to make trouble, they went. They guided us to a river seven leagues from this place, with wonderful banks, and, although level, so densely wooded that the trees formed thick and wide groves. Here we found a small fruit the size of the wild pear or yellow sapodilla, of very good flavor. The river contained an abundance of very good fish, and although at some points it had good fords, in other parts it was extremely deep and vessels could sail on it with ease. It flowed due east, and its waters were fresh and pleasant to taste. Here the land was fertile and much better than that which we had passed. The pastures were so good that in many places the grass was high enough to conceal a horse.

The following day, the Spaniards encountered three to four hundred warriors from another tribe who were hostile to the Escanjaque, and whom the Escanjaque traveling with them identified as the people who had massacred the 1594 *entrada*. They told Oñate that "in this region they had murdered the Spaniards, surrounding them with fire and burning them all."

Oñate nevertheless successfully endeavored to make peace with them. He refers to them as Rayado, though this term may only have meant that they were people who tattooed their faces. The Rayado people then generously offered the Spaniards corn, the first they had seen since entering the Plains, as well as loaves of cornbread which Oñate recalls as being "as large as shields and three or four fingers thick."

That night, the three factions bedded down warily for an uneasy night's sleep.

At dawn, the situation began to devolve toward a violent confrontation when a Rayado chief named Catarax stepped forward. Counterintuitively, the Spaniards took him prisoner, but despite this, he defused a situation that would have otherwise been a bloodbath. Oñate writes that "it was remarkable to note how they obeyed him and served him, like a people more united, peaceful, and settled. As evidence of this it is enough to say that while they might with justice have become aroused because of his arrest, they did not do so, merely because he signaled to them that they should withdraw."

Taking Catarax with them, the Spaniards forded the Arkansas River and continued on. Within just a few miles, they were at the edge of what was almost certainly the Quivira of Coronado. Oñate writes that:

> We came to a settlement containing more than 1,200 houses, all established along the bank of another good-sized river which flowed into the large one [probably the Arkansas, at last]. They were all round, built of forked poles and bound with rods, and on the outside covered to the ground with dry grass. Within, on the sides, they had frameworks or platforms which served them as beds on which they slept. Most of them were large enough to hold eight or ten persons. They were two lance-lengths high and had granaries or platforms. . . . They entered them through a small grass door. They ascended to this platform by means of a movable wooden ladder. Not a house lacked these platforms. We found the [city] entirely deserted but not lacking maize, of which there was much and of good quality.

The place where multiple large rivers come together could have been any of a number of places. It may have been where Cow Creek joins the Arkansas in the vicinity of present-day Hutchinson, Kansas, about 50 miles east of Big Bend. Meanwhile, there is archaeological evidence of a large-scale settlement east of Wichita, near where the Walnut River enters the Arkansas. Looking at the map and noting that one of the closest towns is El Dorado, Kansas, one might be tempted to say that Oñate made it so far and came so close. Of course, this El Dorado is not *the* El Dorado, and would not come into existence for another 270 years.

The large number of houses indicated that the Spaniards had reached some portion of the sprawling series of riverside villages which constituted the Quivira visited by Coronado and by the Leyva-Humana *entrada*. As noted previously, it is still the supposition of ethnographers and archaeologists that the people who dwelt here were the Wichita.

When Oñate stopped the Escanjaque from burning the abandoned houses, they told him that they feared these house-dwelling people, and "accordingly persuaded us that under no circumstances should we proceed, saying that the people who had withdrawn from this settlement had done so in order on the third day to assemble their friends, who were so numerous that in the course of a whole day they would not be able to pass by their houses, and that undoubtedly, our number being so small, they would soon put an end to us, not a single person escaping."

Oñate admitted that, while this cautionary note only spurred him on, he was in fact concerned that a large number of people were assembling to confront the Spaniards. Leaving the Escanjaque at the site of the first group of houses, the Spaniards pressed on, but only for one day. Thinking long and hard, and staring at the distant horizon, the Last Conquistador called it quits.

In his *relación* of this *entrada*, which he penned back in Nueva México several months later, he rationalized having not achieved his ultimate goal of finding a city of gold. He wrote at length about the fruits of the expedition, the discovery of rich agricultural land, and "learning the wonders of this land," suggesting that the king ought to find this inter-

The name "Quivira" lives today in the name of Gran Quivira, a long-abandoned pre-Columbian pueblo and trading center on a 6,500-foot plateau in central New Mexico. Both Coronado and Oñate passed nearby long before it had this name, but it was not the place which they sought.

esting in light of the potential for future settlement, but he made no mention of his having abandoned the quest for the treasure which he sought more than anything else, and for which he had come so far.

Oñate knew how far he had come, but had no idea of the size of the continent he had tried to cross. He assumed that he was just a short distance from the Atlantic Ocean, writing that "The carts went over the country to the settlements very nicely, and so far as the nature of the land was concerned they could have gone as far as the North Sea [the Atlantic], which could not have been very far, because some of the Indians wore shells from it on their foreheads." In fact, the carts still would have had more than 1,300 miles left to go if Oñate had decided to continue to the Atlantic.

The trip back began on a far more treacherous note than the trip out. When they had gotten back to where the Escanjaque were staying in the Quiviran houses, the Spaniards discovered that their attitude had changed completely. As Oñate writes, "unsuspecting any treason, we found the Indians who at first had pretended to be friends, now converted into cruel enemies, and entrenched within the same houses, ready to carry out their evil intent."

The Spaniards raised their hands in a sign of peace, but were met by a hailstorm of arrows, and the battle was joined. Oñate writes, probably exaggerating, that they were attacked by 1,500 Escanjaque. The Spaniards circled their wagons and began fighting a defensive battle.

In his vivid account of the action, Oñate writes that: "The battle continued and the Indians became more furious than at the beginning, keeping it up for more than two hours with the greatest of courage, although at their own cost, for they proved the valor of the Spanish nation. At the end of this time, the greater part of our men being wounded, though not dangerously in any case, the *adelantado* and governor [Oñate himself], seeing the great barbarity of our enemies, and that many of them were dead, and that they were not to be frightened and would not turn their backs, ordered his men to retreat; and, freeing some women whom the soldiers had captured, he would not consent that they be further injured."

It is not clear from Oñate's report whether the women had been captured during the battle or had been taken by the Spaniards some time earlier. If the latter, this may have been the reason that the Escanjaque turned hostile in the first place, and why they broke off the fight as soon as the women were released.

Juan de Oñate returned to San Gabriel on November 24, 1601, five months and a day after he began his trek, and two months after the fight with the Escanjaque on the Arkansas River. He had traveled more than 1,500 miles. He finished writing up his *relación* on December 14 and dispatched it to Viceroy Alvaro Manrique de Zúñiga in Mexico City. It would end up in the archives in Seville, but it is unknown whether the eyes of King Philip III ever fell upon it.

20

THE LAST CONQUISTADOR

The difficult day of the conquest has just ended in a blaze of gold and blood. Ora y sangre—a funereal apotheosis! Night descends upon the battlefield of the Conquistadors, and silence follows. But at dawn, into the shadows that slowly pale, phantoms slip one by one. Then day is here, and the morning light falls gradually upon these new beings, lighting their res-olute features with its silver gleam. They wear neither helmet nor breastplate, but robes of monkish home-spun or the sober doublets of men of law. They carry no swords, but in their hands is the mason's trowel or the ivory staff of the alcalde or the cavalier's lance. At first there are only a few, but soon a numberless crowd emerges from the shadows. They gather up the dead and bury them. The battlefield has become a cemetery. Then, in serried ranks, elbow to elbow, like the Spartan phalanxes, they move off westward. These are the colonists.

—Jean Descola (Seville, March 1951)

IT HAD BEEN FIVE YEARS since he had written so eagerly about the pearls, and three years since his return from the dis-appointing adventure at the Quivira of Coronado. Juan de Oñate was finally ready to undertake another major expedition. On October 7, 1604, he set out from San Gabriel, bound for the South Sea, the Gulf of California at the mouth of the Colorado River.

He initially followed the same route as he had in 1598, first to the Zuni pueblos, and next to the Hopi Three Mesas. He was traveling light, with only thirty lightly armored soldiers. They were accompanied by Padre Francisco de Escobar, the commissary, or superior, of the missionaries in Nueva México. His practical value to the expedition was that he was a gifted linguist.

He would also be the man who chronicled Oñate's quest for the South Sea, though his diary was not rediscovered in the Archivo de Indias in Seville until around the turn of the twentieth century. For nearly four centuries, Padre Gerónimo de Zárate Salmerón's extensive history of Nueva México from 1538 to 1626, published in the latter year, was considered to contain the definitive story of Oñate's 1604 *entrada*. When the Escobar diary was located, it was found to have been Zárate's primary source.

Oñate had never been west of the Three Mesas. The last time he had been there, he had sent Captain Marcos Farfán de los Gados to find the mines reported by Antonio de Espejo— and he had. Six years on, Oñate wanted to see for himself.

Coming within sight of the snow-capped San Francisco Peaks, Oñate and company began meeting the Yavapai people who had been so cordial to Farfán on his earlier visit. Escobar writes that Oñate found that "the men are well-featured and noble; the women are handsome, with beautiful eyes, and they are affectionate." The latter seems rather suggestive for a Franciscan padre.

Though Farfán did not mention it, Escobar reports that some of these people, whom he called Cruzados, wore crosses tied to their hair above their foreheads. As a Franciscan, Escobar would notice such a thing. He concluded that "many years ago there traveled through that land a [Franciscan missionary] who told them that if at any time they should see men bearded and white, in order that they might not molest or injure them they should put on those crosses, which is a thing esteemed by them. They remembered it so well that they have not forgotten it." Neither Escobar nor Zárate would venture a guess as to *who* that might have been.

Oñate went on to visit some of the mines, probably in or near the Verde Valley area west of Prescott, which had been "discovered" by Farfán's party. Herbert Bolton believes that they saw the San Andreas mine, the richest of those reported by Farfán. In this area, Oñate also met people who knew about the South Sea, and were able to give him directions. They told him that it was twenty days' journey to the south through the land of the Amacava (Mojave) people. They said that he should follow a river with little water, probably the Bill Williams Fork, which flowed into a larger river. This was the Colorado, which Escobar called the Río de la Buena Esperanza, the River of Good Hope.

Heading south along the banks of the Colorado, they met the Amacava, and heard stories of another tribe who wore, according to Escobar, "bracelets of gold, on the wrists and on the fleshy part of the arms and in their ears."

They spoke a language similar to that of the Indian servants whom the Spaniards had brought all the way from Nueva Vizcaya. However, these people did not come from the south, in the direction of Nueva Vizcaya, but from the *north*. They were said to be fourteen days' journey in that direction, near a lake which was called Copalla.

A few days later, as they continued south, the Spaniards passed though the land of the people whom he dubbed Bahacecha, a tribe who spoke a language similar to the Amacava. Adolph Bandelier supposes that they may have been the Hualapai, but their exact identity is uncertain. Their leader, a man called Otata, "came out with a great following to the road to receive the Spaniards and to beg them not to pass on that day, but to remain overnight in his pueblo."

Around the campfire, Otata "told of many things and secrets of the land," and when talk turned to Copalla, he responded by showing them a gold toothpick. He put it to his wrist "as if putting it around, giving to understand that the Indians of this lake wore bracelets of that material."

Though Oñate apparently dismissed these stories without a second thought, a lake labeled "Copalla" does show up occasionally on Spanish maps from later in the seventeenth century. The location is that of the freshwater lake south of the Great Salt Lake that was later named Lake Timpanogos, and which is now called Utah Lake. It is indeed north of the lower Colorado River, but by more than fourteen days on foot. Zárate may have been aware of this lake when he compiled his narrative of Oñate's *entrada*.

These people also told the Spaniards of a place closer by where people possessed gold. As Escobar writes:

> At a distance of nine or ten days' journey, there was a lake on whose banks lived people who wore on their wrists yellow manacles or bracelets, which they made us understand, from [lapel clasps] of gold and of brass which we showed them, putting them on and wearing them on the wrists or arms, they said they were the same as that metal which those Indians wore on the wrists, and afterwards two old Indians asserted the same. When shown a small bar of brass they gave us to understand that the other metal was darker and that they called it anopacha, which name afterwards other Indians, who were three or four and more leagues distant from these, gave to a little brass watch which I carried, without being asked any questions at the time about this matter, from which it is clearly to be inferred that there is yellow metal in this country. Indeed, there is a name common in all the nation which signifies this yellow metal, but only among the Indians of the Bahacecha and Amacava nations, for when I asked about it of the other Indians whom we saw on the same river nearer the sea, they could tell me nothing about it, either because they did not understand me or did not know it. But in Bahacecha and Amacava there were so many who said it that they almost convinced me beyond doubt that there are both yellow and white metal in the country, although it is not certain whether or not the yellow may be gold and the white silver, for of this I have very grave doubts.

For the sixteenth-century hunter-gatherers of the Mojave Desert to have mastered the art of alloying brass would have been more remarkable than their possessing gold.

Pointing toward the south, the Bahacecha also showed Oñate some coral, which seems to have delighted him more than the promise of golden bracelets.

Another story which especially fired Oñate's imagination was of an island in the sea which Zárate called "Zinogaba," and which could be reached only by an all-day journey in a large boat. They told the Spaniards that the people on the island had pearls.

Among the other "secrets of the land" which Otata shared around the campfire were stories of a tribe downstream who slept standing up, another who slept underwater, and yet another comprised of one-legged people. Lest we conclude that Otata was now merely pulling the legs of the Spaniards, it should be mentioned that he also told of a race of giants who lived near the South Sea. This corresponds with the giants whom the Melchior Díaz expedition had claimed to have seen when they traveled overland from the interior to the South Sea in 1540—although neither Escobar nor Zárate make this connection. Escobar does say that when he later mentioned the race of giants near the South Sea to people at the Hopi Three Mesas they claimed to be familiar with such a tale.

As they continued southward along the Colorado, the Spaniards met more tribes speaking different languages. Some of these tribes were as friendly as the Bahacecha, and some were not. Escobar, the linguist, mentions having counted ten separate languages being spoken along the lower 150 miles of the Colorado. Whatever the language, though, they always knew what was meant when the Spaniards communicated with them about the large body of salt water, and they always pointed south. There was sufficient mention of coral that Escobar began to speak of the area at the mouth of the river as the "Coral Coast."

Escobar writes that it was on the Feast Day of the Conversion of St. Paul (January 25, 1605) that they finally reached the South Sea, although Zárate suggests that they discovered a broad bay on this date, and that they had reached the sea a couple of days earlier. Of the bay, Escobar happily reports that: "We arrived with great joy . . . where we saw, according to the declaration of seamen, the finest bay, or port (for it is called by both names) which any of them ever had seen. We called it the Port of the Conversion, since it was discovered on that day. It is formed by the Río de la Buena Esperanza, where it enters the sea, with a mouth three or four leagues wide, according to the statements of the seamen who with me saw it."

Oñate took possession of the port in the name of King Philip III, and began asking the people whom they met along the shore about where he could find the pearls.

The accounts of both Escobar and Zárate end rather abruptly, quickly jumping to a mention of the Oñate *entrada* returning to San Gabriel exactly three months later, on April 25. As this was a shorter period than the outbound journey, we can conclude that little time was spent exploring the South Sea or the area around the mouth of the Colorado.

Oñate almost certainly found coral, and he probably returned to Nueva México with some pearls. However, while Escobar writes that some "shells and stones" gathered on the journey were shown to the viceroy in Mexico City in October 1604, he does not mention pearls. After the latter being so much a part of earlier Oñate narratives going back to 1599, one wonders why neither chronicler discussed pearls in detail at this point. There is no mention of an excursion to the mysterious Island of Zinogaba, nor of actually meeting the giants. From this, we can conclude that the Spaniards did neither.

Though the Oñate *entrada*, like so many sixteenth-century Spanish expeditions, failed to bring back tangible evidence of great wealth to rival that pillaged from the Aztec and the Inca, it was nevertheless historically important. His was the only group of Europeans to visit the lower Colorado and the upper Gulf of California in the 161 years between the visits by Hernándo de Alarcón and Melchior Díaz in 1540, and the arrival of Padre Eusebio Francisco Kino in 1701. It would be centuries before people of European descent came to settle in large numbers in this remote region.

As for Don Juan de Oñate himself, it was his final expedition and the last milestone in a career that was on the verge of imploding. Though he spent a good deal of time in San Gabriel between expeditions, his absences were not conducive to managing the province with which the viceroy had charged him. Despite his rave reviews of rich soil and a cor-

In 1605, returning from the entrada which took him to the mouth of the Colorado River, Juan de Oñate carved his name at A'ts'ina (Place of Writings on the Rock). Later called Inscription Rock, A'ts'ina is an ancient petroglyph site on the route, well traveled by pueblo people and conquistadors alike, between the Zuni pueblos and the upper Rio Grande valley. It is located about 30 miles east of the Zuni pueblos in what is now El Morro National Monument. Oñate's is the oldest dated inscription here. The three lines read: "Paso por aq[u]i el ade-lantado don ju[an] de oñate del descubrimiento de la mar del sur a 16 de Abril del 1605." This roughly translates as: "Passed this way the advance man don Juan de Oñate from the discovery of the south sea on 16 April in 1605." The term "adelantado," literally meaning advance man, was a title granted to certain conquistadors who functioned as military governors or magistrates in areas recently acquired or claimed on behalf of the Spanish monarchy. This photo was taken by Edward Curtis in about 1927.

nucopia of fruits and vegetables, the land in the upper Rio Grande Valley was found not to be favorable for large scale agriculture. The province was also proving to be a financial drain on the crown.

Many of the settlers who had come north in 1598 and thereafter had grown discouraged and gone back. With them went tales of Oñate's cruelty to the indigenous people of Nueva México. The brutality of the actions taken at Acoma in 1598 continued to fester as an ever blacker mark on his career. (Indeed, the memory of this incident remains alive in the Southwest today. In 1997, the City of El Paso hired the well-known sculptor, John Sherrill Houser—the son of Ivan

Houser, the assistant to Gutzon Borglum in carving Mount Rushmore—to create a monumental equestrian statue of Oñate. Completed in 2006, the statue became the flashpoint of divisive protests by people who took offense to the city's official commemoration of a man who had been so cruel to the indigenous people of the region.)

Philip III ordered an investigation into Oñate's misman-agement, but before word of this reached Nueva México, Oñate resigned. He was succeeded by his son, Cristobal de Naharriondo Pérez Oñate y Cortés Moctezuma, who took office in 1608 as the first elected governor of Nueva México. Two years later, Cristobal was succeeded by Don Pedro de Peralta, who had recently founded the city of Santa Fe, and to which he moved the capital of the province. Santa Fe is still the capital of the state of New Mexico, the oldest state capi-tal in the United States, and the third oldest city in the coun-try founded by Europeans.

Juan de Oñate returned to Mexico City and finally faced charges of abuse of power and of excessive force in the Acoma rebellion. Found guilty, he was fined and banished forever from Nueva México. He wound up in Spain, the land of his father, where he died a forgotten man in 1626.

His daughter, Maria de Oñate y Cortés Moctezuma, mean-while, married her cousin, Oñate's old sergeant major from the Quivira expedition, Vicente de Zaldívar.

OÑATE WAS VERY MUCH the "Last Conquistador," the end of an era. He was a contemporary of Sir Walter Raleigh, who would make his one final quest in Oñate's lifetime, and join Raleigh as the last of a dying breed of men. Oñate's career had included the last major *entradas* sanctioned by the Spanish crown that went into the Southwest to chase phantom tales of cities of gold. So much of *terra incognita* had been explored that the willingness to believe the stories had faded.

A century had now passed since the conquistadors first started probing the periphery of the New World, and the Spanish presence had now matured.

As the Last Conquistador crossed El Paso of the Rio Grande for the last time, it was not merely the end of an era of exploration, but it was like the notes which introduce the *rondo*, the final act, of a symphony. In this case, the symphony was the *Siglo de Oro*, the Golden Age of Spain as Europe's leading power.

Financed by Inca gold and the silver of Potosí and Zacatecas, it had been an epoch of unprecedented wealth and cultural richness. The plundered loot had financed great art (Velásquez and El Greco), great architecture (El Escorial), and great literature (Cervantes).

However, the *Siglo de Oro* had another side. There was an economic reckoning to all that wealth, which depressed the value of gold and silver by its mere abundance. As Jean Descola writes:

> But the wealth of Spain was only temporary, and she was not long in feeling the drawbacks of such prodigious wealth. The abundance of gold caused a rise in prices, without an equivalent stimulus to production. A large part of the monetary wealth remained sterile. The great landed proprietors, enriched by speculation, preferred to live on their capital rather than invest it in agricultural works. . . . Certain hidalgos of high rank were even to become moneylenders at high rates of interest, instead of increasing the revenues of their estates. . . . Nothing is more costly than a politique of grandeur. This does not mean that Spain died of hunger on its heap of gold, but in order to live on the level of a Great Power—that is, to keep her rank in Europe, and especially to provide for the needs of her American Empire—she had to buy abroad what she could not make at home: Flax and hemp from Normandy, canvas from Brittany, sailcloth from Saint-Brieuc, cloth from England, and hardwood for shipbuilding from the Baltic. Thus the gold and silver imported from America were exported, in the form of coins, to France, England, and Holland to pay for the merchandise necessary to the homeland and the empire.

The Spanish imports of goods were so considerable that they had the effect of stimulating the industry of the three enemy nations and contributing to their prosperity. Simultaneously the foe and the client of France, England, and the Low Countries, Spain was to end by being nothing but a dumping ground for gold between the Atlantic and the Pyrenees until such time as the power founded on the metal yielded irremediably to the power founded on industry.

Meanwhile *New* Spain entered the seventeenth century having become a flourishing entity unto itself, populated by people whose parents had been born there, and who had never even seen "Old" Spain. For a generation, the region had been ruled by Spaniards who overthrew the indigenous nobility, but by the seventeenth century, the ruling caste was an amalgam of both worlds, at least culturally.

Maria and Cristobol Oñate were the children of the post-conquistador seventeenth-century generation. While Juan de Oñate had been born there to the nouveau nobility of New Spain, they were, like his mother, Spaniards in whose veins ran the blood of Aztec royalty.

21

An Ambassador from the Enlightenment in El Dorado

The Spaniards have had a confused notion of this country, and have called it "El Dorado"; and an Englishman, whose name was Sir Walter Raleigh, came very near it about a hundred years ago; but being surrounded by inaccessible rocks and precipices, we have hitherto been sheltered from the rapaciousness of European nations, who have an inconceivable passion for the pebbles and dirt of our land, for the sake of which they would murder us to the last man.

—The 172-year-old man to Candide, in Voltaire's *Candide, ou l'Optimisme* (1759)

HAVING MADE THE LONG and arduous journey to fabled El Dorado, Candide and his valet Cacambo entered a house that was characterized by Voltaire as being "very plain . . . for the door was only of silver, and the ceilings were only of gold, but wrought in so elegant a taste as to vie with the richest. The antechamber, indeed, was only encrusted with rubies and emeralds, but the order in which everything was arranged made amends for this great simplicity."

The old man, who received the strangers on a sofa stuffed with hummingbird feathers, treated them to liqueurs served in diamond goblets. He then chuckled at the "inconceivable passion" which the Europeans had for the mere pebbles and dirt of El Dorado.

Voltaire's fictional allegory, penned two centuries after Sir Walter Raleigh had first gazed upon the South American continent, serves to underscore how deeply and permanently the legends of Gonzalo Pizarro's El Dorado, Raleigh's Manoa, and Coronado's Cibola had become ingrained in mainstream European popular culture.

Throughout the sixteenth century, the legends had inspired men such as these to risk their lives, but in the years after Raleigh's last disastrous voyage, and after the Last Conquistador was banished from Nueva México, the adventurers hung up their spurs and handed the legends to the mythmakers and the spinners of yarns.

Though John Milton called El Dorado the "great citie" of "yet unspoil'd Guiana" in *Paradise Lost* (1667), the English spent the seventeenth century ignoring the temptation. They were now building colonies in the New World, and exploiting more tangible resources than unproven and undiscovered cities of gold—resources such as tobacco, in which Raleigh himself had a hand in popularizing.

By the eighteenth century, the American colonies of both the Spaniards and the English had matured to the point where they had become sufficiently sophisticated culturally that they could think of themselves as nations rather than colonies.

In the drawing rooms of Europe—as well as of Boston, Philadelphia, Virginia, and Mexico City—the late eighteenth century was the Age of Enlightenment, also called the Age of Reason, an era in which reason guided the intellectual, scientific, and cultural experience. The great philosopher Immanuel Kant wrote in his seminal 1784 essay *Answer to the Question: What Is Enlightenment?* that the Enlightenment was "Mankind's final coming of age, the emancipation of the human consciousness from an immature state of ignorance and error." This was the era in which the great intellectuals and philosophers were vigorously hammering nails into the lid on the coffin of superstition, fantasy, and far-fetched theories such as mystical cities of gold.

Or so it seemed.

One of the great scientists of the Enlightenment was the Prussian naturalist Alexander von Humboldt, the brother of the philosopher and linguist Friedrich Wilhelm von Humboldt, who served as the Prussian education minister and who founded Humboldt University in Berlin.

Alexander was active in fields from botany to geography, and is still recalled for his groundbreaking studies of the interconnected nature of the forces in the natural world. A university student in Frankfurt at the time Kant wrote his essay, Humboldt went on to make his mark as one of the first important observational scientists to embody Kant's idea of emancipation from ignorance. His method was highly empirical, dependent on accurate observation and precise measurement. Thomas Jefferson considered him to be the most important scientist he had ever met.

As a globe-trotting scientific observer of the natural world, Alexander von Humboldt preceded Charles Darwin by more than three decades. Humboldt penned many books about his scientific work, but one of his best known is his tome about his American trip, entitled *Relation Historique du Voyage aux Régions équinoxiales du Nouveau Continent* (*Personal Narrative of Travels to the Equinoctial Regions of America*). This 1799–1804 expedition, which took him to both North and South America, came about through a succession of random events.

The voyage, which was ultimately very important scientifically, happened only because he and botanist Aimé Jacques Alexandre Bonpland failed in an effort to book passage on a ship out of Marseilles. The two well-heeled gentlemen scientists were supposed to have been part of Nicolas Baudin's voyage around the world, but when this expedition was postponed, they decided to go to Egypt to link up with Napoleon Bonaparte's incursion. As part of a complex geopolitical chess game, Napoleon had invaded Egypt to thwart British intentions in the Mediterranean, but he also took a coterie of scientists to Egypt with him—this was the expedition during which the Rosetta Stone was discovered—and Humboldt and Bonpland yearned to be in on this action.

When they couldn't get their boat to Egypt from Marseilles, the two went instead to Madrid, where they crossed paths with Spanish Secretary of State Mariano Luis de Urquijo, who had the ear of King Carlos IV. Against the backdrop of the Enlightenment, scientific expeditions were beginning to have a certain cachet among politicians and kings. The Spaniards saw the prestige that could be derived from such a venture, so Carlos decided to bankroll Humboldt and his associate for a scientific expedition to the Spanish dominions in the New World.

The two scientists-turned-explorers set sail from the northern Spanish port city of A Coruña in June 1799. It was both ironic and auspicious that their ship was named for the first family of Spanish adventure and misadventure in South America—the *Pizarro*.

In Guiana, Humboldt followed in Raleigh's footsteps, or rather his canoe path, traveling upriver on the Orinoco, and on its main tributaries, the Caroni and the Rupununi.

Though much of his book reads like the dispassionate discussion of natural phenomena one would expect from a scientist of the Enlightenment, we also glimpse the wide-eyed delight of a man failing to hide the fact that he'd been bitten by the same old-fashioned gold bug that had infected so many back in the impulsive sixteenth century.

Humboldt made notes about the indigenous people he met, the hydrology of the rivers, and about how the land ought to be rich enough to support European agriculture, noting that "the example of Germany and Mexico proves, no doubt, that the working of metals is not at all incompatible with a flourishing state of agriculture."

In his next sentence, though, this scientific ambassador from the Enlightenment tells his readers that "according to popular traditions, the banks of the Caroni lead to the lake Dorado and the palace of the gilded man; and this lake, and this palace, being a local fable, it might be dangerous to awaken remembrances which begin gradually to be effaced."

He goes on to say that as late as 1760, the Carib people were still selling gold dust to Dutch traders, adding that the watershed of the Caroni "must have auriferous [gold-bearing] sands, [because] in summer, when the waters retire, pieces of gold of considerable weight are found there." He also writes of traveling the headwaters in a place "where the mountain of Ucucuamo rises, [which] the natives still call the mountain of gold."

Alexander von Humboldt.
(*Bill Yenne*)

Humboldt also mentions Raleigh and his city of Manoa frequently, and specifically discusses the expeditions in the 1530s and 1540s on the Cundinamarca Plateau by his countrymen, Georg von Speyer and Philipp von Hutten, as well as those of the de Quesada brothers, Hernán and Gonzalo. Humboldt excitedly observes that their accounts "furnish, amid much exaggeration, proofs of very exact local knowledge."

He writes of Gonzalo's son-in-law and heir, Antonio de Berrío, the Spanish governor who had seduced Sir Walter Raleigh with wild tales of the visit to the golden city by Juan Martínez, the fable which was later discredited as a hoax.

Though Berrío was probably deliberately misleading Raleigh, Humboldt thinks either that Berrío may have actually believed the golden tales, or even that he had *seen* the golden city himself. Humboldt writes that "it is difficult to distinguish what this conquistador had himself observed in going down the Orinoco from what he said he had collected in a pretended journal of Martínez. . . . Berrío mentions [a place in the Orinoco watershed] between the confluence of the Meta and the Cuchivero [rivers], where he found many little idols of molten gold, similar to those which were fabricated . . . east of Coro [in present-day Venezuela]."

Humboldt suggests that the "pretended journal" in the Juan Martínez hoax was based on earlier tales about the area spun by Juan Martín de Albujar, and that Berrío didn't necessarily realize that it was a fraud at the time he shared it with Raleigh. Even as he recognizes Raleigh's having been taken in by a hoax, though, Humboldt teases his readers with mention of a treasure map "that was constructed by Raleigh, and which he recommended to Lord Charles Howard [Lord High Admiral under Elizabeth I and James I and commander of the English fleet in the victory over the Spanish Armada] to keep secret." He admits to not knowing the secret contents, but for a scientist to even mention such a thing betrays his being under the spell of the gold bug.

Early in his own efforts to unravel the legend of Guiana's golden city, Humboldt writes that: "All fables have some real foundation; that of El Dorado resembles those myths of antiquity, which, traveling from country to country, have been successively adapted to different localities. In the sciences, in order to distinguish truth from error, it often suffices to retrace the history of opinions, and to follow their successive developments."

As Humboldt discusses the history of the sixteenth-century quests for El Dorado at length, he adds details of his own search in the headwaters of the Orinoco and the Caroni for the elusive Laguna Parima, the inland sea which Raleigh thought to be so large as to rival the Caspian. Indeed, Humboldt was probably aware that Jean-Baptiste Bourguignon d'Anville, who was one of the favorite, no-nonsense geographers and cartographers of the Enlightenment, had included Laguna Parima on his 1748 map of the Americas.

Of Laguna Parima, Humboldt writes: "The town of Manoa and its palaces covered with plates of massy gold have long since disappeared [from the agenda of current active searches]; but the geographical apparatus serving to adorn the fable of El Dorado, the lake Parima, which, similar to the lake of Mexico [Lake Texcoco upon which Mexico City was built], reflected the image of so many sumptuous edifices, has been religiously preserved by geographers. . . . The fabulous traditions of El Dorado and the lake Parima having been diversely modified according to the aspect of the countries to which they were to be adapted, we must distinguish what they contain that is real from what is merely imaginary."

Humboldt himself spent much observational time in South America trying to deduce that distinction, and to disprove the existence of the lake. In the course of these observations, Humboldt found the legends to be as alive and well as they had been in Raleigh's time, as he found himself in the colonial cantinas listening to that same breed of old prospectors whose storytelling had been seducing conquistadors since the sixteenth century. He mentions that in a town near Quito: "I met with some men, who were employed by the Bishop [José Carrión y] Marfil [Auxiliary Bishop of Santa Fé in Nueva Granada] to seek at the east of the Cordilleras [the mountains of central Colombia], in the plains of Macas [in what is now southeastern Ecuador], the ruins of the town of Logrono, which was believed to be situate[d] in a country rich in gold. We learn by the journal of [German surgeon, Nicolas] Hortsmann [who explored the region], which I have often quoted, that it was supposed, in 1740, El Dorado might be reached from Dutch Guiana by going up the Río Essequibo [longest river in Guyana, and the largest river between the Orinoco and Amazon]."

For each of the stories such as that of Bishop Marfil's men, which Humboldt regards as vaguely credible, he throws in one that he considers obviously preposterous, if only to demonstrate that he had not lost his scientist's healthy skepticism. He writes of Don Manuel Centurion, the governor of Santo Thome del Angostura, who was taken in by "Arimuicaipi, an Indian of the nation of the Ipurucotos, [who showed the Spaniards] in the southern sky the Clouds of Magellan, the whitish light of which he said was the reflection of the argentiferous [sliver-bearing] rocks situate[d] in the middle of the Laguna Parima. . . . Another Indian chief, known among the Caribs of Essequibo by the name El Capitan Jurado, vainly attempted to undeceive the governor Centurion. Fruitless attempts were made by the Caura and the Río Paragua [in Venezuela]; and several hundred persons perished miserably in these rash enterprises, from which, however, geography has derived some advantages." It was just like the man from the Enlightenment to find that science could derive "advantages" from the wreckage of rash enterprises.

As though splashing cold water on his face, Humboldt snapped out of the sweet delusions of the imaginary and the unprovable to leave posterity with what may be the first detached scientific study of Spanish South America. An intellectual imbued with the aloof and analytical ideals of the Enlightenment, he could see the future of the region in the remaking of South America in the image of rational and civilized Europe. He concluded that "Gold extracted from the bosom of the earth is far more alluring in the eyes of the vulgar, than that which is the produce of agricultural industry."

After four years in Spanish America, Humboldt traveled onward to the United States, where he was inducted into the American Philosophical Society in Philadelphia. While there, he met with Charles Willson Peale and asked for an introduction to Thomas Jefferson.

They dined with the president at the White House in June 1804, one month after Jefferson had sent his Virginia neighbor, Captain Meriwether Lewis, to command the greatest scientific expedition yet conceived in the far west of the United States. In a letter to Jefferson dated June 27, Humboldt beamed that "I have had the good fortune to see the first Magistrate of this great republic living with the simplicity of a philosopher who received me with that profound kindness that makes for a lasting friendship."

The lasting friendship would continue in correspondence over two decades, punctuated often by letters discussing the Lewis and Clark expedition. In his *Political Essay on the Kingdom of New Spain*, published in 1811, Humboldt wrote that "Captain Lewis undertook this admirable journey with the support of Mr. Jefferson, who has again won the gratitude of all scholars everywhere for this important service to science."

To a man of the Enlightenment sitting in his salon in Potsdam, a service to science was as good as gold, but to an explorer in the inky darkness of his tent, listening to the wind blow through the rugged, remote Cordilleras, even Humboldt's thoughts had turned inescapably to that country rich in fantastic gold called El Dorado.

22

A Fantastic Mirage in the Brazilian Jungle

Uma miragem fantástica, pela qual diversos intelectuais dedicariam todos os esforços para tentar solucioná la. (A fantastic mirage, for which diverse intellectuals would dedicate all their efforts to try to solve.)

—Johnni Langer, in *Revista Brasileira de História* (*Brazilian Magazine of History*) (2002)

IN 1839, THE NATURALIST Manuel Ferreira Lagos began reading an old travel narrative which had been gathering dust in the public library in Rio de Janeiro, the Livraria Pública da Corte, for eighty-five years. The opening page spoke of travelers coming across a crystal mountain, "so beautiful that none could take their eyes from the reflections." This fanciful description got his attention, so he read on.

He had discovered it, probably by chance, in the institution that became the Biblioteca Nacional, the National Library of Brazil, the national archives of the country, which today houses a collection of around nine million books, and nearly a million manuscripts, many of these dating back to Brazil's early days as a Portuguese colony. It was in these files that Lagos came across the mysterious Manuscript 512.

This document is the *relación* of a 1753 expedition into the Bahia region of Brazil north of Rio de Janeiro. In 1940, researcher Hermann Kruse determined that it was authored by the well-documented eighteenth-century soldier of fortune (called a *bandeirante*) João da Silva Guimarães. He and his companions were riding in search of rumored wealth, specifically the silver mines of Muribeca, whose exact location had stymied treasure hunters in the region for at least a decade.

As Lagos read on, he found that the *bandeirantes* had been marveling at the way the sun's rays caught the shimmering quartz on the cliff while trying to find a pass through a mountain range described as the "Alps and Pyrenees of Brazil." Just as they were pondering an alternative path to giving up, one of their slaves stumbled across a partially concealed cleft between mountains while chasing a deer. The theory that it was a man-made opening was supported by their discovery of a trail beyond the opening. Following the trail, to the top of the pass, they looked out on the broad valley beyond. A couple of miles away, they could see a great city.

They sent one of their Indian guides to scout the place, and after two days, he returned to tell them that the great city was abandoned. Moving out at daybreak, they cautiously approached the city. As Johnni Langer of the Universidade Federal do Paraná (Federal University of Paraná, UFPR) writes in *Revista Brasileira de História*, they passed beneath "three arches of great height," and found themselves on a broad street bounded by stone buildings with sculptured façades.

The *bandeirantes* entered several of the buildings, which had interiors so vast and so empty that Guimarães made note of the echoes of their voices as they spoke. He noted that the floors were blackened as though by a fire, and that there were no furnishings whatsoever. Guimarães also observed that the buildings were covered by symbols which he interpreted as letters in an unfamiliar alphabet. He jotted these down, and later transcribed them in the *relación* which became Manuscript 512.

Continuing on the broad street, they came to a vast plaza with a black obelisk at the center. At the top was a statue of a man, with his left hand on his hip, and right hand pointing toward the north. A similar image was found in bas relief on a nearby building. Facing the plaza was the largest building in the complex, whose interior was infested by a considerable number of bats.

Beyond the plaza was a broad, deep river, and past the river were open clearings that looked to the *bandeirantes* as though they had once been cultivated fields. Guimarães writes that there were "green and flourishing fields, and so blooming with a variety of flowers that it seemed as if Nature, more attentive to these parts, had laid herself out to create the most beautiful gardens of Flora."

In his 2002 assessment of these observations, Langer writes that Guimarães may have been influenced by the recent popularity in Europe of rediscovering Roman ruins, which was quite popular at the time. He writes that the description leads him to believe that "the author of the story was deeply fascinated by the archaeological and cultural discoveries that were affecting Europe at the beginning of the eighteenth century." By 1753, most Spanish and Portuguese *bandeirantes* would have been aware that archaeological excavations had been ongoing at Pompeii and Herculaneum for more than a decade.

Langer adds that "elements in the narrative are much more part of old [colonial] folkloric traditions . . . the resplendent mountain ranges, associated with precious metals and stones . . . the myth of the Lost Paradise . . . [and] also many narratives of imaginary cities . . . made with precious metal, as for example, El Dorado."

Leaving the city, the *bandeirantes* traveled downstream on the river as it flowed into another river, where they found a great waterfall, with a series of caverns beneath it. Nearby was a large building with a great portico and a vast interior room. As with the buildings at the city, it was inscribed with symbols resembling an alphabet.

Langer has pointed out hieroglyphs not unlike those recorded by Guimarães were also noted in the 1730s by Martinho de Mendonça de Pena, an academic turned colonial bureaucrat and amateur archaeologist, who was a member of the Royal Academy in Lisbon. Pena's symbols were widely circulated before Guimarães's 1753 discoveries. Langer notes many similarities between the symbols reproduced by Pena, those in Manuscript 512, and the Roman alphabet.

"We marveled," Guimarães writes, "that this place had been abandoned by those who had formerly inhabited it; for, with all our careful investigations and great diligence we had met no person, in this wilderness, who might tell us of this deplorable marvel of an abandoned city, whose ruins, statues and grandeur, attested its former populousness, wealth, and its flourishing in the centuries past."

As an inspiration to treasure hunters and El Dorado seekers through the coming decades, he adds that "we went down to the banks of the river to see whether we could find gold, and without difficulty, we saw, on the surface of the soil, a fine trail promising great riches, as well of gold, as of silver."

As with the mysterious civilization which he claimed to have discovered, Guimarães himself was swallowed by the jungle. His *relación* having found its way to the Livraria Pública a year after the discovery, Guimarães continued to explore the remote hinterlands until 1764, the last year that there is any mention of him in surviving records.

Having discovered the manuscript, Manuel Ferreira Lagos approached the Instituto Histórico e Geográfico Brasileiro (Institute of Brazilian History and Geography). Founded only the year before, in 1838, the IHGB is one of Brazil's most prestigious academic institutions. Just as Guimarães's manuscript had been written against the backdrop of a surge of interest in recently uncovered Roman antiquities, Lagos brought the document to light as the world was enthralled with the recent discoveries of Mayan ruins in Mexico. The time was right, the IHGB decided, for Brazil to publicize its own ancient ruins.

The nineteenth-century investigators began collecting information from travelers who had been in the interior of the Bahia, and sifting through centuries of folklore of what Langer calls traditions of "magic cities" and such "old colonial myth metamorphoses as El Dorado."

During the 1840s, there were numerous expeditions in search of Guimarães's lost city, some coming from as far away as · Denmark. The German botanist Carl Friedrich von

Martius, who had made his own expedition into the Bahia interior and the upper Amazon between 1817 and 1820, also weighed in. From Munich, he wrote that he believed such an advanced civilization had once existed in the Brazilian *terra incognita*. He said that the cultural memory of such pre-Columbians could be found in the mythology of the people still living in the interior, as well as in the archaeological vestiges which Guimarães mentioned. Like El Dorado in the sixteenth century, this magic city took on a life of its own, and was starting to seem real. However, as Langer cautions, "the credibility of the lost city, despite its great academic acceptance, was not an absolute fact."

In 1840, the members of the IHGB decided to send a man to look for the lost city. José de Carvalho e Cunha was professor and a specialist in eastern languages, and he had served as a priest under Archbishop Romualdo Seixas of Bahia. The archbishop was an honorary member of the IHGB, and very interested himself in Guimarães's lost city. Langer mentions that "the reasons for the interest of Seixas with the lost city are obscure. The most likely one is that he liked to keep a control on all the scientific facts and cultural direction in his province." As for the fantastic nature of Guimarães's ruins, Carvalho shrugged that he was not interested in the gold, only in the archaeology.

Carvalho began by unraveling the meager geographical data provided by Guimarães and correlating it to actual locations. He calculated his mountain range to be the Serra do Sincorá, and the rivers to be the Paraguaçu and/or its tributary the Una. The Paraguaçu begins in the Chapada Diamantina uplands in central Bahia and follows the Sincorá before entering the Atlantic in the Baía de Todos os Santos near the city of Salvador.

Arriving in the coastal fishing village of Valença in February 1841, Carvalho began asking around about people who might have more information about the mysterious interior. To his amazement, the first man with whom he spoke, an old-timer named Antonio Joaquín da Cruz, confirmed the existence of a large waterfall with deep caverns beneath it. He said that he had heard stories of a city, but had been afraid to venture into the wilderness to investigate. Carvalho deduced that the local legends of this lost city probably predated Guimarães's time.

He also mentioned that the legend included a dragon that prowled the jungle in the vicinity of the lost city. Traveling upriver, someone had probably seen an anaconda or other large snake upriver, but stories do get out of hand. Dragons were so much a part of the accepted nature of *terra incognita* that Carvalho dutifully mentioned such a serpent in his report to the IHGB and in an article in the institute's journal. Once they become integrated into a myth, imaginary dragons are harder to kill than real ones.

In November 1841, the IHGB president, Viscount Leopoldo, went to Brazilian emperor Dom Pedro II to arrange financing for the expedition. The emperor, who had been crowned only four months earlier, was eager to make his mark, and national identity was high on his list of priorities. Knowing this, Leopold sold the *entrada* to Pedro, not as a treasure hunt, but as a scientific expedition that would provide new information about the previously unexplored "lands not yet defined in the interior of Brazil . . . spaces unknown, inaccessible, isolated, dangerous, dominated by rude nature and inhabited by barbarians, heretics, infidels, where they did not have . . . religion, civilization and culture."

Who better to lead such an expedition bringing civilization to Brazil's heartland, Leopoldo asked the emperor rhetorically, than the priest José de Carvalho?

It only took Pedro II four days to accept Leopoldo's proposal. More than the idea of bringing nineteenth-century civilization to the barbarians, Pedro had seized on the idea that finding the ruins would prove that Brazil had been home to an advanced civilization long before Portugal exported its culture to these shores.

Carvalho was in the field in early December, but by February 1842, the initial euphoria was over. The IHGB was receiving letters from him complaining that the funding was insufficient to sustain the expedition. Thereafter, communication was spotty at best. A dispatch from Carvalho reached the IHGB in August, and then nothing was heard until the middle of 1843. In June 1844, Carvalho wrote that he had given up the search on the Paraguaçu, and had moved to the Orobó.

Two years turned into three, and by 1845, Carvalho had failed to accomplish what Guimarães seems to have done so effortlessly in a few months. After 1845, the communications between Carvalho and the IHGB ceased altogether and funding stopped.

From letters that the priest did write to Archbishop Seixas, however, it seems that he remained in the interior, probably in the Serra Sincorá, until around 1848. There were rumors that he had gone mad and was hearing the sounds of bells. Carvalho is confirmed to have shown up, exhausted and frustrated, in the city of Salvador in 1849. He apparently died the same year.

In the meantime, the idea of this lost city still had its true believers. In July 1848, Major Manoel Rodrigues de Oliviera even upped the ante, advancing an amazing theory in the IHGB journal. He suggested that the lost civilization in the center of Bahia included an anchorage on the Paraguaçu, and a road to quarries in the mountains at which people once obtained the marble for their statues and monuments.

With the death of the tenacious priest, however, the belief that the lost city could be found began to unravel. In 1849, Brigadier General José da Costa Bittencourt Camara published a sound rebuttal to Oliviera's fantastic speculation in the magazine *Razão*. He asserted that the original 1753 manuscript was entirely fictional and that Oliviera's embellishment was preposterous.

The manuscript went back into the file in the Livraria Pública da Corte, where it had slept for the eight decades between Guimarães and Lagos, to slumber again and to await the hand of a future generation, when it would be touched again, as the eager man touches the bottle containing the genie.

23

ESPEJO'S CHILDREN

> Expectations awakened and cherished in the beginning
> of the sixteenth century, not fulfilled but never com-
> pletely dispelled, have in past years prepared for the
> failure of many enterprises in the Southwest of the
> United States. These expectations were built upon the
> basis of a misunderstood fact.
>
> —Adolph Bandelier, *The Gilded Man* (1893)

FOUR CENTURIES HAD COME and gone since Antonio de
Espejo had stopped looking for cities of gold and had gone to
Arizona looking for the mines which were the source of gold
and silver. Over the next couple of centuries, few had followed his lead. By the nineteenth century, though, people
who followed his dream would be coming back to pick up
where his footsteps left off.

During that time, there had been little enthusiasm in the
Vice royalty of New Spain for struggling across the inhospitable Sonoran Desert on a gamble, especially when the silver fields of Zacatecas were so fruitful, and so much closer to
home. Nor had there been, over those centuries, an overwhelming desire to settle these lands in the north. Aside from
the trading center at Santa Fe, which became especially prof-

itable only after it was linked to the U.S. economy by the Santa Fe Trail, there were no major population centers in what is now Arizona and New Mexico.

The nineteenth-century settlement of the Southwest would come not from New Spain, but from the United States. Whereas there had been an urge among Americans to "go west" since before Daniel Boone led his party though the Cumberland Gap in 1775, there had been no parallel urge to "go north" among the people of New Spain before 1821, nor of Mexico after it achieved independence in 1821.

Mexico had even encouraged Americans with an urge to "go west" to settle in Texas, but took umbrage when the Texans declared independence themselves—*from* Mexico—in 1836. Nine years later, Mexico fought another war to get Texas back, but only because the Texans now wanted to join the United States. Farther west, in California, the settlers were also more likely to be from the United States than from Mexico.

Against this backdrop, big changes were due in a region that had evolved very slowly for centuries. In the space of nine days in 1848, two events—taking place nearly 2,000 miles apart—radically altered the history of the American West forever.

On January 24, a carpenter named James Wilson Marshall was constructing a sawmill on property owned by the Swiss-born rancher and entrepreneur John Augustus Sutter on the American River in the Sierra Nevada foothills about 40 miles east of Sacramento, California. Wilson did a double take when he saw some pieces of brightly colored metal mixed into the gravel at his feet. He saw a few more pieces, and then a lot more. It seemed to be everywhere. He started picking up the pieces.

Was it? It couldn't be? It was. The pieces turned out to be gold.

John Sutter wanted to keep the discovery quiet, but it was impossible. Within a matter of weeks, Sam Brannan, publisher of the *California Star* newspaper in San Francisco got hold of the story. According to California historian Hubert Howe Bancroft, he walked through San Francisco holding a glass vial and shouting "Gold! Gold! Gold from the American River!"

What happened over the next four years has been called the biggest voluntary mass migration in so short a span since humans began documenting their history. Nearly a quarter million people more than quintupled California's population, most of them arriving in 1849—it took that long for the news to reach the outside world—as a human tidal wave of "Forty-Niners." Those who arrived early were overnight millionaires, staking claims and picking gold nuggets out of the placers and sandbars of the foothill rivers that ran from the Sierras.

Those who arrived later became millionaires by panning or digging—or by setting up commercial enterprises that sold goods that the prospectors needed. Estimates of the current dollar value of the first few years of the California Gold Rush run into tens of billions. This excitement being reminiscent of all those sixteenth-century dreams of El Dorado come true was lost on virtually no one. The word appeared often in press accounts, and a California county formed in 1850 in the heart of the gold fields was named El Dorado.

On February 2, nine days after James Marshall started picking up nuggets, the United States and Mexican governments signed the Treaty of Guadalupe Hidalgo, ending the twenty-one-month conflict once called the Mexican War, and recently referred to by the more descriptive appellation, Mexican-American War.

By the terms of this agreement, the Mexican government lost a war and lost face—but was paid the current-dollar equivalent of about a third of a billion for mostly unpopulated frontier land that had remained largely ungoverned since Mexico had sent the last Spanish viceroy packing in 1821. In places where there was a significant population—such as in Texas and California—the descendants of Spanish settlers were far outnumbered by immigrants from the United States. Texans considered themselves Texans, and in California, the grandchildren of Spaniards, who saw virtually nothing of the Mexican government but its tax collectors, considered themselves "Californios" rather than Mexicans.

In addition to Texas and California, the treaty gave the United States the territory that became the states of Nevada, Utah, New Mexico, and parts of Arizona, Colorado, Oklahoma, Kansas, and Wyoming. We might also add that the United States now encompassed those city-states from the Zuni and Tiwa pueblos to the Hopi Three Mesas which had so fascinated the conquistadors in the sixteenth century—as well as that vast swath of territory explored by the conquistadors from Francisco de Coronado to Juan de Oñate.

With the California gold rush, the emphasis was on the riches of the Sierra foothills. Even after the obvious gold was picked up, and mine shafts were being sunk to get at underground veins, people spoke of the mystical "mother lode," the source of all the nuggets that had created an army of overnight millionaires. In fact, today, in the twenty-first century, one can go into those same foothills and easily run across prospectors who are still confidently searching for it.

As the California gold rush matured, the gold fever was refreshed by the Pike's Peak gold rush in Colorado in 1858, and by the Comstock Lode silver boom which began the same year in western Nevada. These discoveries, both made by people en route to the California bonanza, were merely the two largest of many smaller "rushes" that occurred across the West in the wake of the Forty-Niners' westward migration.

The psychological effect of these tremendous finds was analogous to Francisco Pizarro's discovery of the Inca cities sheathed in gold. If fabulous wealth had been found in this place *and* that, why not over here, or over there as well?

It was not long before prospectors were rediscovering the old sixteenth-century tales, and following Espejo's trail into Arizona and New Mexico. Though the climate which had daunted Spanish settlement for centuries was far less inviting than the cool streams and Ponderosa forests of the California gold fields, claims were staked and discoveries were made— some of them significant. Places such as Silver City, New Mexico, became boomtowns.

Just as many sought the mother lode in California, many sought the elusive big bonanza on Espejo's trail. There were few places in the era after the great rushes of 1848–1858 where prospectors searched harder. They found just enough to keep them going, but as Adolph Bandelier laments in the epigraph to this chapter, there was more than enough disappointment and disaster to go around. Nevertheless, by the

1860s, the Espejo trail in the Southwest had become the American equivalent of the sixteenth-century folklore surrounding El Dorado.

As folklorist and treasure hunter J. Frank Dobie wrote in *Coronado's Children* (1930), "the human imagination abhors failure. Hope and credulity are universal among the sons of earth, and so when English-speaking men took over the *sitios* and *portiones* of Spanish lands in the Southwest, they acquired not only the land that Spanish pioneers had surveyed but the traditions they had somehow made an ingredient of the soil itself."

Though some are lost forever, and many are waiting to be found on dusty shelves of roadside used book stores, or on yellowed pages in deep archival file drawers, there is no end to the stories that comprise this folklore.

Lost too, are the mines themselves. Like El Dorado, they are shadowy places that more people know *about* than know how to find. As with the traces of evidence that pointed the knaves and conquistadors ever onward toward El Dorado, the best stories of the best mines are those wherein tangible evidence has been seen and touched. Compared to the folklore of the sixteenth century, the protagonists in the nineteenth-century tales were solitary characters, not leaders of armies. They were more like Cabeza de Vaca or Marcos de Niza than Francisco de Coronado.

As with Cabeza de Vaca, many came across their discoveries, and their roles in the Southwest treasure folklore, accidentally.

One such man was an old prospector named Charles Breyfogle, whose name became a verb to describe the search for lost treasure. He came west as a Forty-Niner, failed to strike it rich in 1849, but managed to eke out a living following the placers of the Sierras. In 1864, he was prospecting in the wastelands of Death Valley, about a day's ride west of the Black Mountains where Espejo may have first found gold.

He and two companions were ambushed by Indians one night, and only Breyfogle managed to escape. He found himself lost, alone and without water in the hottest place in the Western Hemisphere. A temperature of 134 degrees Fahrenheit was recorded in Death Valley in 1913, and it is frequently above 120 degrees in this 3.3 million-acre wilderness. During the ensuing days of wandering, he nearly died of thirst. Eventually, he staggered into a remote trading post shoeless, with his clothes in shreds and his bald head so severely sunburned that people thought he'd been scalped.

His tales of finding a ledge with a wide vein of solid gold sounded like a hallucination—until his caregivers discovered that his pockets were filled with the richest gold ore anyone had ever seen. As the story goes, he was never able to find the ledge again. Over the decades many attempts were made to find the "Lost Breyfogle Mine," so many that by the beginning of the twentieth century, the word "breyfogling" became synonymous with looking for lost mines.

Probably the most famous treasure story in American folklore is that of the Lost Dutchman Mine. There are a number of lost Dutchman mines throughout the West, but there is only one Lost Dutchman Mine in the Superstition Mountains of Arizona. A source of incomparably pure gold ore in staggering quantities, this mysterious mine has been the subject of several dozen books, and countless articles in various periodicals. It has served as the general prototype for numerous grade-B Western movies, and has fueled countless late night debates around desert campfires and in Phoenix hotel bars.

The story naturally begins with a Dutchman, who was not Dutch, but rather "Deutsche," meaning German. His name was Jacob Walz, although in some tellings his surname is spelled Waltz or Weitz, or any number of similar variations. The Akimel O'odham (Pima) people called him "Snowbeard," a name which indicates that his appearance was archetypal of the grizzled old prospector.

According to the legends concerning the origins of Jake Walz, the Dutchman was born at the end of the first decade of the nineteenth century in or near the town of Oberschwandorf in the German state of Württemberg, the home of the conquistador Philipp von Hutten.

He landed in New York around 1845 in the midst of the first major wave of German immigration to the United States. He was in his mid-thirties and anxious for adventure and his share of those riches which European immigrants were supposed to find in the New World.

The Dutchman found the streets of New York not to be paved with gold, but he heard stories of the big gold strike down in North Carolina, and followed them. As almost invariably happens in gold strike stories, the facts were but a ghostly shadow of reality and most of the sites had either been worked to death or claimed. Walz followed other gold strike stories south into Georgia, and later west to California, where he was among the Forty-Niners who reached the foothills in that bonanza year.

Having worked the placers around and near El Dorado County for nearly a decade, he followed the news of gold being found in the San Gabriel Mountains in 1858, and remained in Southern California until 1861, when he became a naturalized citizen of the United States.

Sometime over the next two years, the far away look in the Dutchman's eyes took him from the more and more crowded Golden State to the rugged mountains and deserts of Arizona Territory. He filed the first of several claims in Prescott in September 1863 for a site in the Bradshaw Mountains near where Antonio de Espejo was shown the Indian mines 320 years earlier.

It was in 1868 that Walz, now nearing the age of sixty—and probably wearing the whiskers that earned him the name "Snowbeard"—arrived in the proximity of *the* legendary mine. It is known that in that year he homesteaded in the Río Saltillo (Salt River) Valley on the north side of the Superstition Mountains.

The same Akimel O'odham people who called the Dutchman Snowbeard called the mountains Ka-atak-tami, which meant, as deciphered by the Anglos, that something up there was associated with the supernatural. The English-speakers called this forbidding wilderness the "Superstition Mountains" and that name is still used today.

Long before any Dutchman ever dreamed of this place, indeed long before the Akimel O'odham people ever dreamed of this place, the prehistoric Mogollon (pronounced "Muggy-own") people lived here. A few of their cliff dwellings are here, but no one remembers what they called the Superstition Mountains.

Most stories about the Dutchman agree that he spent most of the next twenty years prospecting in the Superstitions,

although he may have also traveled seasonally around Arizona
Territory working for wages to
support himself while searching
for the fortune that history tells
us he eventually found. It was in
1870, during one of these so-
journs that he met another
"Dutchman," Jacob Weiser, probably while working at Henry
Wickenberg's Vulture Mine.

At some point, the two Jakes
left Wickenberg's employ and
struck out on their own. Somehow, somewhere, they struck it
rich in the Superstitions and were
seen around Phoenix, paying for
drinks and dry goods with bags of
gold nuggets. Some historians
have suggested that the gold may
have been stolen while they were
still working for Wickenberg,

The "cities" of ancient cliff
dwelling people look down
upon the gold seeker hiking
deep into the Mogollon
Mountains today.

although there is a consensus that it was of higher grade than
had been found at the Vulture.

Various stories have circulated about how they found their
mine. One has it that they shot and killed two Mexican
prospectors whom they mistook for Indians, and discovered
they'd been digging gold. Another tale, widely told during
the twentieth century, is that they were shown a treasure map
by a Mexican landowner named Miguel Peralta whose life
they saved in a saloon knife fight. Rewarding them with a
look at his treasure map, the man made the two Jakes his
partners, and after they had taken out a great deal of the gold,
the two Dutchmen bought out their partner's interest.

Somewhere over the years, Jake Weiser disappeared. Some
say he was killed by Apaches, but others say it was Jake Walz
who did him in. Still others claim that there was but one
Jake, and people had used so many variations on the surname
that it seemed like Walz and Weiser were different people.

Jake Walz remained in view, at least occasionally. Long
periods of time would go by with no one seeing him, and

then he would be around Phoenix again, paying for drinks with gold nuggets. The story is that the Dutchman's saddle-bags were filled with the richest gold ore that local assayers had ever seen.

For the rest of his life, Jake Walz moved back and forth between Phoenix and the undisclosed location of his secret mine. He never filed a claim, probably figuring that it was ultimately more dangerous to tell the location on a claim form than to just protect the site with obfuscation and deception.

The winter of 1890–1891 found an aging Jake Walz befriending Julia Elena Thomas, an old Mexican widow who owned a small bakery in Phoenix. There was talk of a romance, and most versions of the tale report that he told her the whole story of the mine. Late in the summer of 1891, he promised to take her there "in the spring."

But for the Dutchman, the spring would never come. He died at Julia Elena's home on October 25, 1891. They found a sack of rich gold ore beneath his deathbed.

Immediately after Jake Walz slipped out of Phoenix that last time, a number of people who knew the bits and pieces of the story rode into the hills to find the elusive mine. There are numerous stories of people who devoted decades of their lives to the unsuccessful search for the Dutchman's secret. Despite the fact that they are within 20 miles of the edge of the Phoenix metropolitan area, the Superstition Mountains are an almost hopeless labyrinth of dead end gullies and box canyons in which the entrance to a cave might easily be concealed against even the most exhaustive search.

Meanwhile, there were major gold discoveries just west of the Superstitions on the way to Phoenix. The strike that would become the Black Queen Mine occurred in November 1892, and within four years of its discovery in April 1893, the legendary Mammoth Mine gave up $3 million worth of ore.

Early in the twentieth century, an American veterinarian named Erwin Ruth helped smuggle a Mexican family into the United States, one step ahead of the Mexican Revolution. These people, as the story goes, were Peraltas related to the original partner of the two Jakes. For his trouble, they gave

Ruth a copy of the original map. Ruth gave it to his father, Adolph Ruth, a federal clerk in Washington, D.C.

In 1931, Adolph Ruth retired and went to Arizona to find the treasure. He hired a pair of cowboys to take him into the mountains. Several days later, Tex Barkley, the rancher for whom the cowboys worked, began to worry about the elderly city slicker out in the hills in the summer heat, so he went to look for him. Barkley found Ruth's camp, but not the man. A six-week search turned up nothing. In December, a skull was found in West Boulder Canyon, five miles from where he'd made camp. It had what looked like two bullet holes in it. It was identified as Ruth's.

Ruth's death attracted national media attention to the Lost Dutchman Mine, and led to numerous attempts to find it. Since that time, a continuous succession of treasure seekers have gone into the 159,700-acre Superstition Wilderness Area, which encompasses the mountains. Many have not come out alive, and some have not come out at all.

To paraphrase Adolph Bandelier, the expectations awakened and cherished in the beginning of the sixteenth century are still alive in the twenty-first century. Like those of the nineteenth century which Bandelier bemoaned, they have usually been met with failure—or worse. In January 2011, the *Arizona Republic* reported the discovery of the remains of three men who had gone in search of the Dutchman's secret during the summer of 2010. One of them had been reported missing while breyfogling in the Superstitions in 2009, but was later found alive.

He was not so lucky the second time around. The trio were presumed to have gotten lost in the maze of canyons which have frustrated so many for so long, and to have succumbed to the scorching heat after their water ran out. They will not be the last.

24

INTO THE VALLEY
OF FANCIFUL THOUGHT

> If the Adams gold is a negative, the illusion has at least
> been magnificently positive. The tradition is a part of
> the vast land of mountains and silences, of silent peo-
> ple and vistas, of hidden life and hidden death in
> which the Lost Adams Diggings still lie lost and still
> lure on men who dream.
>
> —J. Frank Dobie, *Apache Gold and Yaqui Silver* (1939)

ACROSS THE SOUTHWEST, 250 miles east of the
Superstition Mountains, lies the great inland sea of black lava
which the Spaniards called "El Malpaís," or "the badlands,"
and which geologists now call the Zuni-Bandera Volcanic
Field. This was the formation of razor-sharp rock, which had
forced the sixteenth-century conquistadors from Coronado to
Oñate to detour widely as they made their way between
Acoma and Cibola. As this writer has seen firsthand, it is a
rugged escarpment with narrow vents which can swallow an
unsuspecting hiker.

J. Frank Dobie eloquently describes: "Coves of boulder-
strewn earth and outjutting headlands of fire-blackened lava
make the outline of the area as irregular as the fjorded and
promontoried coast of Norway. . . . Toward the north of it
there are numerous extinct volcanoes, from which the seas of

fire once flowed. . . . In it are pits of glazed walls so steep that only a creature of four padded feet would attempt descent to their barren floors. Horrific chasms, made by the lava's contracting when it cooled, cut and crisscross the beds so that a person trying to progress in a certain direction will be twisted into labyrinthian isolation. Such places are impassable even for burros. . . . That lava will cut a pair of rawhide shoe soles to shreds in a day's walking."

However, El Malpaís is also in the region of the mountains which Antonio de Espejo insisted "give promise of mines and other riches." Indeed, one of the great mysteries of a fantastic world of gold found in the nineteenth century takes us to this place.

The "Lost Adams Diggings," was, and potentially still is, a placer so rich that gold could be picked up by the fistful. While such hyperbole is not uncommon, especially in tales originating in the Southwest, the Adams site is either more widely corroborated or it is a rumor more consistently and more widely spread than most fabrications. It is either the subject of the tallest of tales, or one of the richest unexploited placers in the world. It is named for Adams, not because he found it first or profited most, but because of those who were there, he was the one to survive and to tell the tale.

Before Adolph Ruth's body was found riddled by bullets, and the Lost Dutchman became internationally famous, the Lost Adams was the most talked-about golden hoard in the American Southwest.

Adams, who went by a single name, earned his living running freight wagons between Tucson and California. Born in Rochester, New York, in 1829, he came west in 1861 to get into the freight business, or out of fighting in the Civil War, or both.

The yarn begins in August 1864—the same year that Breyfogle entered the folklore—with Adams heading west out of Tucson with two wagons and a 12-horse team. Breaking camp one morning near Gila Bend, Arizona, he was attacked by a group of Apache set on stealing his horses. Grabbing his rifle, he fought back and managed to kill one of the intruders before the others stampeded his team. Having returned to his camp from rounding up his horses, he found his wagons burned, his provisions stolen, and the bankroll he kept under his wagon seat missing.

He headed north to an Akimel O'odham settlement on the Gila River, hoping to barter for food, and arrived to find the Indians entertaining a group of prospectors. There were several Americans and a German named Emil Schaeffer, who is the "Dutchman" of the Adams story, as Southwest treasure stories usually seem to have one.

Also in the group gathered around the campfire was a Mexican with a deformed ear, who was telling a story about how he and his brother were kidnapped as boys by the Apache, and about how they had grown up as Apache slaves. His brother had been killed in a fight with an Apache, and the young man had retaliated by killing the murderer. Knowing that a slave who killed a man had no future, he ran. He was on his way to Mexico, when he ran into the prospectors shortly before Adams rode up.

Having grown up among the Apache, he was unaware that the shiny metal called "gold" had great value as a trade item. When he learned this, he told the prospectors that he knew of a canyon where the ground was littered with this yellow stuff. Some of the pieces, he said, were the size of turkey eggs. He said that a man could pick up more in a day than his horse could carry.

This revelation naturally got the attention of the prospectors, who wanted to know where this canyon might be. The young fellow with the shriveled ear gestured to the northeast, indicating that the place was about "ten sleeps" in that direction. He added that the canyon was *bien escondido* (well hidden), and let that phrase hang for a moment.

He may have grown up far from conventional "civilization," but he knew intuitively how to bargain. He knew that they wanted the yellow stuff, and he knew that they needed him to get there. He said he would help them in exchange for a saddled horse, and a gun and ammunition. He gave them a promise of satisfaction guaranteed, and told them that if they weren't happy with the *bien escondido* canyon, they not only didn't have to pay him, they could shoot him.

Adams, who had arrived accidentally at a most auspicious moment, found himself an important part of the expedition because he still had most of his twelve-horse team, and the prospectors needed horses.

How far they traveled toward the northeast is not known. There is no journal, only a story retold many times. It may have been "ten sleeps," more or less, but it is hard to estimate how far they traveled between sleeps. As anyone who has traveled long distances in the West on horseback knows, the speed of a large group is governed by the slowest horse, usually the pack horse with supplies.

In the story, originally told by Adams himself, the Mexican pointed out mountains as landmarks. Many who have tried to reconstruct the route have suggested that the prominent El Morro mesa (now El Morro National Monument), about halfway between Acoma and the Zuni pueblos, may have been one such landmark—but this is just a guess. Also mentioned is a wagon trail leading to a fort, which is thought to be Fort Wingate, located about 12 miles east of Gallup, New Mexico.

El Malpaís figures prominently in the various retellings of the tale, and it encompasses a number of canyons which can be described as *bien escondido*. The miles of sandstone cliffs which surround the lava beds are also part of the narrative.

The penultimate "sleep" was at "the pumpkin patch," a place on a stream where Indians had once grown squash. Around noon the following day, the expedition halted as the Mexican disappeared behind a boulder that seemed like part of the wall. Here, a virtually invisible "hidden door" led to a narrow Z-shaped canyon. Nobody in the party had noticed the entrance until the man entered it. The portal was so naturally camouflaged that it was virtually invisible.

Secret doors have long been elements in folk legends from throughout the world. Rife with subconscious or deliberate symbolism, they have been used as metaphors for everything from rights of passage to mysteries that really should be kept secret. For those men who rode through that secret door in the New Mexico badlands on that fateful September day, nothing would ever be the same.

The trail beyond the secret opening was extremely narrow, twisting and turning as it led steeply downhill. At the bottom, there was a flat open area with a small stream running through it. In the gravel bars at the side of this small stream, the ground really was littered with gold nuggets—some the size of turkey eggs. Still more was found to be buried just under the surface. The more Adams and the prospectors dug, the more gold they found. It was unlike anything any of them had ever seen.

They paid the Mexican as promised, and even gave him a second horse as a bonus. He left immediately and was never seen again.

Except for Schaeffer, the Dutchman, who worked alone and distant from the others, the prospectors agreed to work cooperatively and pool their haul in a single cache. They constructed a log shack above an ancient Indian grinding rock and piled their gold in this place.

It was now late September. The days were growing shorter and the weather colder. Winter can come early in the mountains of New Mexico, and El Malpaís has an elevation above 8,000 feet. There were probably discussions of the amount of gold that could be taken out before the snows came.

There was also a certain amount of concern when the prospectors discovered that they were not alone. The men had made contact with a group of Chiricahua Apache, which included the well-known leader Kas-tziden, known to the white men as Chief Nana. They were camped above a falls in the stream in another part of the same canyon, which Kas-tziden called Sno-ta-hay. The Apache agreed that they would not bother the prospectors if they stayed below the falls and away from their camp.

Ten days after they began their excavations, food was running low, so the prospectors decided to send six men, including an individual named John Brewer, to find the wagon trail and go up to the trading post at Fort Wingate to get supplies, including tools. There was ample gold to make their purchases.

As this was being arranged, Schaeffer whispered to Adams that he feared the inevitability of trouble between the Apache and the prospectors. He had decided to ride out with Brewer—taking his own separate gold stash with him—and he would not be coming back.

Looking out from the sandstone cliffs west of Acoma toward the lava beds of El Malpaís, New Mexico.

Perhaps it was a matter of the grass being greener, but the notion developed among the prospectors that the biggest gold deposits lay upstream in the end of the canyon from which they had been banned by the edict of Kas-tziden.

As Frank Dobie, who researched the life and times of Adams in more detail than anyone, writes, they had become convinced that the "the ledge—the mother lode with nodules of ore 'as big as wild turkey eggs'—was located above the falls, and they wanted to work it. Yet Adams kept them in hand. He realized how serious a violation of the Apache instructions might be. One day a man who had gone after two strayed horses gave Adams an especially fine nugget to keep for himself. He said that in trailing the horses above the falls he picked it up. Adams reprimanded him and put the nugget under a chip at the base of a certain stump. Several stealthy pannings in the Indian territory followed. One man brought back a coffeepot half-full of gold."

At this point, the story of Adams became like the story of Adam in Genesis. Just as Adam and his companion were tempted to eat the forbidden fruit from the forbidden tree, Adams and his companions were being tempted to take forbidden gold from the forbidden end of Sno-ta-hay. Adam balked and urged her not to, but Eve ate. Adams balked, but despite his admonishments to the contrary, the men started sneaking into Kas-tziden's realm.

Though the potential danger from this situation seemed not to have bothered them, the men had other concerns. With a week having come and gone and no word from Brewer's supply party, the men grew nervous. Adams and another man named Davidson agreed to go out of the canyon and search for them. They saddled up and rode back out through the Z-shaped, zigzag canyon and passed through the "secret door."

The Dutchman's premonition had come true. To their horror, Adams and Davidson almost immediately stumbled over the bodies of five men amid scattered tools and broken flour sacks. The ambush had apparently taken place only an hour or so earlier. John Brewer's mortal remains, however, were not to be found.

Adams and Davidson placed the five bodies in rock crevices and covered them with pack-saddles to preserve them from coyotes until they could be properly buried, and hurried back to tell the others. When they reached the bottom of the canyon, they heard a commotion up ahead—there was the popping sound of gunshots and the screams of frightened, injured men coming from the direction of the log shack above the grinding rock.

Creeping to a vantage point from which they could observe what was going on, they hid themselves among the boulders and looked on aghast as their fellow treasure hunters were massacred and mutilated by a group of Apache. Adams and Davidson assumed correctly that the Apache would make a head count of the deceased prospectors and discover that two were missing, so they released their horses, hoping the animals would divert the Apache search parties long enough for them to make their escape.

When night had fallen, the two survivors sneaked into the camp to get a drink of water, and to grab some of their gold. The cabin, which had been burned by the Apache, still smoldered and was too hot to touch so they couldn't get to the gold in the grinding rock. They were afraid to splash water on it for fear of alerting the Apache, but Adams had hidden one or more large nuggets outside the cabin and was able to recover this. Unfortunately, however, they were able to find only two canteens in the dark. Filling those, they escaped from Sno-ta-hay Canyon before dawn.

Adams and Davidson headed southwest, back toward Arizona. Traveling only at night for fear of being seen by the Apache, they stumbled through El Malpaís, running scared and tearing their boots on the rocks and lava outcroppings. Days melted into a week as they fretted with the coming of the frost and the first light snows. They had guns and gold, but they had no soles left on their shoes and very little to eat. They survived on acorns and piñon nuts, but finally, when he could stand it no longer, Adams decided to shoot a rabbit.

The smoke from their first campfire since Sno-ta-hay curled into the sky, and they were spotted by a group of riders. Fortunately, these men turned out to be U.S. Cavalry troops who took them to a military post in Arizona.

Meanwhile, John Brewer had survived the ambush at the "secret door," and he too sneaked back into the canyon one night after the ambush. He saw Adams and Davidson creeping through the shadows and mistook them for Apache, but they did not see him. He crept out of the canyon before they did and was long gone when they emerged.

As Adams and Davidson had gone southwest, Brewer hiked eastward, hoping to reach one of the trading posts along the Rio Grande. After several days, he passed out from sunstroke and exhaustion, but was discovered by a group of people from one of the Rio Grande pueblos. After having recuperated, he joined a pack train headed for Santa Fe and eventually worked his way back to Missouri over the Santa Fe Trail. For years he thought he was the only survivor.

There are various stories about what happened next to Adams. One tells of him showing up in Tucson at some point with $22,000 in gold nuggets. Another has him still at a U.S. Army post when he killed an Apache whom he recognized as being part of Kas-tziden's group in the canyon. He was arrested for murder, but escaped, and eventually settled down in southern California.

Davidson was not so lucky. Adams was only thirty-five, but Davidson was a somewhat older man, and he never really recovered from his ordeal in the desert. The legend tells that he died soon after, without ever having revealed the location of the diggings. Of the survivors, Schaeffer, who had ridden out with Brewer, left the United States vowing not to return, and he kept his promise. John Brewer would not see New Mexico again for a quarter of a century, and being wanted by the U.S. Army, Adams was in no hurry to go back in search of the gold.

Over time, Adams's tongue gradually loosened—aided perhaps by the occasional nip of brown goods—and he began relating tales of gold, guns, and human bones. Gradually the *"bien escondido"* canyon of Sno-ta-hay became known as the Lost Adams Diggings.

In 1874 an old Canadian mariner known as Captain C. A. Shaw paid Adams $500 to stop talking and start walking. The captain had amassed a nest egg which he planned to invest in a treasure hunt that he was betting would net him enough to retire in luxury to Guam, an island he had visited during his years at sea, and which was the end of his rainbow.

Adams took Shaw and a party of sixteen to Arizona, where he attempted to reconstruct the original trip from the Akimel O'odham village on the Gila River. They rode northwest across the desert, with Adams trying to recall landmarks from a decade before.

However, in 1874, relations between the Apache and the whites had become even more violent than in the 1860s, and the threat of hostile action by the Apache made Adams nervous. He led Shaw and his party aimlessly through the wilderness of dusty hillsides and pine forests, scratching his beard and shaking his head with a sense of confusion about him. Finally, he simply gave up. As Dobie explains: "The men with him were exasperated at his failure to remember landmarks. On subsequent hunts, as will be seen, similar exasperation almost cost Adams his life. He would appear to remember, and then waver. His explanation to critics was boiled down into five words—words that became a saying over the Southwest: 'The Apaches made me forget.'"

The specter of Kas-tziden, his firm warning, and the massacre still cast a long and distinct shadow across the hopes and dreams of the aging prospector. Indeed, one version of the story tells that while on this expedition, Adams chanced to come face to face with Kas-tziden at a trading post near the San Carlos Reservation. Maybe it was Kas-tziden's expression, or the hard, cold glint in his eye that froze Adams's spine and make him eventually admit that "the Apaches made me forget."

When Adams forgot, most of those in the expedition turned back to California, but Captain Shaw stayed on in New Mexico. He visited Fort Wingate and was able to confirm that in 1864, six men had in fact come into the fort's trading post to buy—using gold nuggets—supplies for a small placer mining activity they claimed was in El Malpaís. Shaw also apparently met a clerk at a trading post on the Warm Springs Agency who had discussed gold with Kas-tziden and who had written the word "Sno-ta-hay" in his ledger.

Convinced of the veracity of Adams's story, Shaw became like a man possessed. The Lost Adams Diggings became his personal obsession. He never again laid eyes on the ocean, much less his beloved Guam. Year after year, until his death in 1917, Shaw rode the hills and canyons of western New Mexico, following leads and extrapolating what he could from every shred of evidence. Shaw probably never found the Lost Adams Diggings, but what he did find helped to corroborate Adams's tale and to add fuel and substance to the legend.

Adams himself spent a good deal of time in New Mexico during his later years, but more of it in the role of the grizzled prospector talking about the diggings than looking for them. In September 1886, he had a heart attack while on a hunting trip and died shortly after he got home to Los Angeles.

After Adams's death, the legend took on a life of its own. Just before he died in El Paso in about 1927, a businessman named John F. Dowling, who had been in the mining industry for many years, claimed that he had been in Sno-ta-hay Canyon in 1881. He had met the U.S. Army post surgeon who cared for Adams back in 1864, and who had seen Adams's gold nuggets with his own eyes. The doctor returned in later years, hired Dowling to help him find the canyon, but eventually gave up. However, Dowling and another man later did find it. Dowling vowed to return, but he left the country for work, later went blind, and never did go back. In turn, his story became part of the growing legend.

In the 1920s, at about the same time that blind John Dowling was dreaming his last dreams of Lost Adams gold, stories were going around southern New Mexico about an old cowboy named Aamon Tenney who had met John Brewer in 1888. He had come back to Arizona unaware that Adams had spun out the legend in those same parts for a dozen years before he took his last ride home in 1886.

Just a boy at the time, Tenney had tagged along with Brewer on some of his rides in search of lost wagon tracks, a pumpkin patch, and a secret door. The old man filled the kid's head with the same stories that had haunted his own for a quarter century. He could remember details like the feel of the egg-sized nuggets in the palm of his hand and the terror of watching men hacked to death—that made the story exciting for a boy and memorable for an old prospector—but he could not remember details like the shape of the rock that hid the secret door.

Brewer died disappointed and Aamon Tenney grew up and grew old with his own unique perspective on the Lost Adams legend—which he was only too glad to pass down to later generations of impressionable youngsters.

Another curious character who is part of the Adams lore was a devotee of Indian herbology named Doc Young. Two generations before the peyote-eating Carlos Castaneda excited impressionable youngsters in the 1960s with his quasi-anthropological series of best-sellers about hallucinogenic plants, mystic superpowers, and the mythical "Don Juan Matus," Doc Young claimed to have tasted herbs that made him ageless, psychic, and able to fly with eagles.

Among the stories told by Doc Young was that he had traveled to Heidelberg in 1900, where he tracked down the last survivor of the original expedition, Emil Schaeffer. The elderly "Dutchman" reportedly confirmed the story of the canyon and the nuggets, and told how he had managed to get to Hamburg with $10,000 worth of gold.

Doc Young also claimed to have met old Captain Shaw and that he saved the old sailor's life. Throughout the 1920s and the 1930s, he regularly claimed to know the exact location of the Lost Adams Diggings, and that he would be going there "next summer." Like both Adams and Shaw, the ninety-two-year-old doctor ran out of next summers, and long before he passed through the secret door.

Among the most intriguing characters in the folklore of treasure legends are the people who have no need for gold. The Muisca chief encrusted with gold dust was one. James B. Gray was another.

In 1937, when he was researching the location of the Adams Diggings, J. Frank Dobie chanced to meet a man in Albuquerque who knew where they were, but didn't care. Gray was a cowboy turned photographer who had worked on the 3H Ranch in Arizona and had ridden with Teddy Roosevelt's Rough Riders in Cuba. He had worked in North Africa and the Middle East. He fought as a soldier of fortune in China and with the French Army during World War I. Looking for lost mines had apparently once been a hobby of his, and he said he discovered the Lost Adams Diggings in the 1880s. He had almost been killed by the Apache himself

in the process. He found it, but by 1937 when he met Dobie, he had no interest in it because, being a Rosicrucian, he had "sworn off money."

Dobie also speaks of crossing paths with Nat Straw, the legendary mountain man, who spent most of his eighty-five years as a trapper and grizzly hunter in the Mogollon Mountains. Before Straw passed away in 1941, Dobie asked him about the Adams Diggings, but he declined comment. "He never told me that he went to live with the Navajos and married one of their women for the express purpose of learning the tribal secret of the Adams gold," Dobie writes. "This I heard elsewhere. Though he told me a lot he learned from the Navajos, he swore he had never looked for the Adams Diggings."

The Adams Diggings are a perfect allegory for the lasting legacy of the whole notion of mankind's obsession with cities of gold and the stuff from which they are made. As Dobie points out, it is the *tradition*, not the gold, which still lures on those who dream. The last words belong to Nat Straw, by way of Dobie's final thoughts on the man:

> One time while he was prospecting—just prospecting in general, he said—high up in the Mogollons among the mountain tops, he came upon a giant aspen tree. Its smooth whitish bark seemed to ask for carving. He opened his pocket knife and, reaching up above his head, carved a human hand pointing skyward. Then under the hand he engraved these lines:
>
> *The Adams Diggings is a shadowy naught,*
> *and they lie in the valley of fanciful thought.*

THE GREATEST
ARCHAEOLOGICAL
DISCOVERY OF THE AGE

The beauty of the white granite of this structure sur-
passed in attractiveness the best Inca walls in Cusco
which had caused visitors to marvel for four centuries.
It seemed like an unbelievable dream. Dimly, I began
to realize that this wall and its adjoining semicircular
temple over the cave were as fine as the finest stone-
work in the world. It fairly took my breath away.
What could this place be? Why had no one given us
any idea of it?

—Hiram Bingham, on his first look at Machu Picchu
(July 24, 1911)

IF THE SIXTEENTH CENTURY had been the century of
exploration in the service of exploitation, the nineteenth century, the one which began with Alexander von Humboldt,
was the century of exploration in the service of science. The
new word for "conquistador" was "archaeologist."

Though the concept had been around for a very long time,
archaeology as we understand it today was born in the nineteenth century—though its early practitioners in those years

bore a closer resemblance to sixteenth-century chroniclers such as Pedro de Castañeda, than to twenty-first-century tenured professors and graduate students.

Even as the lone prospectors of the nineteenth century pursued the ghosts and dreams of the Spanish conquistadors across the American Southwest on their own whim, gentlemen explorers were fanning out across the globe under the auspices of such philanthropically endowed and scientifically minded institutions as the Royal Geographical Society in London and the American Museum of Natural History.

Founded in 1830 for "the advancement of geographical sciences," the Royal Geographical Society was among those which sponsored expeditions to the remote corners of the world from which the phrase *terra incognita* had yet to be retired. The society sent explorers into distant places ranging from "Darkest Africa" to the poles. The list of people who were supported or sponsored by the society was a who's who of nineteenth- and early twentieth-century exploration that includes Richard Francis Burton, Charles Darwin, David Livingstone, Robert Falcon Scott, Henry Morton Stanley, and Ernest Shackleton.

Across the ocean, the American Museum of Natural History in New York sponsored or lent its scientific credence to numerous worldwide expeditions between the 1880s and the 1930s. Also in the United States, Charles Eliot Norton founded the Archaeological Institute of America to explore and preserve archaeological sites.

Meanwhile, the administration of President Millard Fillmore had taken an official interest in the mysteries of the *terra incognita* of a continent closer to home. In 1851, the Navy Department, under the scientific authority of the Naval Observatory, ordered Lieutenant Lardner Gibbon and Lieutenant William Lewis Herndon of the USS *Vandalia* on a mission to explore the rivers of the upper Amazon. They traveled as far upstream as the mouth of the Ucayali. Their report to President Fillmore, dated February 9, 1853, mentions both Paititi and El Dorado by name, though the report carries no mention of an effort by the U.S. Navy to seek out these places.

A generation later, an act of the U.S, Congress in 1879 formed the Bureau of American Ethnology (now part of the

Department of Anthropology within the Smithsonian's National Museum of Natural History). The bureau's founding director, John Wesley Powell, was a quintessential nineteenth-century conquistador of science. Though he had lost most of his right arm in the Civil War, Powell was a tireless explorer who led a series of geographical and ethnographic expeditions into corners of the American West which were still unexplored in the mid-nineteenth century. The 1869 Powell Geographic Expedition, a milestone in the exploration of the West in the name of science, marked the first time that non-Indians had floated down the Colorado through the Grand Canyon.

During the latter decades of the nineteenth century, thanks to entities such as the American Museum of Natural History, the great "lost cities" of the American Southwest— the Anasazi pueblos at Mesa Verde and Chaco Canyon—were first systematically studied by archaeologists, and first brought to the attention of the outside world.

Even President Theodore Roosevelt, an archetype of the adventurous American, joined the list of intrepid adventure travelers of the age, making his own scientific trip to the Amazon in 1913–1914 with the support of the Museum of Natural History.

It was about the science, they insisted, but this was still an era when explorers were adventurers first and scientists second. Indeed, many, if not most of the great explorers of this era (Darwin excepted) were as thin on their academic resume as they were long on ambition, fortitude, and practical skills.

It was about the science, they insisted, but bubbling just beneath the austere, academic façade was a boiling soup of adrenaline and testosterone, stirred by a little boy's yearning for adventure and a madman's obsession with knowing the unknown. These were still the days when venturing into an unsurveyed wilderness was a very dangerous thing to do. As we know, these explorers were cut from the same hardy cloth and driven by the same eagerness as Coronado or Raleigh, and they suffered and triumphed in the same punishing environments as their sixteenth-century forebears.

A man whose name appears frequently on the title pages of numerous publications of the Bureau of Ethnology, and the

Museum of Natural History, as well as the American Institute of Archaeology, is Adolph Francis Alphonse Bandelier. Quoted widely in this book, he was one of the first men to combine an academic study of lost cities—from El Dorado to Cibola—with serious dirt-under-the-nails fieldwork. Born in Switzerland, he immigrated to the United States as a young man, and cut his teeth in his ultimate career under the mentorship of anthropologist Lewis Henry Morgan. He began his fieldwork in the American Southwest, where he became a leading expert on the pre-Columbian civilizations in the area. One of the ancient Anasazi sites in New Mexico that he explored is now a national monument named for him. In 1892, Bandelier headed south to the Andes, where he studied ancient Inca sites for the American Museum of Natural History, and became one of the first to scientifically investigate the legend of El Dorado.

At the same time this new generation of explorers was taking to the field, there was a parallel effort to find, dust off, and translate the narratives of conquistadors and explorers which lay forgotten in darkness for centuries.

In the United States, men such as Frederick Hodge and George Parker Winship of the Bureau of Ethnology, sought out, translated, edited, and published many original narratives of early American history, including those of Cabeza de Vaca and Francisco de Coronado. In London, across town from the Royal Geographical Society, another organization was born in the fertile renaissance of interest in the world's *terra incognita*. Founded in 1846, the Hakluyt Society took its name from Richard Hakluyt, a contemporary of Sir Walter Raleigh who had been a collector of sixteenth- and seventeenth-century accounts of journeys and expeditions of that era. The Hakluyt Society, which, like the RGS, is still going strong in the twenty-first century, translated and published the true and the alleged-to-be-true tales that had long before been pigeonholed in the depths of places such as the Archivo de Indias in Seville.

Just as the Royal Geographical Society and the American Institute of Archaeology provided the means by which fieldwork would be possible, the publication of long-lost accounts inspired further quests for long-lost cities—with and without lost gold. In that sense, they served the same function as the yarns told by the proverbial old prospector to inspire imaginations to believe that great things lay just beyond the horizon.

In the realm of inspiring imaginations, however, nothing served this cause better than the print media, which by the late nineteenth century was becoming increasingly important in crafting the public mood. Newspapers turned the explorers into pop culture icons, just as the ventures of the explorers sold newspapers.

At the same time that they were serving science and their own personal urge to attack the unknown, this new generation of explorers was also serving the growing lust of their public for exciting newspaper accounts like those in the popular *Illustrated London News*. The media followed, and even obsessed about the intrepid adventurers. It is well known in popular memory that when Stanley undertook his famous expedition in search of Livingstone in Africa, he did so as a journalist for the *New York Herald*.

When the National Geographic Society, America's answer to the royal society, was formed in Washington in 1888, its journal, *National Geographic*, began as a means of bringing news of the society's expeditions to the membership, but soon it evolved into one of the most popular and most famous travel magazines in the world. Just as the "reality television" of the twenty-first century celebrates human endeavors in extreme climates and extreme geographic locations, so too did the news media of the nineteenth and early twentieth centuries.

Lust for gold was replaced by lust for something which money often cannot buy—media attention.

On the morning of June 15, 1913, people opened the *New York Times* to the headline:

LOST CITY IN THE CLOUDS FOUND AFTER CENTURIES Prof. Hiram Bingham of Yale Makes the Greatest Archaeological Discovery of the Age by Locating and Excavating Ruins of Machu Picchu on a Peak of the Andes in Peru

For all those who were under the misapprehension that lost cities were illusions fabricated from mist and shadow, Machu

Picchu was a wake-up call. For all those who believed that lost cities still awaited discovery in the valley just beyond the horizon, Machu Picchu was proof of life in the oft-told, oft-lampooned legends.

Hiram Bingham III was an archaeologist-adventurer who combined the eager interest in fieldwork of a Bandelier with the heavily academic background that men such as Bandelier lacked. Born in Hawaii when it was still an independent kingdom, he was the son of a Protestant missionary and earned degrees from both Yale and the University of California, as well as a Ph.D. in history from Harvard. In 1908, three years out of Harvard, Bingham took a side trip to Peru while attending a conference in Chile, and was bitten by the bug of interest in the mysterious lost cities of the Inca. In 1911, he returned as director of a Yale University scientific expedition. Many people have suggested, though Steven Spielberg declines to confirm it, that Bingham, as an academic archaeologist equally at home in the field, is one of the prototypes for the character of Indiana Jones.

Conquistadors had spent a century searching for El Dorado, Manoa, and Paititi. The eight years that José de Carvalho e Cunha had spent thrashing about in the Bahia rain forest looking for a lost city had killed him. Hiram Bingham found a lost city he did not know existed, and he did it in less than a day.

As Bingham was asking around about Inca ruins in the highlands northwest of Cusco, he met a local boy named Melchor Arteaga. He spoke only Quechua, but told Bingham through a translator that he knew of such a place. For a Peruvian silver dollar, he agreed to take Bingham there. How many times, in the history of the quest for lost cities in the Andes, had someone promised such a thing to a gullible outsider?

They started out at midmorning, Bingham, Arteaga, and the translator, a police sergeant named Carrasco. The going was difficult. As Bingham relates: "For an hour and twenty minutes we had a hard climb. A good part of the distance we went on all fours, sometimes holding on by our fingernails. Here and there, a primitive ladder made from the roughly notched trunk of a small tree was placed in such a way as to help one over what might otherwise have proved to be an impassable cliff. . . . In another place the slope was covered with slippery grass where it was hard to find either hand-holds or footholds. Arteaga groaned and said that there were lots of snakes here. . . . There were no ruins or *andenes* [paved walkways] of any kind in sight."

Hiram Bingham III. (*Bill Yenne*)

At the top of the cliff, they were rewarded with spectacular views of valleys far below, and cursed by dense underbrush that made the progress slow and laborious. However, shortly after noon, according to Bingham:

> Suddenly without any warning, under a huge over-hanging ledge the boy showed me a cave beautifully lined with the finest cut stone. It had evidently been a Royal Mausoleum. On top of this particular ledge was a semi-circular building whose outer wall, gently slop-ing and slightly curved bore a striking resemblance to the famous Temple of the Sun in Cusco. This might also be a Temple of the Sun. It followed the natural curvature of the rock and was keyed to it by one of the finest examples of masonry I had ever seen. Furthermore it was tied into another beautiful wall, made of very carefully matched ashlars of pure white granite, especially selected for its fine grain. Clearly, it was the work of a master artist. . . . The flowing lines, the symmetrical arrangement of the ashlars, and the gradual gradation of the courses, combined to produce a wonderful effect, softer and more pleasing than that of the marble temples of the Old World.

Taking another step forward, Bingham beheld the great, and now iconic, panorama which "seemed like an unbelievable dream" and which took his breath away.

Hiram Bingham was not the first outsider to gaze upon this place called Machu Picchu, which means "Old

Mountain" in Quechua. For at least half a century, prospectors and missionaries had been passing this way, but their stories were not widely told, and when they were, they were regarded merely as the sorts of shadowy "lost city" stories that had been a staple in the cantinas of South America since the Pizarro brothers first perked up their ears.

What is especially amazing, until one ponders the difficulty of the climb, is why the Pizarros and their successors never found Machu Picchu in the sixteenth century. "Why," Bingham asks, "had no one given us any idea of it?"

Unlike the stories of lost cities seen in the mist only one time by a lone, half-crazed explorer, Machu Picchu would never be lost again. Bingham returned in 1912 and 1915, now with armies of scientists and the backing of both Yale and the National Geographic Society. The latter devoted the entire April 1913 issue of their yellow-bordered magazine to the site. With this, the world took notice and Machu Picchu was on its way to becoming the global icon and tourism magnet that it is today.

Bingham himself went on to a career in politics. He was elected lieutenant governor of Connecticut in 1922, and governor in 1924. However, Bingham would end up serving as governor for just a day before going to the U.S. Senate to serve out the term of Frank Bosworth Brandegee, who had committed suicide. In turn he was re-elected to a six-year term in his own right in 1926. By now, he had hung up his climbing boots for more urbane footwear.

As for the growing popularity of Machu Picchu as an object of curiosity, the rest, as they say, is history. However, what of Machu Picchu in pre-Columbian times, before the conquistadors and the university-endowed explorers? Through the years, there have been various theories about what Machu Picchu had been in its glory days.

Hiram Bingham believed that it was, as Paititi was supposed to be, "selected perhaps a thousand years ago as the safest place of refuge for the last remnants of the old regime, becoming the capital of a new kingdom, giving birth to the most remarkable family which South America has ever seen, partially abandoned when Cusco once more flashed into glory as the capital of the Inca Empire, it was again sought out in

Machu Picchu photographed soon after Hiram Bingham had announced the location of a lost city of the Incas. Views of the ruins from this vantage would soon become among the most recognizable achaeological images in the world.

time of trouble when another foreign invader [Pizarro] arrived—this time from the north—with his burning desire to extinguish all vestiges of the ancient religion."

Recently, it has been theorized that it was used as a retreat by the emperor Pachacuti, who ruled until 1472, two decades before Columbus. Most archaeologists agree that it was abandoned by the latter part of the sixteenth century, though nobody is sure exactly why, nor how, an inhabited Machu Picchu could have coexisted with the Spanish occupation for many decades without them knowing about it.

Bingham's own final theory, more romantic than one might expect from a U.S. senator, was that during the early sixteenth century, Machu Picchu was used as a secret sanctuary for an order of priestesses, analogous to the Vestal Virgins of ancient Rome, who were known as the "Chosen Women of the Sun."

The academically trained son of a missionary speculates that after the Spaniards captured Cusco, Machu Picchu became "The home and refuge of those Chosen Women whose institution formed one of the most interesting features of the most humane religion of aboriginal America. Here, concealed in a canyon of remarkable grandeur, protected by nature and by the hand of man, the 'Virgins of the Sun,' one by one passed away on this beautiful mountain top and left no descendants willing to reveal the importance or explain the significance of the ruins which crown the beetling precipices of Machu Picchu."

26

THE MAN
WHO FOUND THE
LOST CITY OF FX11

Whether we get through, and emerge again, or leave
our bones to rot in there, one thing's certain. The
answer to the enigma of Ancient South America—and
perhaps of the prehistoric world—may be found when
those old cities are located and opened up to scientific
research. That the cities exist, I know.
—Percival Harrison Fawcett to his son Brian, 1925,
from *Lost Trails, Lost Cities*, Brian's collection of his
father's letters (1953)

A VICTORIAN GENTLEMAN turned grizzled prospector sat
at a table inside the palatial Biblioteca Nacional in Rio de
Janeiro looking at the same document which had fired the
imagination of Manuel Ferreira Lagos and José de Carvalho e
Cunha a century earlier. In this crumbling, yellowed document dated 1753, he studied strange and cryptic hieroglyphs
and read of a lost city with broad streets and grand plazas. He
read tantalizing suggestions of great wealth.

A long slumbering document had come to life once again
after all those years, and having been touched, it once again
yielded up a genie who whispered of wonderful things.

Percy Fawcett was on the cusp of a life-changing moment which would make him a celebrity known for elusive lost city quests, and drive him to the edge of a madness so many had suffered in the jungles of South America.

He was the antithesis of Hiram Bingham, who had usually kept at least one foot firmly planted in the reality of the twentieth century. Fawcett was a man of this new era, and a world very unlike the era of Pizarro, Coronado, and Raleigh, yet deep inside his being, he was much more like them than he was like Bingham.

Having served in the British Army in colonial Ceylon (now Sri Lanka) Fawcett had cut his teeth on solo adventuring as a British spy in Morocco in 1901. In that same year, he followed in his father's footsteps to become a member of the Royal Geographical Society. Five years later, Fawcett, now approaching forty, was dispatched on his first expedition to South America by that society. The purpose was to survey indistinct and contested borders in the area where Bolivia, Brazil, and Peru meet. The purpose behind the purpose was that the region was rich in rubber trees. At the dawn of the twentieth century, with the Industrial Revolution entering its mechanized stage, rubber was the equivalent to the spices sought in distant lands by the Europeans at the dawn of the sixteenth century. In 1906, there was a lot of money in rubber.

As Fawcett notes, "Again and again I was asked—even begged—to map private rubber concessions for staggering fees, and had I nothing else to do I might have done it. I was once offered the equivalent of [half a million in today's dollars] for a survey that would have taken about three weeks to complete. A map of a concession was always required before it became legally valid. The regular surveyors were far too scared of diseases and savages to risk their lives in these regions, even though they could have made their fortunes in very little time."

Heading into the jungle from La Paz and the Andean foothills, Fawcett and his colleague Arthur Chivers were stunned by the steamy jungle which had greeted unsuspecting Europeans since Gonzalo Pizarro and Francisco Orellana crossed the mountains in search of El Dorado in 1541.

They encountered many of the same terrors as their predecessors. Of traveling the Río Abuna, Fawcett writes of being admonished by a local man that "you'd better look out for yourselves on the Abuna. . . . The fever there will kill you—and if you escape that, there are the [Pacahuara people]. They come out on the banks and make a boat run the gauntlet of poisoned arrows. . . . Not so long ago 48 men went up the Río Negro—that's an effluent of the Abuna—in search of rubber. Only 18 came out, and one of them was stark, staring mad from the experience!"

After six months of being driven crazy by the bugs, snakes, and fear of cannibals, Fawcett was ready to give up, but he pondered the question and deliberately did not. He had succumbed to an obsession, addicted now to the adrenaline rush of cheating death in a strange and fascinating land.

He confides in his journal that "at least once in every man's lifetime death looks him straight in the eyes and passes on. In forest travel it is never far off. It shows itself in many aspects, most of them horrible, but some apparently so innocuous that they scarcely win attention, though none the less deadly for that. Time and time again the concatenation of events leads up to the very edge of disaster, and halts there."

Fawcett had embraced his counterintuitive fixation with the "green hell" which would rule his actions for the rest of his life. He was driven by the same excitement of being in regions unexplored by Europeans that had fired the imaginations of the previous Royal Geographical Society explorers. It may have been scientific when you were studying maps and charts back in London, but the first time you closed your eyes in the jungle, and contemplated the sounds, the smells, and the true hazards of the place, you either succumbed to the fear or you embraced it. Fawcett embraced it.

Most outsiders who entered the Amazon basin and came back to tell the story never tried again. Theodore Roosevelt entered his venture with his typical enthusiasm, but he suffered an infected leg wound on the ominously named Río da Duvida (River of Doubt) and nearly died. Shaken by his experience, he never returned. As many other explorers came, looked, saw enough, and turned back, Fawcett went back again and again, as if he could not see enough. After his first visit Fawcett made five further expeditions into these same jungles between 1908 and the 1914, the year that World War I began.

Fawcett's accounts of his travels are punctuated with many of the elements that feature prominently in all *relacións* of travels in the South American jungles going back to the conquistadors. There is the broadness of the rivers, the harshness of the climate, the fear of cannibals, the very large reptiles, and of course, the horribly large number of predatory insects. Remarkably, his journal also records something to which Sir Walter Raleigh had devoted a lengthy passage in his own account. That is, one specific, stunningly beautiful woman.

While it is not unusual for men traveling in distant places without their significant other (both Raleigh and Fawcett were married) to notice the ladies they might encounter, it is noteworthy that both men would fixate at length on one woman. Of a particular chief's wife, Raleigh had written that "in all my life, I have seldom seen a better favored woman."

Fawcett went even further, calling his focus "the most beautiful woman I have ever seen." He added that she possessed "long silky black hair, perfect features, and the most glorious figure. Her large black eyes alone would have roused a saint, let alone an inflammable Latin of the tropic wilderness. I was told that no less than eight men had been killed fighting for her, and that she had knifed one or two herself. She was a she-devil, the living prototype of the 'jungle girl' of novel and screen, and dangerous to look at in more ways than one."

Perhaps in both cases, the woman in question was a sort of psychological allegory for the singular treasure the man sought, a treasure beyond all others, but a treasure which was surrounded by seen and unseen peril, and which he knew deep inside was unobtainable.

Percy Fawcett became well-known for his travels into the unknown, one of the characters the pictorial press came to love. In fact, he is said to have been the prototype for the fictitious Professor George Edward Challenger in Sir Arthur Conan Doyle's 1912 novel *The Lost World*, a story of the discovery of a place in the Amazon jungle so remote that dinosaurs still thrived. Indeed, Doyle used Fawcett's Amazon field notes as a reference for his book. Fawcett may also have been another of the prototypes for Indiana Jones.

Along the way, Fawcett's imagination, his observations, and the stories he heard from the old prospectors convinced him—or seduced him— into the belief that there had once been a major civilization, a great city, in this vast rain forest. As with El Dorado, Manoa, and all the other legendary cities of this mysterious land, it lay unseen by European eyes. A scientific man raised in the no-nonsense world of Victorian England, Fawcett had long since assured himself that

Percival Harrison Fawcett. (*Bill Yenne*)

El Dorado was a mere allegory, and that lost cities should not be defined—as Machu Picchu certainly was not—solely as cities of gold.

As his lost city had no name in folklore, and it should not in his mind be called by one of the usual names, he stated "I call it 'Z' for the sake of convenience."

How Fawcett came to be convinced that such a place existed was probably the cumulation of several factors. Naturally, the lost city stories circulate in cantinas across the continent. He was also aware that another, earlier Royal Geographical Society member, Richard Burton, had been there in the late 1860s and had described his adventures in his 1869 book *Explorations of The Highlands of Brazil*. Then too, Fawcett had learned of that certain scrap of paper in Rio de Janeiro.

If there was one moment that altered the course of the rest of Fawcett's life, it was holding the ancient document at the Biblioteca Nacional.

In his recent book, *The Lost City of Z*, David Grann tells the story of Fawcett's quest, beginning his own field survey of the Fawcett legend in the place where Fawcett became convinced of the reality of this place he named Z. Grann went to the Biblioteca and viewed the manuscript for himself. He marveled at the hieroglyphs, realizing that he had already seen them—in Fawcett's own journals. Like the original author in 1753, Fawcett had been mesmerized by the strange alphabet.

Who was the man who wrote this enticing memo, and first transcribed these symbols? As noted in a previous chapter, Hermann Kruse decided in 1940 that the author was the *bandeirante* (soldier of fortune) João da Silva Guimarães. In his account, Fawcett did not mention Kruse or Guimarães, but called the man Francisco Raposo, adding cryptically, "I must identify him by some name." Raposo is a common Brazilian surname with the double meaning of "Fox," as in "cunning-like-a." Grann mentions neither name, but notes the word *bandeirante*, and reports that the name on the manuscript is illegible. However, all parties agree that most of the document has been as readable since Fawcett's time as it was when Manuel Ferreira Lagos first saw it in 1839.

The city called Z, though given a name that was not its own, was not a metaphor—but it was still theoretical. As a scientific man, Fawcett considered it his job to prove the theory. As a man obsessed he never gave a second thought to disproving the theory.

The task was a daunting one. For the public, El Dorado had been a metaphor since before Voltaire's time. For the archaeological and anthropological community, El Dorado was a ridiculous fantasy. No civilization of any size or sophistication, they asserted, had ever existed, nor could it exist in the interior of the Amazon watershed. The people who lived here were hunters and gatherers of the most primitive kind, and they had always been hunters and gatherers of the most primitive kind. The soil could not, they were convinced, support agriculture, and without agriculture, there could be no great civilization.

What about the other old manuscripts that had been entering the light of day thanks to the Hakluyt Society and other like-minded nineteenth-century translators? Writers from Gaspar de Carvajal (who chronicled the Pizarro-Orellana *entrada*) to Sir Walter Raleigh had mentioned seeing huge numbers of people and deliberately planted orchards. These observers, the modern scientists insisted, were simply mistaken.

This notion that no city could ever have existed in the Amazon basin was not only the prevailing theory held from the nineteenth century though most of the 1920s, it was unquestioned dogma. For Percy Fawcett, getting people to take Z seriously was like paddling upstream on the Amazon itself.

After the discovery of Machu Picchu, the twentieth-century scientific community couldn't categorically say that there were no more lost cities awaiting detection in South America, but they did insist that these could not be found in the Amazon basin. Anyone who, like Fawcett, asserted otherwise was, in a word, an "amateur."

Fawcett had come out of the jungle after the summer of 1914 planning to get resupplied and go back as soon as possible. Instead, he discovered that while he was away, he had missed the biggest global crisis of his age, and this crisis had propelled his nation and the world into World War I. Though well over conscription age, Fawcett nevertheless felt honor-bound to reenlist in the British Army and ended up leading an artillery brigade on the front. The war, which most people thought would be over in months if not weeks, lasted more than four years. It cost Britain nearly a million lives and took a terrible emotional toll on the lives of the Britons who survived—Fawcett included. The major expedition to locate Z wound up being postponed for more than a decade.

In the meantime, Fawcett made a three-month trip into the Brazilian interior in 1920–1921, approaching from the Atlantic rather than from the Andes as he had previously. His purpose, as he describes it, was to "penetrate the veil of the primeval—to eliminate false clues and make sure of the right route." During his prewar expeditions, Fawcett had explored the headwaters of the Amazon in northern Bolivia, as well as the area around the river that forms the border between Bolivia and Brazil—which is known as Río Iténez to Bolivians and Río Guaporé to Brazilians. After surveying the latter, he decided that Z was located about 600 miles northeast of this area, and west of the Bahia jungles where João da Silva Guimarães claimed to have found his abandoned metropolis.

Fawcett placed Z in the headwaters of the Xingu River, an Amazon tributary, and the Araguaia River, the primary tributary of the Río Tocantins, which in turn runs into the Atlantic in parallel with the Amazon. Z was roughly in the geographic center of Brazil, in the region called Mato Grosso (Thick Woods), which includes the Brazilian state of the same name. The area was largely unexplored by people of European descent well into the twentieth century, and much of it remains so in the twenty-first. "There are," Fawcett wrote, "curious things to be found between the Xingu and the Araguaia."

His point of departure into the jungle this time was the exact center of the continent at the city of Cuiabá, the capital city of Mato Grosso. As Fawcett observes in his account, Cuiabá was once the center of a gold mining boom, and after a heavy rain, you could still pick up nuggets in the town's plaza, washed downstream from some unseen mother lode.

It was here that Fawcett began crossing paths with those staples of our narrative, the wily old prospectors. There was one man—"just call me Felipe"—who knew the stories of the lost city intimately, and who had agreed to guide Fawcett in 1921. There were also the mysterious Indians with wonderful tales of a city whose houses were perpetually illuminated with phosphorescent "stars," and of other "fair complexioned Indians with red hair," who lived in Cidade Encantada (Magic City) in the Gongogi basin which vanished as you reached it. Fawcett also mentions that the Botocudo people "preserve a legend of the Aldeia de Fogo—the Fire City—so called because its houses are roofed with gold."

Fawcett came away in 1921 almost mesmerized with the possibilities. Having penetrated the veil of the primeval, he muses that he had "found enough to make it imperative to go again. . . . I have probed from three sides for the surest way in; I have seen enough to make any risk worth while in order to see more, and our story when we return from the next expedition may thrill the world!"

This time, Fawcett came home to find, not a war, but the opposite. The "Roaring Twenties" were at full volume, and a hunger for excitement in the air. It was the Jazz Age, and the era of moving pictures, dance crazes, speakeasies, and Great

Gatsbys. Aviation was new, and the tabloids overflowed with the thrilling exploits of daring airmen—and daring air-women. Continents were crossed, and so too the oceans and the poles. In 1924, two U.S. Army biplanes circumnavigated the globe, and the race was on for the first solo nonstop flight across the Atlantic, which came with Charles Lindbergh.

In the meantime, Howard Carter made a discovery in the Egyptian desert that piqued the interest and the imagination of the tabloid press and its readers around the world—ancient golden treasure. In 1922, as the news of the fantastic wealth and splendor of King Tutankhamen's tomb began to flood onto the front pages of the world's newspapers, it spawned an enormous thirst for more tales of the gold of ancient civilizations.

Percy Fawcett was in the right place at the right time, and because of his earlier expeditions, he was at the height of his visibility. Indeed, *Time* magazine later called him "a popular sensation during the booming 1920s." Unfortunately, he was not alone.

Alexander Hamilton Rice, Jr., the son of millionaire and former Boston mayor Alexander Hamilton Rice, had announced that he was headed to South America with an expedition of his own. Fawcett understood, with no small measure of jealousy, that Rice's deep pockets could provide him with resources and equipment that were far beyond what financial support he could expect from the Royal Geographical Society.

In terms of equipment, Alexander Hamilton Rice was going all out. He announced that he planned to take a seaplane aboard his ship and to survey the mysterious interior of the continent for the first time from the air. By the end of the nineteenth century, the two threads of exploration and media attention to it were thoroughly entwined. By the 1920s, a third thread was woven into that same bundle. This was the thread of innovation in both transportation and communications technology. One could now fly over the poles more easily than taking a dogsled to them. One could now speak by radio from the remotest parts of the world, from which it once took uncertain weeks to relay a message.

Rice planned to apply this technology boldly to the terrain which had frustrated everyone from Gonzalo Pizarro to Percy

Fawcett. With an airplane, he could cover the span of Fawcett's three-month 1921 expedition in a couple of days. Fortunately for Fawcett, Rice had his sights set on the Orinoco, the land over which Sir Walter Raleigh had obsessed. To Fawcett's relief this was about 1,500 miles north of the place where he pictured his City of Z.

Rice's large, well-financed expedition would be accompanied by the famous German anthropologist Theodor Koch-Grünberg, as well as the filmmaker Silvino Santos, whose 1922 silent production *No País das Amazonas* (*In the Country of Amazon*) had been the first major documentary about the area. The second film which Santos planned to shoot in the Amazon had the working title *No Rostro do Eldorado* (*On the Trail of El Dorado*). The media loved the idea.

Fawcett, meanwhile, might have been accompanied by a celebrity of his own. Colonel T. E. Lawrence, better known as Lawrence of Arabia, heard about the trip and asked Fawcett if he might join him. However, Fawcett turned Lawrence down, confiding to friends that he didn't feel that someone accustomed to the Arabian desert could handle the harsh climate of the Amazon jungle. Instead, Fawcett took his twenty-one-year-old son Jack, and Jack's friend Raleigh Rimell.

The American media was thrilled by Rice's expedition, but did not ignore Fawcett. Selling his story to the North American Newspaper Alliance not only guaranteed publicity from the likes of the *New York World*, *Los Angeles Times*, and the *Toronto Star*, it netted Fawcett badly needed cash to fund his trip.

Fawcett knew that it was make or break time. He was fifty-eight years old, and he knew that this would be his final expedition. One of the last things he wrote was an admission that: "I am growing too old to pack at least forty pounds on my back for months on end. . . . If the journey is not successful my work in South America ends in failure, for I can never do any more. I must inevitably be discredited as a visionary, and branded as one who had only personal enrichment in view. Who will ever understand that I want no glory from it—no money for myself—that I am doing it unpaid in the hope that its ultimate benefit to mankind will justify the years spent in the quest?"

As Fawcett and the boys reached Rio de Janeiro in February 1925, their every move was dogged by a battalion of reporters, but their numbers soon thinned as the explorers headed inland. They took a train as far as the city of Cuiabá, then headed in country on horseback, the same method of travel used by Pizarro and Orellana 384 years before.

They departed from "civilization" on April 20, planning to use couriers to send back progress reports that would be forwarded to the world via the North American Newspaper Alliance. This lasted for only a month. Fawcett and the boys disappeared without a trace.

DESPITE THEIR AIRPLANE and their radios, it had not been easy going for the Rice expedition either. Though they lost radio contact with the outside world for a time, they finally made it out alive—all except Koch-Grünberg, who died of malaria. The Santos film, *No Rostro do Eldorado*, was released and was reportedly successful, but no prints of it are believed to survive today. The El Dorado which was the subject of the film was the metaphorical one. Like Milton and Voltaire, Santos understood the resonance of the word.

Meanwhile, the world and its media waited with baited breath for Fawcett to reappear. When months, then a year, passed with no sign of him, his disappearance became the biggest "lost-while-exploring" story in the world, earning a distinction in that subcategory of folklore which it would hold until it was superseded by that of Amelia Earhart in 1937.

As with Earhart, there were flurries of speculation about what may have happened to Fawcett's company. Over the years, these ranged from the theory that they had been eaten by cannibals, to the idea that they had settled down and were living happily in a jungle paradise.

As with Earhart, there eventually were flurries of sightings. The occasional traveler from the interior claimed to have seen them, but no evidence was forthcoming. In 1928,

George Miller Dyott, a fellow member of the Royal Geographical Society, who had led the second outsider expedition after Roosevelt's to travel the River of Doubt, went looking for Fawcett.

Even as Dyott was still in the jungle, *Popular Science* magazine commissioned Francis Gow Smith, an explorer and ethnologist with the Museum of the American Indian (then run by the Heye Foundation, and today by the Smithsonian), to write on the topic for its March 1928 issue. Smith, whose own exploring credentials included the Amazon rain forest, presumed that Fawcett and company were being held captive by the indigenous inhabitants of the deepest Mato Grosso, and assumed that Dyott would be successful in locating them.

In his article, Smith wrote fancifully that the Fawcetts and Raleigh Rimell "have become a pagan tribal trinity, and as such they are safe, well cared for, worshipped with weird rites and fed on outlandish dainties like iguana eggs and roasted ants. . . . I could describe their daily life in detail, for I was for a short time, a similar captive-guest among the Carajas on the Island of Bananal [in the Araguaia River]."

Smith confidently predicted that within a matter of months, if not weeks, Dyott would stride into the camp with an outstretched hand, uttering the phrase, echoing that of Henry Morton Stanley when he found Livingstone—"Colonel Fawcett, I presume."

It never happened. Dyott came back empty handed.

If not Dyott, there were others. Newspaper accounts occasionally published reports by people who claimed to have seen and spoken with Fawcett. A Brazilian prospector, Roger Courteville, emerged from the jungle in early 1932 to report that he had found Fawcett alive and well, cultivating a small farm. He had lost interest in the outside world. Meanwhile, a Swiss trapper named Stephen Rattin reported to Arthur Abbott, the British consul-general in São Paulo, that he had spoken with Fawcett in October 1931.

Even as the luster of his Roaring Twenties popularity was overshadowed by other events, Fawcett still made headlines. On January 24, 1944, at the height of World War II, *Time* magazine ran with a Fawcett story, noting that "recently

Brazilian reporter Edmar Morel returned to civilization with a ghost-pale savage named Dulipé, who he claimed was Jack Fawcett's son by a Kurikuro Indian woman." *Time* added that "as photographed, Dulipé has all the characteristics of an albino, a not uncommon freak among South American Indians."

Through the years, various stories have been told, various items have been found, and most of both have been eventually debunked. There was a compass that turned out to have been one that Fawcett gave away in 1921. Some bones were given to Orlando Villas Boas in 1951 by some Kalapalo people, who claimed that they belonged to Fawcett. Taken to England to be examined, they were determined not to be his.

After World War II, Fawcett's younger son Brian gave it a try, hoping at the least to find his brother Jack still alive. Traveling both by plane and on foot, he tried to reconstruct the path taken by his father and brother, but his hopes, like theirs, were swallowed in a trackless rain forest. David Grann writes that Brian Fawcett discovered evidence in his father's papers that by 1924, the elder Fawcett had turned the corner on believing that Z was an archaeological site, and thinking of it as the magical playground of a supernatural priesthood.

Grann writes that "Fawcett had filled his papers with reams of delirious writings about the end of the world and about a mystical Atlantean kingdom, which resembled the Garden of Eden. Z was transformed into 'the cradle of all civilizations' and the center of one of [nineteenth-century spiritualist and accused charlatan Madam Helena] Blavatsky's 'White Lodges,' where a group of higher spiritual beings helped to direct the fate of the universe. Fawcett hoped to discover a White Lodge that had been there since 'the time of Atlantis,' and to attain transcendence."

Throughout the history of quests for lost cities in South America, the point at which people came to think of a place as a metaphor rather than a physical reality was the point at which they stopped risking their physical body trying to find it. If the papers which Brian discovered are Percy Fawcett's true conclusions on the eve of his 1925 *entrada*, then he is perhaps the first man to mount an expedition in search of a shadow which he actually believed to be just that.

Like a trail into the jungle, the interest in Percy Fawcett and his fate reached a fork. One trail was pursued by those who believed that Fawcett did make contact with the Great White Lodge or the Great White Brotherhood imagined by many followers of Blavatsky and her Theosophical believers. The other trail was followed by explorers and adventurers who sought physical evidence that would resolve merely the mystery of a prominent missing person, who almost certainly had long since passed away.

In 1953, Brian Fawcett edited and published a collection of his father's manuscripts and letters. In it, he likened his father to a "New Prester John." Indeed he was by then a man who, like John, had become a myth. He presided over a magical kingdom deep in the unapproachable heart of *terra incognita*, a kingdom that was both allegorical and real enough for people to still spend time searching for him.

In the 1960s, the Danish travel writer Arne Falk-Rønne was among many who claimed to have met somebody who knew somebody who knew what happened. In this case, he was told that the Kalapalo people had killed the three outsiders. In 1996, James Lynch, a banker from São Paulo, put together a seventeen-man team, including his teenaged son, and went into the jungle. Having studied the Fawcett legend in minute detail, he was sure he knew what he was doing. Detained by Indians, Lynch and his team bought their freedom after three days of captivity by surrendering their mountain of equipment, including boats and radios. They got out and never went back.

In 2005, David Grann followed the Fawcett legend for an article in the *New Yorker*, spoke with Lynch, and even traveled to the place where he had been taken captive. He met the Kalapalo people who supposedly had killed Fawcett. They explained that it was not them, but a rival tribe.

Like Stanley locating Livingstone, Grann located the anthropologist Michael Heckenberger, of the University of Florida, who had been working in the headwaters of the Xingu River for more than a decade. Heckenberger promptly, and almost anticlimactically, took Grann to Z.

First, Heckenberger showed Grann a moat, then canals, then roads, then a great plaza. He showed him the remnants of a city on the scale of the one reported by João da Silva Guimarães, albeit without the great stone buildings. Heckenberger scratched the ground randomly and turned up copious shards of pottery. Though Heckenberger, like many before him, considered Fawcett an "amateur," he had confirmed the existence of his Z. An enormous city had existed in the place where Fawcett was searching—hidden in plain sight.

As David Biello wrote in *Scientific American* in August 2008: "In 1925 British adventurer Colonel Percy Fawcett disappeared into the wilds of the Amazon, never to be heard from again after going there in search of a lost city he called Z. But decades later, a city of sorts—actually a series of settlements connected by roads—has been found at the headwaters of the Xingu River where Fawcett went missing in an area previously buried beneath the dense foliage."

But Heckenberger and his modern colleagues don't call it "Z." They call it "FX11." The initials stand for "Formadores do Río Xingu" (Headwaters of the Xingu River).

The FX11 site is also known as the Kuhikugu Cluster, which Heckenberger himself described in *Scientific American* in 2009 as "the largest pre-Columbian town yet discovered in the Xingu region of the Amazon."

But it is just one of many major residential centers. FX11 is only part of a vast archipelago of similar, FX-designated "lost cities" spread across an area larger than Connecticut and Rhode Island combined. The Kuhikugu Cluster supported a huge population in the heartland of South America from about the ninth to the sixteenth century—even as the conquistadors were running around the continent searching for cities of gold.

FX11 serves as the hub, which, according to the University of Florida Upper Xingu Project, is "directly linked to three secondary centers (FX21, FX35/36, FX38), which are themselves tied to small third-order satellite [sites]" and so on. Based on Heckenberger's research, David Biello reports that as many as 50,000 people lived in more than two dozen towns, and the cities boasted plazas 490 feet across. The site was eerily reminiscent of the Omagua cities which Francisco Orellana had seen along the Amazon in 1541, and which

Philipp von Hutten attacked in the headwaters of the Río Meta in 1543.

Heckenberger has joined the list of twenty-first-century archaeologists and anthropologists, such as Anna Roosevelt and Clark Erickson, who have discovered convincing evidence for very large civilizations in the rain forests of central South America where twentieth-century academics had once insisted that it was impossible.

There were no great stone structures as in Peru or in Mexico's Yucatan, because wood was plentiful, and stone was hard to get. The wood structures deteriorated into dirt in the steamy climate, as though they had never been there. There were, however, vast fields of pottery fragments, as well as the vast networks of roads, plazas, and moats, which were virtually invisible—unless you knew what to look for.

What better description than this for the kingdom of the New Prester John?

27

THE MAN
WHO FOUND
EL DORADO

Like the priesthood, treasure hunters burn with a faith
and trust incomprehensible to the man in the street.
Once he sees a treasure map, he will believe even his
worst enemy, let alone a friend. I was here because of
that belief, and here was a real map to substantiate that
faith and hope. I simply had to find that lost land of
treasure, El Dorado, no matter what it had cost others
in disappointment and tragedy.
—Leonard Clark, *The Rivers Ran East* (1953)

A MAN WALKED into a cantina not unlike the one in
Panama City where Francisco Pizarro had first heard of the
gilded cities of the Inca in 1522, or that one in Quito where
his little brother had first heard of El Dorado nearly two
decades later. He was a man not unlike the Pizarro brothers,
or Ambrosius Ehinger, or Francisco Vásquez de Coronado, or
Sir Walter Raleigh.

Of the twentieth-century explorers who lifted the veil of
South America's mysteries, Hiram Bingham had been a cool-
tempered scientist in the service of science. Percy Fawcett had

been an increasingly obsessive gentleman explorer who insisted to the last that he too was in it for the science. Leonard Clark was a soldier of fortune. He was in it for the gold.

Lewis Gallardy, the United States consul in the jungle outpost of Iquitos, Peru, who knew him, said of Clark that he was "not of the same class as other modern-day explorers—that is, geologists, botanists, ethnological collectors, etc.—but that rare Victorian type, the trail-breaker: the true explorer whom all others must follow."

It was late June 1946, and Clark had been pacing the back streets of Lima for a couple of weeks, waiting impatiently for a man with a map.

If Hiram Bingham was the academic with the dirt of field work under his nails who was the "yin" of Spielberg's Indiana Jones, then Len Clark could easily have been the "yang." He had authored the book *A Wanderer Till I Die* in 1937, and was one of those men who also walked the walk. In World War II, he was tempered in that crucible of mid-twentieth century American adventurers, the Office of Strategic Services, the storied predecessor to the Central Intelligence Agency. The brainchild of General "Wild Bill" Donovan and Franklin D. Roosevelt, the OSS was a collection of mavericks and adventurers, turned government-sanctioned spies, saboteurs, and hit men.

As an OSS agent, Clark had operated behind Japanese lines, coordinating underground operations, guerilla organizations, and espionage rings throughout China, Mongolia, and elsewhere. His own memoirs recall his leading an 18,000-man Chinese cavalry contingent against Japanese railroads like a latter-day Lawrence of Arabia. Clark had also been, as Gallardy recalls his resume, "private advisor to the Arab League in Egypt, and to various princes and lamas in Mongolia and Tibet and to at least five warlords in China. He personally took the unofficial surrender of Formosa from General [Rikichi] Ando three months prior to its occupation by Chiang Kai-shek and the American Forces."

The war had now been over for less than a year, and Clark was pursuing another project as a solo operator—El Dorado.

Percy Fawcett had said that he wanted no glory, no money for himself from his pursuit. He wrote that he was doing it unpaid in the hope that its ultimate benefit to mankind would justify the years he had spent in the quest. Clark, meanwhile, had written "I simply have to have that gold."

Having made and lost a fortune in Asia as a soldier and soldier of fortune, Clark had been down to his last thousand dollars, when he met somebody who knew somebody who had a map. The latter somebody was a wily old prospector, albeit from Peru's landed gentry, named Miguel Maldonaldo.

Clark writes that after his searching and waiting, "Maldonaldo finally returned to Lima, and after swearing on his mother's grave as to its authenticity, gave me a yellowed, badly cracked and very old Spanish parchment map of El Dorado, in exchange for a $100 bill. Of course, there was no way possible of crosschecking such a document; I simply had to take his word for it, and the hunch of my old friend back home, and go."

And so he went.

His goal was near the confluence of the Río Marañón and the Río Santiago, deep in the headwaters of the Amazon, where according to the notations on the map, Padre Juan Salinas, a Jesuit missionary, had found cities of gold in 1557.

On the map, there was an explanation of how Salinas had descended the Santiago and had run the rapids of the Pongo de Manseriche, the gorge on the Marañón which separates the Andean foothills from the Amazon basin.

While he had been waiting for Maldonaldo, Clark had put his time in Lima to use researching the gold mines of Río Santiago. He discovered information not widely disseminated which portrayed the Río Santiago as having been an important gold mining area in the sixteenth century. This fact had apparently been a secret that was closely guarded by the Spaniards back then in order to prevent interlopers from jumping the claim.

Clark read that between 1558 and 1652, the average payment of the 25 percent share of the profits due the Spanish monarchy ranged between 500 and 800 kilos of 23-karat gold, and this from a single placer. Another record showed that in each of the four consecutive years from 1570 to 1574, the average payment had been 9,700 kilos of gold, meaning the total mined during each of these years would have been at least 38,800 kilos, or 1.4 million ounces. At the world gold prices in 1946, the peak annual take from that single placer would have been the equivalent of $49 million. In early twenty-first-century dollars, it would have been around $2.1 billion. There was the reason that the twisting, turning section of the distant upper Marañón was called "La Serpiente de Oro" (The Golden Serpent).

As anyone who has panned gold in places such as the Sierra Nevada foothills of California can tell you, placer gold is refreshed annually, swept downstream each spring by high water from unseen sources in the mountains. In the Sierra, the prospectors and tourism promoters call this the "mother lode."

Clark concluded that a placer untouched by the greedy hands of outsiders for 294 years, and surrounded by still other placers, would be more than worth his while. And he now had a treasure map. This document did not simply tell the vague story of gold "somewhere" up there on that distant and treacherous river, it showed exactly where.

Operating under the cover story that he was planning to search the upper Amazon for medicinal herbs, Clark defied the warnings of all whom he met that he was making this *entrada* at his own peril; he headed out of Lima on July 2.

By train, he crossed the Andes to Oroya, where he linked up with a man named Jorge Mendoza, a friend of a friend, a university graduate and son of a wealthy family, who had worked as a professional hunter in the Amazon jungle. In exchange for expenses, Mendoza would function as an interpreter and the necessary second pair of eyes which jungle travel requires. He was, as Clark later observed, a man who could be trusted, especially not to ask too many questions.

On July 10, reaching the end of the last road passable by wheeled vehicles, the two latter-day conquistadors stepped into the millions of square miles of unknown that had recently swallowed Percy Fawcett and countless others before him. Over the coming days, they made their way though the jungle, marveling at colorful birds and strange-looking fruit bats, cringing at the hissing of enormous half-hidden snakes, fearing the noiseless approach of a jaguar, and warily keeping an eye on the indigenous people who watched them silently from the opposite shore of the river.

It was a world in which "vines crossed like cat's cradles overhead, and hanging from them by long, bushy tails and spidery arms was a jabbering band of coata monkeys. Their shaggy black hair coats had whitish patches, and they squealed in holy terror as they swung off into the towering jungle."

Leonard Clark.
(*Bill Yenne*)

The men made contact with the indigenous tribes wielding nine-foot blowguns with curare-tipped darts, and stood face to face with the *brujos*, or shamans, with painted faces. They sampled the herbal remedies present-ed by their hosts in large thatched buildings, as human skulls and skins peeled from human bodies hung above their heads. They listened to drums and incantations, and met Iye Marangui, a *brujo* who said he was the brother of the serpent. They were entertained by some tribes, but briefly taken captive by another.

With the help of some local people they conscripted along the way, they built a succession of rafts and balsa canoes, with which they descended the Río Perené and Río Tambo. Each of these vessels lasted until smashed on rocks when transiting rapids or waterfalls. In the settlements, they were entertained by the occasional expatriate Europeans, who had abandoned the outside world before World War II, and by Padre Anthony, a legendary missionary who was described as the Dr. Livingstone of the whole region.

One night, while Mendoza was still pretending that he thought that Clark was really here in search of medicinal plants, talk turned to gold. As they sat swatting insects around their campfire, their conversation echoed thousands that had probably been heard in these rain forests in the centuries since a European first spoke the words "El Dorado."

"Gold is as potent a bait today as it was four hundred years ago." Clark observed. "I tell you, it is the very biggest thing in the world."

"It only means, my friend, that you should have had your head examined." Mendoza replied. "Dream stuff. . . . And your people call mine 'romanticos.'"

It was not the first time that a man who had been born here told an outsider that gold was the obsession of a madman.

Reaching the Río Ucayali at the tiny settlement of Atalaya on July 29, they hitched a ride on a forty-foot dugout hauling cargo downstream to the "metropolis of 50 houses" which was Pucallpa. They traveled generally north, though the river zigged and zagged so much that the north arrow on the compass and the bow rarely aligned.

At Pucallpa, the two men parted company. A message caught up with Mendoza telling him that his oldest brother had died, and his presence was required in Lima. They parted, planning to reunite in the jungle, but never did. Mendoza made it to Lima, but found himself now head of the family, with plantations to manage, and a career change. He had found his gold.

As Mendoza headed home overland, Clark caught a seaplane, courtesy of the local Peruvian army commandant, and headed eastward to Iquitos, the "Pearl of the Jungle," that Clark aptly describes as the Timbuktu of the western Amazon. Located near the point where the Ucayali and the Marañón flow together to form the Amazon, Iquitos is the largest Peruvian city in the Amazon basin. It was here that Clark planned to secure a permit to ascend the Marañón and follow Miguel Maldonaldo's treasure map to El Dorado.

In Iquitos, for the first time since Lima, Clark checked into a proper hotel, the Malecón Palace, a place which he describes as a "rookery of the richest patrónes" in town.

It was in Iquitos that Len Clark met the U.S. consul, Lewis Gallardy, who intervened on his behalf when the Peruvian authorities at first denied his request for travel documents. There were rumors of an impending war with Ecuador and the Peruvians didn't want any foreigners running around upstream.

Fortunately, Gallardy knew somebody who knew somebody and the necessary papers were issued. Gallardy's father-in-law also provided Clark with letters of introduction to certain merchants in the river town of Borja, across the Marañón from the sixteenth-century Spanish outpost of San Francisco de Borja. Clark next secured passage upriver to Borja on a Flamingo Oil Company steamer. Now, all he needed was to find an interpreter to replace Jorge Mendoza.

Meanwhile, it was in the dining room of the Malecón Palace that Clark chanced to meet the person who would be his companion for the next leg of his journey.

"We must have been half-way through dinner when Inez Pokorny came into the room," he writes. "She had on a white dress and she was slim. Her small head, the wary shine to her green eyes, the round neatness of her figure and the way she stood for an instant in the doorway, was cool, steady, infinitely appealing. It brought every man at our table to his feet. . . . I asked what an American girl was doing in such wild country and was told that she had been eight months on her way up the Amazon in river-boats." Nobody seemed to know exactly why.

During his stay at the hotel, Clark got to know his fellow guests, mainly businessmen, fairly well and conversation naturally turned to their reasons for passing through Iquitos and where they were headed next. When Clark mentioned to an Englishman named Ian Rokes that he was headed up the Marañón and needed an interpreter, Rokes casually suggested "why don't you take Inez along, she knows the language." Clark responded that this was preposterous, telling him that no female outsider traveling alone had ever been upstream from Iquitos. To this, Rokes reminded him that no such woman had ever traveled alone to Iquitos. Inez thought about it and agreed. The ensuing banter was as though from a movie, with Clark insisting this was no place for a woman and Inez insisting that he needed someone who knew the "river patois."

The issue was decided when Clark's boat left early without him, it was Inez who arranged transportation. She knew somebody, a certain Austrian aristocrat named Baron Walter Frass von Wolfenegg, who had fled the Nazis a decade earlier, and was now working for the Peruvian government. He had a boat, called *La Patria*, which could take Clark upriver—as long as Inez went too. The baron decided to come as well.

Inez would prove to be unexpectedly competent in her role. Clark's description portrays her as an adventurous heroine reminiscent of young Ana de Ayala, who accompanied Francisco Orellana on his second voyage into the jungles of South America 401 years earlier. Perhaps too, one might compare her to the other Inez who traveled these rivers in search of El Dorado—the sixteenth-century Inez de Atienza, the lover of El Dorado-seeker Pedro de Ursúa, whom Clements Markham, the nineteenth-century translator, described passionately as "the heroine of the Amazon." Clark later said proudly that Inez "managed admirably" when he taught her to fire and field strip his Colt M1911 pistol.

By September 3, they were swatting at clouds of mosquitoes on the Amazon and nearing the chocolate-colored Marañón. As Clark described it, the river "turned and squirmed like some living anaconda having its head chopped off, whipping through the flat endless marshes and eternal jungle."

For days they ascended the serpent of a river, catching fish, dodging the omnipresent bugs, and counting the endless miles that separated them from Borja, the last outpost on the conventional map that coincided with the treasure map which Clark kept stashed in his money belt.

Their progress was suddenly and rudely interrupted when *La Patria's* engine seized and they had to put ashore, make camp, and wait for aid from a passing ship. Fortunately, they came ashore near the plantation of an old *patróne* named Don García, who entertained them cordially.

As they languished, the baron's crew became increasingly nervous. The Jivaro people who were indigenous to the headwaters of the Marañón had seen the boat, and the outsiders were hearing the sound of what some interpreted as "war drums." The Jivaro, who still embraced the inimitable "cultural practice" of extracting the skulls of human victims and "shrinking" their heads, had been especially terrifying to Europeans since the days of Pizarro and Orellana.

At last, the baron decided that he would lash *La Patria* to a raft, put into the main channel, and float with the current back to Iquitos. Clark naturally bowed out of this endeavor, telling his companions that he intended to borrow a dugout and a couple of Don García's Cocama employees as rowers and continue upriver. Inez, he said, should go back with *La Patria* to avoid becoming prey to "headhunters." Predictably, she refused. Together, she and Clark waved goodbye to the baron from Don García's veranda. The date was Friday the thirteenth. The patróne never expected to see his dugout again.

As for Len Clark, his black Friday moment came a few nights later when he awoke to the slithering of a coral snake—locally called *nacanaca*—a foot from his face. He whispered to Inez, who managed to get her hand on his gun. Unfortunately, the thing spat venom into his face and sunk its fangs into his neck just before she fired.

The next few hours were a gradual decent into delirium as the poison flooded his body. The next few days were a hellish, if nearly miraculous recovery, as their Cocama companions applied poultices and folk remedies to save Clark's life. He woke up blind, but alive. Passing in and out of consciousness, he woke up the following day able to see light. Feeling himself in a moving dugout, he called to Inez and asked where they were. She told him that they were headed upstream—still on course for Borja.

As Clark's sight slowly returned, they paddled their way through a series of close calls, including one involving a Jivaro man who took a momentary fancy to Inez, and another when their boat was capsized by a collapsing river bank.

On September 25, they met another patróne, a scraggly man named Miguel Rojas, who lived along the shore in a little hut with his Jivaro wife and several children. Their rowers took this as a sign that their job was done, and took off as soon as Clark and Inez were ashore. Rojas shrugged that the Cocama were probably afraid of the *yacumama*, a sea monster or "water spirit."

The next "water spirit" they encountered was a trader headed upstream in a motor launch, so they caught a ride. Stopping at the small settlement of Barranca near the mouth of the Río Morona, they picked up a patróne who offered to sell Clark and Inez three shrunken heads that he was carrying.

He also colorfully explained, flicking his cigarette ash carelessly, the feeding habits of anacondas, telling them that the serpent usually "approaches under water, seizes its victim in its jaws which are lined with powerful teeth. The snake then swims out to deep water, and there drowns the man. If the attack is made on land, the human victim is usually struck on the head by a 'hammer blow' as the front of the snake's head is very hard and bony. Its victim unconscious, the great snake then coils around him and constricts, crushing the bones for convenient swallowing."

The man then offered to bet Clark $1,000 that an anaconda could swallow a domestic pig whole. He offered to supply both the pig and snake to settle the wager. Clark declined. Such was the entertainment on the remaining 150 miles upstream to the mouth of the Río Santiago.

At Borja, Len Clark first unrolled his treasure map for the curious gaze of Inez Pokorny. He revealed to her for the first time his reasons for his obsession with getting to this place—the golden city of El Dorado.

He told her of how the map explained the solution to a monumental mystery, and how it had made its way from Padre Juan Salinas to Miguel Maldonaldo and to the money belt of Len Clark. He told her that Spanish conquistadors extracted millions every year from this place for half a century, and that there was certainly more where that came from.

He admitted that he expected her to mock him for the madness that had consumed him, a madness from the venom of the gold bug, a venom more potent than that of the *nacanaca*.

Instead, Inez revealed a secret of her own. She was, she told him, not just a headstrong adventure tourist, but a fellow treasure seeker. El Dorado was not madness, she smiled, but *her* secret goal as well.

Unlike him, she was not working alone, but at the behest of a well-capitalized, London-based organization that she called the National Gold Bearing Society of El Dorado. She explained that she had come to the Amazon late in 1945 and had spent her time learning the local dialects and picking up secrets about El Dorado which those in the know might be more willing to share with an attractive young woman than a man, like Clark, who had the look of the gold bug's venom in his eyes.

Inez further revealed that several of the Borja merchants to whom Clark had letters of introduction were in on her secret, and were members of the Gold Bearing Society.

Gold was very much a topic in Borja, because Indians would often show up offering to trade nuggets for goods which the merchants could provide. They must be getting it somewhere, and the Gold Bearing Society was keen to know the source. The greedy merchants were anxious for the mother lode.

Though the merchants readily spoke to Clark about gold, Inez apparently did not reveal to them that Clark had a map. Her loyalties may have been switching from those who did not know where to look, to one who did.

However, to complicate matters, Clark learned the following day that his travel permit had been cancelled. His only choices were to take the next steamer back to Iquitos, or to go rogue. He was literally at a point of no return. If he defied the Peruvian authorities who revoked his papers, he could not return the way he had come. If he went on to El Dorado, he would have to hike out of the Amazon basin by going across the Andes into Ecuador. It was an impossible task, but despite the fact that his eyes still burned from the snake venom, he decided to chance it.

Without telling anyone, especially not alerting the Peruvian soldiers who had been ordered to watch him, Clark met with a patróne named Guzman, who was not part of the cabal of merchants, and hired the man to guide him through the treacherous rapids of the Pongo de Manseriche, the gorge on the Marañón which separates Borja from the mouth of the Santiago.

Meanwhile, Inez had been making similar plans of her own. She would not be retreating to Iquitos either. Once again, they joined forces, and in turn, they slipped surreptitiously out of Borja on October 28.

The dawn of the rainy season and high water thwarted their passage of the raging rapids of the Pongo, but like an improbable scene from a Hollywood blockbuster, none other than their old friend, Baron von Wolfenegg, dropped in with a seaplane to fly them across. However, they waited for more than a week for Guzman and his native paddlers to get through with the dugout that they needed to continue their expedition.

Now entering the Andean foothills, the travelers were greeted by a change of scenery to a more mountainous form of unexplored wilderness. They admired the condors by day, and sought refuge from the foul-smelling vampire bats by night. To their relief, the people of the Aguaruna branch of the Jivaro whom they met in large numbers along the way were cordial, offering them food and even demonstrating the grisly art of "shrinking" human heads. Inez Pokorny's natural charm and uncanny ability to easily learn dialects was proving valuable.

On November 27, after many trials and much tribulation, the travelers reached a place in the Jaén de Bracamoros region of Peru where they found themselves surround by old stone fortifications which Clark interpreted as having been erected four centuries earlier by Spanish gold diggers seeking to protect themselves from attacks by the Jivaro. There were, as Michael Heckenberger would find in Bahia half a century later, canals that had once brought water to this settlement. There were long traces of gravel which indicated a long-ago placer mining operation of considerable size.

As Clark and Inez walked these traces, and the sandbars along the river, they began noticing the sparkle of yellow metal like that which must have greeted James Marshall along California's American River in 1848. Occasionally, they saw Aguaruna people with baskets, casually picking up nuggets. Inez smiled, and a group of women generously offered her the use of a basket. Clark filled his pockets with around two pounds of nuggets. He had found his El Dorado.

The next day, Clark traded everything he had, from his razor to his spare ammunition, to the Aguaruna for bamboo tubes packed with gold. On December 2, compass in hand, he and Inez began hiking westward toward the snow-covered Andes. They climbed out of the jungle, onto the windswept plateaus, bought some horses and a pack mule from some Indians they met, and headed into the mountains. It was already winter, and there was every reason to believe that spring would find their bones among those of countless others who had succumbed to the madness of El Dorado's sweet promise in this remote region. They passed through clusters of ruins which Clark believed to be among what he called the "Seven Cities of El Dorado," an analogy which represented a merger of the twin theories of El Dorado and the Seven Cities of Cibola.

They found themselves eating snakes to survive until Clark managed to shoot a deer. He later killed a small bear with his machete. They watched their pack mule play out and falter, no longer able to carry the treasure. Clark buried a couple of the tubes, and shouldered the others himself. Inez adopted a couple of ocelot kittens and led them on a leash.

It was a strange couple who staggered into a mountain town called Bellavista on Christmas eve. Like that other couple long ago, they fell asleep on the stone floor of a stable occupied by donkeys. They slept not with a celebrated newborn child, but with the celebrated gold of El Dorado and two ocelots.

The next day, they discovered that they could take a bus to the Pacific along a winding road, and this was the first leg of a journey that took them to Quito, where Len Clark bade goodbye to Inez, bound for London, at the airport.

They parted with her insisting that the El Dorado they had found belonged to her employers—but knowing that nothing would be sorted out so long as Peru and Ecuador disputed their boundaries. Len Clark sold the gold for $16,000 through a broker, because no bank would touch gold from disputed territory. He had been promised more, but the broker skipped town for Colombia. He dutifully forwarded Inez's share of the profits.

Clark went home to San Francisco and wrote a book about the whole experience, called *The Rivers Ran East*, which created quite a stir when it was first published in 1953, and is highly recommended reading. He is not believed to have ever returned to his Seven Cities of El Dorado.

Clark went on to publish *The Marching Wind* in 1954 and *Explorer's Digest* in 1955. The title of his prewar book, *A Wanderer Till I Die*, was prophetic. In 1957, he died an unexplained death while searching for gold on Venezuela's Río Caroni, the same Orinoco tributary which had confounded Sir Walter Raleigh in 1595. Inez Pokorny vanished into the shadows, although there is a record of a woman of that name, who would have been twenty-eight at the time of Clark's El Dorado expedition, and who died in New York in 1978. If her mysterious syndicate ever went back to exploit the Seven Cities of El Dorado, they kept it very quiet.

28

THE LEGEND
THAT WILL NOT DIE

The treasure which you think not worth taking trouble and pains to find, this one alone is the real treasure you are longing for all your life. The glittering treasure you are hunting for day and night lies buried on the other side of that hill yonder.
—B. Traven, *The Treasure of the Sierra Madre* (1927)

IN A ROOM INSIDE an old library almost within the shadow of St. Peter's Basilica, a man opened an ancient volume entitled *Perúana Historia*, a compilation of documents dating to the years from 1567 to 1625. He was merely doing research for a paper he was writing for Universidad Catúlica in Lima, not looking for anything earth shattering. But this was soon to change.

Mario Polia was no stranger to this place, the Jesuit Historical Institute and Archives in his native Rome, nor to any number of similar institutions between this eternal city and the Instituto Nacional de Cultura del Perú in Lima. Born a year after Leonard Clark and Inez Pokorny found the placers of El Dorado in the headwaters of the Golden Serpent, Polia was a professor of anthropology at the Pontificia Universitá Gregoriana, the Papal Gregorian University in

Rome. He had been studying and lecturing on the ancient civilizations of South America for decades, both in the libraries and in the field by the time that he laid his hands on *Perúana Historia* late in 2001.

He leafed though three dozen of the crisp, yellowed pages of the *Perúana Historia* before his eyes fell upon a letter written by Padre Andrea López, the chancellor of the Collegio dei Gesuiti, the College of the Jesuits, in Cusco, Peru. It was addressed to his supervisor in Rome, Claudius Aquaviva, who became the fifth Superior General of the Society of Jesus in 1581.

As he read the page, Polia discovered that it was more like a page from J.R.R. Tolkien, another of his passions, than a normal memo that one might expect to have been written from a college chancellor to his home office.

It concerned a place which Polia had never seen, but which he knew well. He had heard of Paititi, the lost golden city of the Inca, in the numerous legends that had been told, retold, and written down through the centuries. What he was now reading was not a legend of Paititi, but a first-hand account. López had been there. He wrote of a city of gold, rich also in silver and precious stones, where people had mastered the art of metallurgy as well as of monumental architecture.

López reported that he had personally baptized people in this city of gold, and that Paititi's monarch told López that if he converted to Catholicism, he would build "a church made with blocks of solid gold."

What was this place? Was it Paititi, or some other well-known city of great wealth, such as Potosí?

No. López was certainly not mistaking the reality of Potosí with the oft-told rumors of Paititi. In around 1592, he had served as rector of the Jesuit College in Potosí, so he knew it, and he knew the old cities of the Andes as well as most. Paititi was real. The only thing missing from the López *relación* was a set of directions to get there. The conspiracy theorists naturally whispered of a cover-up by the Vatican, who did not want people to find Paititi.

By February 2002, the worldwide media had seized the story, and run with it. Richard Owen, the Rome correspondent for the *Times* of London, published an article headlined "Jesuit Manuscript May Hold Key to El Dorado Quest."

As the headline illustrates, the metaphor and legend of El Dorado are as alive and well in the popular consciousness of the world in the twenty-first century as they had been in the sixteenth. In the legendarium and epic allegories of J.R.R. Tolkien, a topic on which Mario Polia has published a number of books and articles, the theme is a quest for the real and metaphorical gold of "the Ring." The principal character, the hobbit Bilbo Baggins, sings a song entitled "The Road Goes Ever On."

This is a concept which easily summarizes the road to El Dorado, the road to the cities of gold. Refreshed from time to time by the chance discoveries like that of Mario Polia, the simmering fever is refreshed and the quest goes ever on, as it has for five hundred years.

Just when we are tempted to believe in El Dorado merely as a fantasy metaphor, something happens. At the beginning of the twentieth century, Hiram Bingham found a lost city of a size and scale that stunned even the academics. In the twenty-first century, long after the dogma that no great civilization could have existed in the Amazon was set in stone, Michael Heckenberger and his colleagues are mapping a great complex of population centers in the heart of the rain forest. Then Mario Polia found a manuscript which "proves" that Paititi is real.

Just when one begins to think that no more mysteries can be revealed, someone finds an ancient, shriveled document, lost and forgotten in a distant corner of an archive.

Just when one begins to think that no more mysteries can be revealed, someone sees and touches something unbelievable that has been lost and forgotten for centuries in a distant corner of *terra incognita*.

THROUGHOUT THIS BOOK, we have met adventurers, conquistadors, and madmen who insisted to the very last that their lost city of gold was just across the horizon. We watched them as they gambled their lives, and went to their graves stymied by cruel reality, which they believed to be their own fault for not taking one more step. They were haunted by those, like Bingham, who *did* take one more step and really were rewarded with the fantastic.

Bingham was not the last to make the seekers take that one last step. In 2001, the same year Mario Polia found the *Perúana Historia* document, British explorer Peter Frost and his colleague Scott Gorsuch were surveying a heretofore unknown lost city high in the Andes. As for its being just around the next bend, this city is located a mere 22 miles from Machu Picchu. Frost had first glimpsed it in 1999, clinging to the cliffs at 12,500 feet, drifting like an apparition in the swirling mist that cloaks the peaks at this elevation. D. L. Parsell of *National Geographic* wrote in March 2002 that the "ruins include tombs and several artificially built platforms that suggest the area was an important burial site and ceremonial grounds for sacred rites. . . . The team also found the remains of more than 100 circular buildings." It has been named Qoriwayrachina, which is Quechua for "where wind was used to refine gold."

"It's the Indiana Jones fantasy," Gorsuch told Juan Forero of the *New York Times* for an article published on May 13, 2004. "It's really not more complicated than that. . . . The search for El Dorado, this idea that there are lost cities out there waiting to be found."

Like their tabloid predecessors in the last century, today's journalists cannot get away from the term "El Dorado," and of course few headline writers can resist the name of the favorite swashbuckling adventurer of today's popular mythology.

With each passing year, those lost cities awaiting discovery are indeed being found, both by sober archaeologists and by those people who are traveling the road which goes ever on, and living the Indiana Jones fantasy.

Dr. Johan Reinhard, the archaeologist who has the enviable post of Explorer in Residence at the National Geographic Society, began surveying ancient ceremonial sites on mountaintops in the Andes in the 1980s. He discovered Inca artifacts during an underwater survey of Lake Titicaca, and has found frozen mummies at 22,000 feet in Argentina. In

1995 he found the frozen mummy of a teenaged girl while climbing the 20,700-foot Nevado Amapo in Peru. Known as Momia Juanita or the Ice Maiden, she shared fame and headlines with Reinhard, as well as an enduring place in the folklore of lost civilizations which are no longer lost.

Greg Deyermenjian, a fellow of the Royal Geographical Society and the chairman of the New England Chapter of the Explorer's Club, who has been exploring the mountains of Peru since the 1980s, had his simmering passion for Paititi refreshed and confirmed by Mario Polia's discovery in the *Perúana Historia*. Since 2004, he has led a series of Paititi expeditions into the mountains and high elevation cloud forests north of Cusco. Traveling by both foot and helicopter, he and his team discovered and documented a number of Inca ruins, though nothing which he is yet ready to proclaim as the elusive site of Paititi itself.

Since the Perúvian archaeologist Walter Alva discovered a mummified nobleman in Sipán in northern Peru in 1987, archaeologists have been delving into the Moche civilization which preceded that of the Inca by half a millennium. In 2005, the mummy of a Moche woman warrior was discovered at the edge of Trujillo, Peru's third largest city. While some speak of great treasure being just across the next horizon, this find was just across the street.

Her grave, filled with gold and jewelry, had been undisturbed for a thousand years when the conquistadors passed this way, and it was still undisturbed in the twenty-first century. John Verano of Tulane University, part of the archaeology team on the dig, made the obvious comparison, likening the discovery to that of King Tut's tomb. Scott Norris of the National Geographic Society reported "wooden weapons sheathed in gold" and said that she was "accompanied by numerous necklaces, nose ornaments, and earrings finely wrought in gold, gilded copper, and silver."

Year after year, former lost cities which are no longer lost crop up in the headlines, and with them, tantalizing tastes of treasure. In 2006, a solid gold Moche mask, inlaid with precious stones, which had been pilfered by tomb raiders some years earlier, was recovered in London by Scotland Yard. The value was placed at $2 million, and this was before the price of gold began spiraling upward.

Just when we are tempted to believe in El Dorado merely as a fantasy metaphor, someone shows you an article about a million-dollar golden mask. There is nothing like this to keep treasure hunters interested. From the depths of dusty archives to the heights of Qoriwayrachina to the glitter of Moche gold, the lure of a tangible El Dorado persists as always.

The road goes ever on, and El Dorado is just around the corner.

"I know of two sites that are sort of undiscovered, that I'd like to discover," Peter Frost told Juan Forero of the *New York Times*, refusing to reveal their exact locations. "I feel it's wise not to broadcast intentions."

There are those who believe that Sir Walter Raleigh never found Manoa and Francisco de Coronado never found Quivira because they do not exist. However, if the confirmed discoveries in South America have proven anything, it is that betting against the existence of a lost city is a fool's wager. There are those who believe that Raleigh and Coronado came up short simply because they looked in the wrong places. Through the generations, a great many people have taken this wager.

Through the generations, there have always been—and continue to be—the wily old prospectors with sweet stories of the place over yonder which is the right place to look for a city of gold.

There have always been—and continue to be—crumbling manuscripts cropping up in corners of old libraries where the sun has not shone for centuries.

And then, of course, there are the treasure maps.

Pascual de Andagoya sold one to Francisco de Pizarro. Miguel Maldonaldo sold one to Leonard Clark. If you know somebody who knows somebody who knows where to look, anyone may buy a treasure map. They sell them in the cantinas on the back streets of Cusco. They sell them at roadside shops on the back roads of New Mexico. They sell them on the Internet. Even today, most of them cost much less than the $100 which Len Clark paid in 1946. Of course, most are worthless. Most, but not all. That is, if you believe the yarn which Clark spun—and why not?

✳

INSIDE THAT LITTLE ADOBE CANTINA at the side of the road in the mountains of New Mexico, the fire still burns in the old beehive fireplace built into the corner of the room. Outside, it is so dark and cold that it is hard to imagine leaving the warmth of the crackling logs.

The stranger excused himself so smoothly that we didn't even get a chance to say that we never caught his name.

The tequila, dark and soothing, poured from a bottle that has no label, is gone. On the bar, he has left a single coin. Thinking it a silver dollar, I open my wallet. The stories he had to tell were easily worth the price of a few drinks.

Then I realize that the warm hue of the coin is not from the yellow glow of the fire nor of the lights on the back bar. The coin is not a dollar, nor a coin of a recent century, nor a coin of the same realm as my currency, nor is it mere silver. I guess that the wily old prospector has bought the last round after all.

Discussing all of this with my companion as we examine the coin, we ask in unison, "Where did he say that place was?"

"Just across the horizon," comes the answer.

We agree that at dawn, as the first rays of the new morning sun touch the towering sandstone cliffs, we will be on the road.

And that road goes ever on. J. Frank Dobie, who has been the trail guide for several generations of adventurers and gold-seekers, said it best: "This dream, based on facts, or based on mere hope, imagination, hallucination, aye, plain fertility in lying, who can say? This dream will still be a reality long after the mountain trails its questers now follow have been eroded into gullies and the critical infidels of their credulity have gone to dusty oblivion."

BIBLIOGRAPHY

Bakewell, P. J. *Silver and Entrepreneurship in Seventeenth Century Potosí: The Life and Times of Antonio López de Quiroga.* Dallas: Southern Methodist University Press, 1995.

Bandelier, Adolph Francis Alphonse. *Contributions to the History of the South-western Portion of the United States carried on mainly in the years from 1880 to 1885.* New York and Boston: Papers of the Archaeological Institute of America, 1890.

————. *Documentary History of the Rio Grande Pueblos of New Mexico.* Santa Fe: Papers of the School of American Archeology. 1910.

————. *Final Report of Investigations among the Indians of the South-western United States (1890-1892).* New York and Boston: Papers of the Archaeological Institute of America, 1892.

————. *The Gilded Man (El Dorado) and other Pictures of the Spanish Occupancy of America.* New York, Appleton, 1893.

————. *Historical Introduction to Studies among the Sedentary Indians of New Mexico, and Report on the Ruins of the Pueblo of Pecos.* New York and Boston: Papers of the Archaeological Institute of America, 1881.

Bandelier, Adolph Francis Alphonse, and George Peter Hammond. *A Scientist on the Trail; Travel Letters of A. F. Bandelier, 1880-1881.* Edited by Society Quivira. Berkeley: Quivira Society, 1949.

Bandelier, Adolph Francis Alphonse, Charles H. Lange, and Carroll L. Riley. *The Southwestern Journals of Adolph F. Bandelier.* Albuquerque: University of New Mexico Press, 1966.

Barba, Alvaro Alonso. *El Arte de los Metales* (1640). Translated by Ross E. Douglass and E. P. Mathewson as *The Art of Metallurgy.* London: Chapman & Hall, 1923.

Benzoni, Girolamo. *Historia del Mondo Nuovo (History of the New World).* London: Hakluyt Society, 1857.

Bingham, Hiram. *Lost City of the Incas*. New York: Duell, Sloan and Pierce, 1948.

Bollaert, William, with an introduction by Clements R. Markham. *The Expedition of Pedro de Ursúa & Lope de Aguirre in search of El Dorado and Omagua in 1560-61*. Translated from Padre Pedro Simon's *Sixth historical notice of the conquest of Tierra Firme*. London: Hakluyt Society, 1861.

Bolton, Herbert Eugene. *Coronado: Knight of Pueblos and Plains*. New York: Whittlesey; Albuquerque: University of New Mexico Press, 1949.

————. *Coronado on the Turquoise Trail: Knight of Pueblos and Plains*. Coronado Cuarto Centennial Publications, 1540-1940. Albuquerque: University of New Mexico Press, 1949.

————. *The Spanish Borderlands: A Chronicle of Old Florida and the Southwest*. New Haven: Yale University Press, 1921.

————. *Spanish Exploration in the Southwest, 1542-1706*. New York: Charles Scribner's Sons, 1916.

Braudel, Fernand. *The Wheels of Commerce*. Translated by Sian Reynolds. London: Collins, 1982.

Burton, Richard F., Capt. *Explorations of the Highlands of Brazil; with a full account of the gold and diamond mines, also canoeing down 1500 miles of the great river São Francisco, from Sabará to the sea*. London: Tinsley Bros., 1869.

Cabeza de Vaca, Álvar Núñez. *Naufragios de Álvar Núñez Cabeza de Vaca (Castaways: The Journey of Álvar Núñez Cabeza de Vaca)*. Translated by Fanny Bandelier. New York: Allerton Book Co., 1922.

Carvajal, Gaspar de. *Relación del nuevo descubrimiento del famoso río Grande que descubrió por muy gran ventura el capitán Francisco de Orellana (Account of the recent discovery of the famous Grand river which was discovered by great good fortune by Captain Francisco de Orellana)*. New York: American Geographical Society, 1934.

Castaneda, Carlos. *The Teachings of Don Juan: A Yaqui Way of Knowledge*. Berkeley: University of California Press. 1968.

Castañeda, Pedro de. *The Journey of Coronado*. Translated with an extensive introduction by George Parker Winship, modern introduction, Donald C. Cutter. Golden, CO: Fulcrum Publishing, 1990.

Castellanos, Juan de. *Elegias de Varones ilustres de Indias.* Ann Arbor: University of Michigan, 1847.

————. *History of New Granada.* Madrid: Pérez Dubrull, 1886.

Chavez, Angelico, O.F.M. (translator and editor). *The Oroz Codex.* Washington, D.C.: Academy of American Franciscan History, 1972.

Chavez, Thomas E. *Quest for Quivira: Spanish Explorers on the Great Plains, 1540-1821.* Tucson: Western National Parks Association, 1992.

Cieza de León, Pedro de. *The Discovery and Conquest of Perú: Chronicles of the New World Encounter.* Edited and translated by Alexandra Parma Cook and Noble David Cook. Durham, N.C.: Duke University Press, 1998.

————. *The Incas of Pedro de Cieza de León.* Translated by Harriet de Onis. Norman: University of Oklahoma Press, 1959.

————. *The Second Part of the Chronicle of Peru.* Translated by Clements R. Markham. London: Hakluyt Society, 1883.

————. *The Travels of Pedro de Cieza de León, AD 1532-50, Contained in the First Part of His Chronicle of Perú.* Translated by Clements R. Markham. London: Hakluyt Society, 1883.

Clark, Leonard F. *The Rivers Ran East.* New York: Funk and Wagnalls, 1953; Palo Alto: Traveler's Tales, 2001.

Clissold, Stephen. *The Seven Cities of Cibola: The Early Spanish Expeditions to North America.* London: Eyre & Spottiswoode, 1961.

Descola, Jean. *The Conquistadors.* Translated by Malcolm Barnes. New York: Viking Press, 1957.

Detienne, Marcel. *The Invention of Mythology.* Brasilia: Editora da Universidade de Brasilia, 1992.

Díaz del Castillo, Bernal. *The Memoirs of the Conquistador Bernal Díaz del Castillo, Written by Himself Containing a True and Full Account of the Discovery and Conquest of México and New Spain.* New York: Farrar, Straus and Cudahy, 1956.

Dobie, J. Frank. *Apache Gold and Yaqui Silver.* Boston: Little, Brown, 1939.

————. *Coronado's Children: Tales of Lost Mines and Buried Treasures of the Southwest.* Dallas: Southwest Press, 1930; Austin: University of Texas Press, 2004.

Erickson, Clark L. "Amazonia: The Historical Ecology of a Domesticated Landscape." In *The Handbook of South American Archaeology*, edited by Helaine Silverman and William Isbell. New York: Springer, 2008.

————. "Archaeological Perspectives on Ancient Landscapes of the Llanos de Mojos in the Bolivian Amazon." In *Archaeology in the American Tropics: Current Analytical Methods and Applications*, edited by Peter Stahl. Cambridge: Cambridge University Press, 1995.

Erickson, Clark L. (with James Snead and Andy Darling). *Landscapes of Movement: The Anthropology of Trails, Paths, and Roads*. Philadelphia: Penn Museum Press, 2009.

Erickson, Clark L. (with James Snead and Andy Darling). "Making Human Space: The Archaeology of Trails, Paths, and Roads." In *Landscapes of Movement: Trails, Paths, and Roads in Anthropological Perspective*, edited by James Snead, Clark Erickson, and Andy Darling. Philadelphia: Penn Museum Press and the University of Pennsylvania Press, 2009.

Escobar, Fray Francisco de. *Father Escobar's Relation of the Oñate Expedition to California*. Edited by Herbert Eugene Bolton. Washington, D.C.: Catholic University of America, The Catholic Historical Review, Vol. 5, 1919.

Fawcett, Colonel Percival H. *Lost Trails, Lost Cities*. Edited by Brian Fawcett. New York: Funk and Wagnalls, 1953.

Ferry, Stephen, and Eduardo Galeano. *I Am Rich Potosí: The Mountain That Eats Men*. New York: Monacelli, 1999.

Flint, Richard, and Shirley Cushing Flint, editors and translators. *Documents of the Coronado Expedition, 1539-1542: They Were Not Familiar with His Majesty, nor Did They Wish to Be His Subjects*. Dallas: Southern Methodist University Press, 2005.

Freyle, Juan Rodríquez. *The Conquest and Discovery of the New Granada Kingdom*. London: Folio Society, 1961.

Gallegos, Hernán. *Relación y Conducta del Viaje que Francisco Sánchez Chamuscado con Ocho Soldados sus Companeros Hizo en el Descubrimiento del Nuevo México en Junio de 1581 (Relation and Conduct of the Voyage that Francisco Sánchez the Singed Made with Eight Soldiers, his Companions)*. Seville: Archivo General de Indias.

Gomara, Francisco López de. *Historia de las Indias*. Antwerp: Edicion de Martín Nucio, 1554; Whitefish, MT: Kessinger Publishing, 2007.

Gosse, Edmund. *Raleigh*. New York: Appleton, 1886.

Grann, David. *The Lost City of Z: A Tale of Deadly Obsession in the Amazon*. New York: Doubleday, 2009.

Hackett, Charles Wilson. *Historical Documents relating to New Mexico, Nueva Vizcaya, and Approaches Thereto, to 1773*. Collected by Adolph F. A. Bandelier and Fanny R. Bandelier. Washington, D.C.: The Carnegie Institution, 1923.

Hammond, George P., and Agapito Rey. *Don Juan de Oñate: Colonizer of New Mexico, 1595-1628*. Edited by George P. Hammond. Coronado Quarto Centennial Publications. Albuquerque: University of New Mexico Press, 1953.

————. *The Rediscovery of New Mexico, 1580-1594: The Explorations of Chamuscado, Espejo, Castaño de Sosa, Morlete, and Leyva de Bonilla and Humana*. Albuquerque: University of New Mexico Press, 1966.

Heckenberger, Michael. *The Ecology of Power: Culture, Place, and Personhood in the Southern Amazon, A.D. 1000-2000*. New York: Routledge, 2005.

Herman, Marc. *Searching for El Dorado: A Journey into the South American Rainforest on the Tail of the World's Largest Gold Rush*. New York: Vintage, 2004.

Herrera y Tordesillas, Antonio de. *Historia general de los hechos de los Castellanos en las islas y tierra firme del Mar Oceano*. Madrid: 1601-1615; Whitefish, MT: Kessinger Publishing, 2009.

Hodge, Frederick W., and Theodore H. Lewis, ed. *Spanish Explorers in the Southern United States*. New York: Charles Scribner's Sons, 1907.

Humboldt, Alexander von. *Relation historique du Voyage aux Régions Équinoxiales du Nouveau Continent (Personal Narrative of Travels to the Equinoctial Regions of America)*. Translated and edited by Thomasina Ross. London: George Bell & Sons, 1907.

Kessell, John L. *Kiva, Cross & Crown: the Pecos Indians and New Mexico, 1540-1840*. Albuquerque: University of New Mexico Press, 1987; Tucson: Southwest Parks and Monuments Association, 1995.

Kruse, Herman. *Manuscrito 512 and the Trip to the Search of the Abandoned Population*. Rio de Janeiro: Department of Historic Sites, National Archive, 1940.

Langer, Johnni. "The Lost City of the Bahia: myth and archaeology in the Brazil Empire." São Paulo: *Revista Brasileira de História* (The Brazilian Magazine of History), 2002.

————. "Ruins and Myth: Archaeology in a Brazil Empire." Ph.D. diss. Curitiba: Universidade Federal do Paraná, 2000.

Mann, Charles. *1491: New Revelations of the Americas Before Columbus*. New York: Knopf, 2005.

Maura, Juan Francisco. *Burlador de America: Álvar Núñez Cabeza de Vaca*. Valencia: Universidad de Valencia, 2008.

————. *Nuevas interpretaciones sobre las aventuras de Álvar Núñez Cabeza de Vaca, Esteban de Dorantes, y Fray Marcos de Niza*. St. Louis: Washington University, Revista de Estudios Hispánicos, 2002.

Moreno, Arellano. *Documentos para la Historia Economic de Venezuela (Documents Related to the Economic History of Venezuela)*. Caracas: Central University of Caracas Press, 1961.

Niza, Marcos. *His Own Personal Narrative Of Arizona Discovered By Fray Marcos De Niza Who In 1539 First Entered These Parts On His Quest For The Seven Cities Of Cibola*. Whitefish, MT: Kessinger Publishing, 2007.

Oroz, Padre Pedro. *The Oroz Codex*. Translated and edited by Angelico Chavez, O.F.M. Washington, D.C.: Academy of American Franciscan History, 1972.

Oviedo y Valdes, Gonzalo Fernández de. *Coronica de las Indias. La hystoria general de las Indias y con la conquista del Perú. {with:} Conquista del Perú. Verdadera relación de la conquista del Perú y provincia del Cuzco llamada la nueva Castilla*. Salamanca: Juan de Junta, 1547; San Salvador, El Salvador: Editorial Nuevo Mundo, 2007.

————. *La Historia General de las Indias*. Edited by J. A. de los Rios. Whitefish, MT: Kessinger Publishing, 2010.

Pacheco, Joaquín F., with Francisco de Cardenas y Espejo and Luis Torres de Mendoza. *Colección De Documentos Inditos, Relativos Al Descubrimiento, Conquista y Organización De Las*

Antiguas Posesiones Españolas De America y Oceania (Collection of Unpublished Documents Regarding the Discovery, Conquest and Organization of the Old Spanish Possessions of America). 42 vols. Madrid: Ministerio De Ultramar.

Pastor, Beatriz. *The Armature of Conquest.* Stanford: Stanford University Press, 1992.

Pérez de Luxán, Diego, George Peter Hammond, and Agapito Rey. *Expedition into New Mexico made by Antonio de Espejo, 1582-1583, as revealed in the journal of Diego Pérez de Luxán, a member of the party.* Edited by Society Quivira. Los Angeles: Quivira Society, 1929.

Peterson, Richard. *The Lost Cities of Cibola.* Quincy, IL: Franciscan Press, 1981.

Polia, Mario. *I Signori delle Montagne: Il mondo mitico e religioso delle Ande (The Gentlemen of Mountains: The Mythical and Religious World of the Andes).* Bologna: Instituto Nazionale della Montagna, 2007.

Powell, Philip Wayne. *Soldiers, Indians & Silver: The Northward Advance of New Spain, 1550-1600.* Berkeley: University of California Press, 1952.

Pratt-Chadwick, Mara Louise. *Francisco Pizarro: The Conquest of Perú.* Boston: Educational Publishing Co., 1890.

Raleigh, Sir Walter. *The Discovery of Guiana.* New York: Harcourt Brace, 1960.

Roosevelt, Anna C., John Douglas, and Linda Brown. "Migrations and Adaptations of the First Americans: Clovis and Pre-Clovis Viewed from South America." In *The First Americans: The Pleistocene Colonization of the New World,* edited by N. Jablonski. Berkeley: University of California Press, 2002.

Schmidl, Ulrich. *Wahre Geschichte einer merkwürdigen Reise, gemacht durch Ulrich Schmidel von Straubingen, in America oder der Neuen Welt, von 1534 bis 1554, wo man findet alle seine Leiden in 19 Jahren, und die Beschreibung der Länder und merkwürdigen Völker die er gesehen, von ihm selbst geschrieben (The true story of a noteworthy trip made by Ulrich Schmidel von Straubingen in America or the New World from 1534 to 1554, where will be found all his troubles of 19 years and the description of lands and noteworthy peoples he saw, described by himself).* Frankfurt: 1557.

Silverberg, Robert. *Golden Dream: Seekers of El Dorado.* Athens: Ohio University Press, 1996.

Simpson, J. *Coronado's March In Search Of the Seven Cities of Cibola and Discussion of Their Probable Location.* Whitefish, MT: Kessinger Publishing, 2007.

Stowell, John. *Don Coronado Through Kansas, 1541, then known as Quivira: A Story of the Kansas, Osage, and Pawnee Indians.* Arkansas City, KS: Don Coronado Company, 1908.

Towle, George Makepeace. *Pizarro: His Adventures and Conquests.* London: T. Nelson, 1897.

Traven, B. *The Treasure of the Sierra Madre.* Berlin: Büchergilde Gutenberg, 1927; New York: Knopf, 1935.

Valverde y Mercado, Francisco de, George P. Hammond, and Agapito Rey (editors and translators). *Investigation of Conditions in New Mexico, 1601.* Albuquerque: University of New Mexico Press, 1953.

Vega, Garcilaso de la Vega. *Historia general del Perú o comentarios reales de los Incas.* Imprenta Villalpanto, 1800-1801.

Wassermann, Felix M. "Six Unpublished Letters of Alexander von Humboldt to Thomas Jefferson." London: *The Germanic Review,* 1954.

Wilson, Wendell E., and Alfredo Petrov. "Famous Mineral Localities: Cerro Rico de Potosí, Bolivia." Tucson: *The Mineralogical Record,* January 1, 1999.

Winship, George Parker. "The Coronado Expedition, 1540-1542." *Fourteenth Annual Report of the Bureau of Ethnology, 1892-1893.* Washington, D.C.: Smithsonian Institution, 1896.

Winship, George Parker, Donald C. Cutter, and Pedro de Castañeda de Najera. *The Journey of Coronado, 1540-1542.* Golden, CO: Fulcrum Pub., 1990.

Zárate, Agustin de. *The Discovery and Conquest of Peru.* New York: Penguin, 1968.

Zárate Salmerón, Padre Geronimo de. *Account of all the things that have been seen and learned in New Mexico, by sea as well as land, from the year 1538 until the year 1626.* Translated by Alicia Ronstadt Milich. Albuquerque. Horn & Wallace Publishers, 1966.

INDEX

BILL YENNE is the author of more than three dozen books on historical topics, and several novels. He has been featured on numerous History Channel programs, and he was recently filmed for an upcoming National Geographic Channel program about Sitting Bull.

Mr. Yenne was born in Arizona, grew up in Montana, and has traveled widely in the American West, visiting many of the sites described in this book personally. He lives in San Francisco, and on the web at www.BillYenne.com.